Forensic Methods

Forensic Methods

Excavation for the Archaeologist and Investigator

MELISSA A. CONNOR

A division of
ROWMAN & LITTLEFIELD PUBLISHERS, INC.
Lanham • New York • Toronto • Plymouth, UK

AltaMira Press
A division of Rowman & Littlefield Publishers, Inc.
A wholly owned subsidiary of The Rowman & Littlefield Publishing Group, Inc.
4501 Forbes Boulevard, Suite 200, Lanham, MD 20706
www.altamirapress.com

Estover Road, Plymouth PL6 7PY, United Kingdom

British Library Cataloguing in Publication Information Available

Library of Congress Cataloging-in-Publication Data

Connor, Melissa A.
Forensic methods : excavation for the archaeologist and investigator / Melissa A. Connor.
p. cm.
Includes bibliographical references and index.
ISBN-13: 978-0-7591-0936-0 (cloth : alk. paper)
ISBN-10: 0-7591-0936-2 (cloth : alk. paper)
1. Forensic anthropology--Methodology. 2. Archaeology--Methodology. 3. Crime scene searches--Methodology. I. Title.

GN69.8.C66 2007
614'.17--dc22

2007001115

Printed in the United States of America

∞™ The paper used in this publication meets the minimum requirements of American National Standard for Information Sciences—Permanence of Paper for Printed Library Materials, ANSI/NISO Z39.48-1992.

Contents

List of Illustrations xi

Acknowledgments xv

1 An Introduction to Forensic Science for Archaeologists 1
- A Brief History of Forensic Archaeology 1
- The Forensic Team 4
- The Investigation 5
- The Crime Scene and Physical Evidence 6
- The Chain of Custody 7
- Arrest and Charge 8
- Pretrial Proceedings 9
- The Trial 11
- Expert Witness Testimony 12
- Summary 15
- Glossary Terms 15
- Suggested Reading 15

2 An Introduction to Archaeology for Forensic Scientists 17
- Archaeologists as Detectives 17
- Archaeological Paradigms 17
- Archaeological Language 18
- A Death in Dealer Park: Using Archaeological Concepts 23
- Summary 27

Glossary Terms 27
Suggested Reading 27

3 Before Fieldwork 29
Project Preparation 29
Personnel 33
Equipment 34
Outdoor Safety 38
Physical Health Concerns 40
Dealing with Death and Stress 40
Summary 41

4 Maps and Site Layout 43
Reference Systems 43
Addresses 43
Latitude and Longitude 44
Township and Range (Legal Description) 45
Universal Transverse Mercator 48
Global Positioning System 50
Site Maps 51
Map Basics 51
Determining Direction and Angle 53
Types of Maps 54
Site Layout and Excavation Grids 58
Plan Maps 59
Elevation 62
Summary 67
Glossary Terms 67
Suggested Reading 67

5 Soils 69
Soil Formation 70
Soil Description 71
Color 71
Texture 73
Coarse Components 75
Structure 76
Stratigraphy 76
Soil Profiles and Graves 76
Body Silhouettes and Soil Chemistry 81

Summary 83
Glossary Terms 84
Suggested Reading 84

6 Surface Remains 85
Taphonomic Factors Affecting Remains on the Ground Surface 86
Scavengers 86
Weathering 89
Slope Wash and Water Transportation 92
Trampling 93
Agricultural Activities 94
Human Movement of Remains 94
General Procedures for Collecting Surface Remains 96
Outdoor Burned and Cremated Remains 101
Investigative Strategy 102
Summary 104
Glossary Terms 105
Suggested Reading 105

7 Locating Buried Remains 107
The Grave as an Archaeological Feature 107
Direct Methods of Grave Location 107
Finding the Grave Using a Witness 107
Soil, Topography, and Vegetation Changes 109
Pedestrian Survey 112
Probes 114
Cadaver Dogs 117
Test Trenches 117
Remote Sensing 119
Aerial Photographs 120
Geophysical Techniques 122
Geophysics Case Study 129
Summary 139
Glossary Terms 141
Suggested Reading 141

8 Excavating Human Remains 143
Exhumation Goals 143
The Grave as a Taphonomic Unit 144
Working the Burial Scene 148

Establishing the Scene Perimeter 148
Safety 149
Graves 150
Documentation 160
Removing the Burial 161
Evidence Management 164
Packaging 165
Ancillary Studies 166
Graves Where the Bodies Have Been Removed 169
Latrines, Cisterns, and Wells 172
Landfills and Dumps 173
Summary 178
Glossary Terms 181
Suggested Reading 181

9 Evidence 183
Clothing 184
Medical Appliances 186
Dental Appliances 187
Orthopedic Appliances 191
Firearms Ammunition Components and Explosive Ordnance 192
Summary 199
Glossary Terms 199
Suggested Reading 200

10 Documentation 201
Field Records 201
Grave Assessment Form 202
Supervisor's Journal 203
Survey and Mapping 203
Photographic Records 205
Feature Form 205
Case Excavation Sheet 207
Chain of Custody Form 209
The Final Report 209
Summary 211

11 The Professional Forensic Archaeologist 213
The Role of the Forensic Archaeologist 213

Defining the Forensic Archaeologist 213
The Archaeologist in Death Scene Investigations 216
The Future of Forensic Archaeology 217

Appendix: Supplies and Services 219

Glossary 221

References Cited 227

Index 245

About the Author 249

Illustrations

TABLES

Table 2-1. Archaeological vocabulary useful in forensics. 21
Table 3-1. General project implementation outline. 30
Table 3-2. Items for individual tool kits. 31
Table 3-3. Team equipment. 32
Table 4-1. Common hypotenuse lengths for excavation or collection units with sides between one and ten units. 60
Table 7-1. Difficult conditions for geophysical surveys and the problems that may result. 123
Table 7-2. Advantages and limitations of grave location methods. 140

FIGURES

Figure 2-1. Relationship of an attribute to an artifact to an assemblage and their position on a site. 20
Figure 2-2. Scene map from Dealer Park. 24
Figure 3-1. Sharpening a shovel. 36
Figure 3-2. Using a two-legged shaker screen. 37
Figure 4-1. Latitude and longitude. 44
Figure 4-2. Portion of a topographic map. 45
Figure 4-3. Standard township layout and designation of partial sections. 47
Figure 4-4. Template for determining township and range locations. 48
Figure 4-5. Template for determining UTM locations. 49

Figure 4-6. Sample sketch map. 55
Figure 4-7. Making a baseline map. 59
Figure 4-8. Triangulation of a square to create the corners of a grid. 61
Figure 4-9. Measuring an elevation. 63
Figure 4-10. Changes in elevation shown in a series of plan maps. 65
Figure 4-11. Isometric projection. 66
Figure 5-1. Page from a Munsell soil color chart. 72
Figure 5-2. Flow chart for determining soil texture by feel. 74
Figure 5-3. U.S. Department of Agriculture soil triangle. 75
Figure 5-4. Reading a soil profile. 77
Figure 5-5. Change in soil profile where grave was dug. 78
Figure 5-6. Grave exposed in subsoil. 78
Figure 5-7. Model graves showing changes in soil horizons. 79
Figure 6-1. Tooth marks from rodent gnawing on bone. 87
Figure 6-2. Surface scatter of horse bone, Last Stand Hill, Little Bighorn National Battlefield Monument. 90
Figure 6-3. Weathering on horse ribs from Last Stand Hill, Little Bighorn National Battlefield Monument. 91
Figure 6-4. Detail of deterioration on human bone from Custer National Cemetery. 92
Figure 6-5. Model of a grave destroyed through agricultural activities. 95
Figure 6-6. Decision tree for surface remains protocol. 97
Figure 7-1. Shallow depression delimits a pig grave. 110
Figure 7-2. Methods of pedestrian survey. 113
Figure 7-3. Types of probes and soil sampling equipment. 115
Figure 7-4. Tile probe in use. 116
Figure 7-5. If the probe is near the decomposing remains, the odor of the decomposition fluids will adhere to the soil and to the end of the probe. 116
Figure 7-6. Backhoe being used outside of Sarajevo. 119
Figure 7-7. Aerial photographs showing mass grave burial activity at Branjevo Farm, Donje Pilica, Bosnia-Herzegovina. 121
Figure 7-8. Model airplane with camera attached on the bottom for low-altitude aerial reconnaissance. 122
Figure 7-9. The Noggins system, a ground-penetrating radar unit. 125
Figure 7-10. Geonics EM38 in use. 126
Figure 7-11. EM31 in use by its inventor, Duncan McDonald. 127
Figure 7-12. Electrical resistivity unit in use. 128

Figure 7-13. Fluxgate magnetometer in use. 130
Figure 7-14. Map of the Perschbacher Cemetery, Scott Air Force Base, Illinois. 131
Figure 7-15. Raw scans by GPR unit. 132
Figure 7-16. Interpretation of profiling completed by the GPR unit. 133
Figure 7-17. Magnetic field and gradient data. 135
Figure 7-18. Electrical conductivity data. 136
Figure 7-19. Resistivity sounding profile. 137
Figure 7-20. Interpretation of the combined geophysical analyses at the Perschbacher Cemetery. 138
Figure 8-1. Adipocere on a body excavated in 1998 and on a body excavated in 2004. 146
Figure 8-2. Leaving the bodies on a pedestal and excavating the surrounding soil to a level below the remains allows the workers plenty of room. 153
Figure 8-3. Leaving the remains on a pedestal while excavating allows the excavator to ensure that all material adjacent to and below the body is easily seen. 157
Figure 8-4. Mass grave where the partially decomposed remains were thrown into a pit dug with heavy machinery. 158
Figure 8-5. Mass grave where the bodies were deposited neatly in rows, in body bags. 159
Figure 8-6. Using plaster bandages to help lift fragile bone. 163
Figure 8-7. The Prozor dump, Bosnia and Herzegovina. 174
Figure 8-8. The Plattsmouth County landfill, where a search was conducted for the remains of a missing three-year-old child. 177
Figure 9-1. Cloth impressions on bone. 186
Figure 9-2. Dentures. 188
Figure 9-3. Ball joints used in hip replacement surgery. 189
Figure 9-4. Components used in knee replacements. 190
Figure 9-5. A surgical staple. 191
Figure 9-6. A sample pacemaker and sample heart valve. 193
Figure 9-7. Stents. 194
Figure 9-8. A sample intrauterine contraceptive device (IUD) and an IUD found with skeleton. 195
Figure 9-9. Basic ballistic terminology. 196
Figure 9-10. The head of a cartridge case. 197
Figure 10-1. Grave assessment form. 202

Figure 10-2. Example of a supervisor's journal. 204
Figure 10-3. Sample photographic record log sheet. 206
Figure 10-4. Feature form. 207
Figure 10-5. Sample case excavation form. 208
Figure 10-6. Sample chain of custody form. 210

Acknowledgments

Six forensic archaeology classes, totalling over a hundred students, used earlier versions of this book as a text. Students in each class were vocal about their likes and dislikes, and the volume was repeatedly improved. Doug Scott, my co-instructor and husband, read every version and contributed to each; he contributed substantially to the chapter on evidence. Peter Bleed also read and commented extensively on the volume. Special Agent Michael J. Hochrein, Federal Bureau of Investigation, generously took the time to comment on a manuscript version of this book. Tal Simmons was both personally and professionally supportive as I made the transition from archaeologist to forensic archaeologist.

In writing this book and for case examples, I drew extensively on my experience working with Physicians for Human Rights (PHR) and the International Commission on Missing Persons (ICMP). Clyde Snow is responsible for first asking Doug Scott and me to participate on a forensic project. Snow, Eric Stover, and the late Robert Kirshner formed a triad responsible for incorporating archaeology into the techniques used by forensic teams investigating war crimes and crimes against humanity and genocide, using the success of the Argentine Forensic Anthropology Team as a model. William Haglund stepped into the giant shoes left by Robert Kirshner as the director of the International Forensic Program for PHR. Under Haglund, I worked for, or under the auspices of, PHR in Cyprus, Kosovo, Sri Lanka, and Nigeria. On every project I learned from my colleagues, both the nationals of the countries in which we worked and the internationals who assisted. They are too numerous to cite, but I appreciate each and every one. Clifford Perera of the University of Ruhana gave permission to use photographs of work conducted by the Sri Lankan forensic experts.

I worked in the former Yugoslavia in 1993, 1996, 1998, and 2000 under the auspices of PHR, ICMP, and the United Nations Tribunal for the former Yugoslavia. I worked with the Bosnia and Herzegovina Federation Commission on Missing Persons, the Republika Srpska Commission on Missing and Tracing, and the Federal Commission on Missing Persons on the Croat Side. All have excellent exhumation teams and I only hope they learned as much from me as I learned from them. The International Commission on Missing Persons and Physicians for Human Rights has been generous in allowing me to use images and case examples, where appropriate.

The Plattsmouth Police Department (Plattsmouth, Nebraska) allowed me to participate in the search for Brendan Gonzalez and was gracious in allowing me to take pictures at the landfill for use in teaching and this manual. Plattsmouth Police Chief Brian Paulsen supplied an unpublished manuscript on the case which I was able to use here. The Lancaster County Sheriff's Office (Lancaster County, Nebraska) allowed me to participate in the exhumation, which I was also able to discuss in chapter 6. Stanton Harms, Curator of the Dental Museum at the College of Dentistry, University of Nebraska Medical Center, made available his collection of medical devices from cadavers for photographs. Donna Garbacz Bader and the cardiovascular surgery and general surgery team at Bryan LGH Medical Center, Lincoln, Nebraska, made available numerous examples of medical implants and helped me understand what purpose they served. Steve DeVore, Midwest Archaeological Center, National Park Service, has not only helped teach remote sensing to our classes for years, but helped me understand the Perschbacher Cemetery remote sensing report used as an example in this volume.

1

An Introduction to Forensic Science for Archaeologists

"Archaeologists Are the Cowboys of Science" is a popular saying on bumper stickers sold at archaeological conferences. The Indiana Jones stereotype portrays archaeologists as independent outdoor types, who are impatient with bureaucracy and red tape, but endlessly patient in research and excavation. However, these are not always the attributes of a good forensic scientist.

Forensic archaeologists cannot work independently; they need to work within a complex legal bureaucracy. Working as part of a forensic team requires an adjustment to the "cowboys of science" mindset. The work is important enough, however, to make the adjustment well worth the effort. Forensic archaeologists need as much patience with the bureaucracy as with the exhumation. They may even find themselves applying red tape on every artifact bag (evidence tape to seal the bag), rather than dodging red tape. This chapter is an introduction to that very real and necessary transition.

A BRIEF HISTORY OF FORENSIC ARCHAEOLOGY

Anthropology in the United States shifted away from European anthropology over a century ago. In the 1880s a young German intellectual, Franz Boas, immigrated to America in search of a job. Boas became known as the "the father of American anthropology" and published a series of papers defining anthropology as "the biological history of mankind in all its varieties; linguistics applied to people without written languages; the ethnology of people without historic records, and prehistoric archeology" (Boas 1904). This created the four-field anthropological approach that most U.S. academic anthropology departments follow today. Meanwhile, in Europe, cultural anthropology, physical anthropology, and archaeology separated into separate disciplines. For forensic archaeology, this is important as the cross training between physical anthropology and archaeology proves critical.

Most American anthropologists in the first part of the twentieth century had a strong background in Boasian four-field anthropology, which required basic courses in cultural anthropology, linguistics, archaeology, and physical anthropology, and additional courses in the specialty field. Archaeology came into forensic science through specialists in physical anthropology who had archaeological training as part of the four-field anthropological discipline and who worked on skeletal cases for forensic purposes. As training became more specialized, archaeologists were more commonly involved in forensic sites. In 1983, two field guides to the excavation of human remains were published (Morse, Duncan, and Stoutamire 1983; Skinner and Lazenby 1983). The publication of these guides was a statement of the interest in the use of archaeological techniques in investigation. However, the role of archaeology was limited to the use of field techniques, and it was taught as something easily learned by the nonprofessional.

The concept of archaeological context in forensic work was emphasized by Sigler-Eisenberg (1985), resulting in an expanded use of archaeology that included not just the techniques, but the theory as well. Sigler-Eisenberg called attention to the idea that it is difficult to work under an archaeological paradigm without the entire constellation of skills and abilities gained through an archaeological education and extensive field experience. She stressed that an archaeologist does not work alone in a forensic investigation, but is rather a team player who needs to know the overall picture in order to understand his or her role.

Hunter and others (1996) published a compilation of papers on forensic archaeology that outlined some of the archaeological techniques most applicable to death investigations. In addition to the recovery and recording of human remains, these papers discussed the identification of burial sites, sophisticated three-dimensional spatial recording, knowledge of soils and stratigraphy, and dating methods. These articles embraced a broad array of archaeological field and laboratory techniques, and included case examples of their usefulness in death investigation. More publications on forensic archaeology (Connor and Scott 2001a; Dupras et al. 2006; Hunter and Cox 2005) continue to show this is an expanding field.

In the last two decades, mass grave exhumations have greatly expanded the use of archaeology and archaeologists in forensic investigations. Sophisticated archaeological techniques have been used extensively in the excavation of complex masses of commingled individuals in Latin America, Rwanda, and the former Yugoslavia. This trend began with the appointment of Dr. Clyde Snow by the American Academy for the Advancement of Science Committee on Scientific Freedom and Responsibility to train Argentine medical and archaeological students in forensic investigation (Joyce and Stover 1991; Snow et al. 1984; Stover 1985; Stover and Ryan 2001). The Argentine Forensic Anthropology Team (the Equipo Argentino de Antropologia Forense) works in a number of countries in addition to Argentina and trains others in forensic investigation. They have assisted forensic investigations in Argentina, Bolivia, Brazil, El Salvador, Ivory Coast, Republic of Georgia, Spain, and the Sudan (Equipo Argentino de Antropologia Forense 2005).

Most archaeologists are involved in forensic work so infrequently that they can spend much of a project in a learning mode rather than as a full and useful team member. The exceptions are state- or university-based archaeologists who gather experience on a repeated basis as state law enforcement agencies request their aid. Other exceptions are the archaeologists who are working on the recent exhumations by Physicians for Human Rights (PHR) for the International Criminal Tribunal for the former Yugoslavia and the International Criminal Tribunal for Rwanda, and full-time forensic teams such as the Argentine, Chilean, and Guatemalan Forensic Anthropology Teams and the International Commission for Missing Persons (ICMP).

In the beginning of this new millennium, forensic archaeology is a small, but growing, subfield of archaeology. "Archaeological Crime Fighters" was the title of a recent article in the popular magazine *American Archaeology* (Robbins 2006). International teams sent to investigate human rights abuses now routinely include archeologists or anthropologists with archaeological training. Training for these positions is minimal, however, and archaeologists have little guidance in the application of their knowledge to forensic situations. This volume is a step in the direction of giving archaeologists that guidance.

THE FORENSIC TEAM

Archaeologists will never work at a forensic scene by themselves. Sometimes finding human remains is the start of an inquiry, but more often it is the result of a long-term painstaking investigation. The criminal investigator in charge of a case usually has responsibility for determining who will work on the case, deciding whether specialists like archaeologists are warranted, and for making an arrest when there is enough evidence for one. In some countries (such as the United States), the criminal investigator works with the attorney who will prosecute the case for the state. In other countries (such as Sri Lanka), the forensic team works directly for an investigative judge. Depending on the legal system, either the judge or the prosecuting attorney may be on-site during the investigation.

Most police departments, sheriff's offices, or other law enforcement entities have their own scene investigation teams to investigate at crime scenes. These specialists are trained in collecting trace evidence such as blood residue, body fluids, hairs, fibers, and many other items which most archaeologists rarely find in their excavations and with which they have little or no experience. The investigators also know their protocols for photographing, mapping, labeling, and collecting evidence, as well as the chain of custody, which are all discussed below. Archaeologists need to become integrated with the scene investigation teams and ensure that police protocols are followed. They also must communicate what they find to the investigators. Finding tool marks in the side of the grave may provide investigators probable cause to search a toolshed on a suspect's property.

Whether the remains are skeletal or fleshed, a forensic pathologist will have the responsibility of identifying the remains and determining the cause of death. If the remains are skeletal, a forensic anthropologist may be called in for consultation, but the pathologist has the legal responsibility of signing the death certificate. For this reason, the pathologist may be at the scene during recovery to gather information that may be relevant to injuries he or she sees on the remains. Many pathologists abdicate this responsibility, but when the pathologist is present, he or she should be given the opportunity to examine the remains before the remains are placed in a body bag. The pathologist may also see things that he or she may wish photographed or included in the map, and this also should be done.

Uniformed police officers who may not be part of the scene investigation team will also be present. The scene should be cordoned off and, usually, a uniformed police officer will note who arrives and when, and who leaves the scene and when. The police may also have a media officer present. This person will talk to the media for the team. The archaeologist should not talk to the media without first discussing with the media officer what information the police intend to release. A good rule of thumb is that general archaeological methods can be discussed, but not the specifics of the case.

There are a number of other forensic specialists, any of whom may be contacted if the case warrants it. There are groups that specialize in the location of remains and graves (for example, NecroSearch); these groups have specialized remote sensing equipment and qualified technicians. Cadaver dogs and their handlers are extremely useful in finding graves. Forensic entomologists specialize in the sequence in which specific species of insects inhabit and feed on remains. They may be able to determine how long a body lay in the open and if it was moved, or whether a buried body lay on the surface for a while before burial. Forensic soil scientists may be able to look at decomposition stains in the soil and tell if there had ever been a body in a particular area (Vass et al. 1992). As with other types of archaeology, the forensic archaeologist needs to know enough about these specialties to know when an expert is needed.

THE INVESTIGATION

The investigators need to determine (1) if a crime was committed, and (2) who was responsible. At the time a body is exhumed, the investigators may still not know if a crime was actually committed. The archaeological evidence may help them determine whether the death involved a crime.

In addition to the physical evidence that the archaeologists deal with, the investigators will be working with two other classes of evidence: witness testimony and written documentation. They will be interviewing witnesses who may include the suspect; people related to the victim, suspects, or scene; accomplices; informers; and experts other than the archaeologist. Investigators will meticulously document each interview and outline potential leads so they can follow up on them. The investigators will also be examining the potentially voluminous documentary evidence—any records that may pertain to the case. These can include telephone records, computer disks, e-mail records, and videos, as well as paperwork such as bills, letters, and notes that document the minutia of our everyday life.

All evidence, whether physical, witness, or documentary, must be obtained legally to be admissible in court. So, in addition to the other aspects of the case, the investigators will be working within the complicated parameters of the legal system. For instance, in the United States, to obtain entry to private property for a search (including a search for human remains), the investigators must either obtain a search warrant or the owner's consent to search the property, or there must be an exigent circumstance that requires immediate action. In most buried-body cases, they will need a search warrant, which requires them to have probable cause that there is evidence related to a crime on the property. Usually a warrant will be specific as to the places that may be searched. If the warrant specifies that a specific property may be searched for a buried-body site, the adjacent property may not also be searched without probable cause and a second warrant.

THE CRIME SCENE AND PHYSICAL EVIDENCE

It would be simple to equate the crime scene with the archaeological site and evidence with artifacts, but it would be incorrect. Evidence is anything a judge permits to be offered in court to determine the question at hand (Osterburg and Ward 2004:631). As discussed above, evidence can be physical (also called real evidence), testimonial evidence given orally by a witness, or documentary/written evidence.

Each type of evidence can also be direct or circumstantial. Direct evidence relates to the matter at hand without inference. For instance, eyewitness testimony would be direct evidence. Circumstantial evidence is evidence based on inference and not personal knowledge (Houck and Siegel 2006:53). Most physical evidence is circumstantial evidence. For example, finding a possession of the defendant's at the scene is circumstantial evidence. From that, one could infer that the defendant was at the scene, but it does not place him or her there in the direct manner that eyewitness testimony could.

A case based on circumstantial evidence is more difficult to build than a case based on direct evidence. The investigators must be able to show that the defendant, and only the defendant, had the means, motive, and opportunity to commit the crime. The prosecutor must be able to argue this to the jury so that the jury has no reasonable doubt whether the defendant committed the crime.

A crime scene relates no more to an archaeological site than evidence does to artifact. The crime scene is the area containing evidence relevant to the crime that potentially occurred. Some jurisdictions have protocols that define the scene as including an area so many feet from the evidence. Frequently though, definition of the scene is based on witness testimony or physical boundaries such as walls. In a homicide case, the scene may include the place the person was murdered, the car used to move the body, and the burial location. In a sense, the crime scene is a series of activity areas that all relate to the same crime.

THE CHAIN OF CUSTODY

As a rule, archaeologists keep good track of the artifacts they find. However, the forensic archaeologist must help ensure that there is a paper trail for every piece of material related to a case from the time that piece is found to the time the case goes to court. Anyone who had an item in their possession may be called on to testify that the item in court is the same one they recovered and bagged on the scene. Any disruption in this chain of evidence or chain of custody may result in the evidence not being admitted in court.

Most police departments have protocols that specify how physical evidence should be marked, transported, and stored. Archaeologists should, whenever possible, use these protocols on a forensic case, rather than their own artifact procedures. There should be an evidence technician on-site, or one archaeologist should act as the evidence technician. The evidence technician will take custody of each artifact as it is uncovered, ensure that the provenience is documented, and enter the artifact into the evidence log under the proper protocol. This begins the chain of custody. When the evidence technician turns the material over to a specialist who will study it or to a secure facility, that action needs to be documented on a chain of custody form (a sample of which is provided in chapter 10).

On many archaeological sites, artifacts are gathered together at the end of the day or when the excavation unit is finished and then entered into the artifact log. This is not appropriate on forensic sites. Items need to be entered into the evidence log immediately when they are found. They should not be placed to the side to be dealt with "in a minute," or put in a pocket or in a backpack. Taking an artifact off the scene (for example, sticking it in a pocket during a lunch break) and then entering it into the evidence log when returning to the scene breaks the chain of custody and can give a defense attorney cause to suggest the material was planted or altered.

ARREST AND CHARGE

As the investigation proceeds, the criminal investigator works with the prosecuting attorney to determine when there is enough evidence against an individual to present a case to a judge. If the judge agrees that the evidence is compelling, he or she will issue an arrest warrant and the individual will be arrested.

In many states and in federal courts, an indictment must be handed down by a grand jury before a person can be tried for a felony. An indictment is a written list of the charges brought against the defendant. The grand jury certifies whether there is enough evidence to conclude that a crime was committed, that it is likely that the accused may have been responsible, and that there should be a trial. Witnesses may be asked to testify in front of the grand jury and investigators familiar with the case present the case as he or she is asked questions by the attorney(s). Then, if the grand jury feels that there is sufficient evidence, it will issue an indictment against the defendant.

In other states, there may be a preliminary hearing rather than a grand jury hearing to determine whether there is enough evidence to charge the suspect. During a preliminary hearing a judge hears arguments by lawyers for the two sides and then issues an "information" with his decision. Preliminary hearings are usually open to the public, where grand jury proceedings are usually closed. Preliminary hearings are adversarial in that both a prosecuting and defending lawyer are present; in a grand jury hearing usually only the prosecutor presents information.

A case including a dead body can result in different charges (Kurland 1997:44–46):

- *Murder in the first degree* is willful, deliberate, and premeditated. "Felony murder" is a killing during the commission of a felony, which is specified by a state statute (and usually includes armed robbery, kidnapping, arson, and rape), and is often treated as first degree murder.
- *Murder in the second degree* is a killing that reflects malice beforehand, but premeditation is absent. Murder committed during a felony other than those specified by state statute is frequently considered second degree murder.
- *Manslaughter in the first degree* is intentional killing without either premeditation or malice. Killing another person in a fit of anger or jealousy may be manslaughter in the first degree.

- *Manslaughter in the second degree,* also called involuntary manslaughter, is killing someone as a result of gross negligence or a reckless act that carried a high probability of killing another. Killing a person while driving drunk may be considered manslaughter in the second degree.
- *Justifiable homicide* is generally used in self-defense cases where the defendant him- or herself would have been seriously injured or killed unless he or she killed the deceased. Homicides committed by officials in the course of their duties may also be considered justifiable.
- *Accidental death* is the result of an accident without premeditation, malice, negligence, or a reckless act.

The difference between murder and manslaughter is intent and premeditation. The difference between accidental death and murder or manslaughter is malice. The archaeologist needs to be sensitive to physical evidence that may show intent or malice. Physical evidence can be used to infer intent and malice and the forensic archaeologist must be aware of this and why certain pieces of evidence are particularly important.

Bindings, ligatures, blindfolds, or gags attached to the deceased can be used to show intent and malice. Natural rope fibers may decay, but the position of the body (for instance, the arms behind the body with the wrists crossed) may suggest that the body was originally bound. Objects associated with the deceased and found outside of their usual context may be used to show intent (for instance, a kitchen knife found in the woods). Tool marks in the floor or wall of a grave may also imply intent or planning, as again, the tool would probably have to have been brought to the site. The perpetrator would have to have thought ahead in order to have this object available.

PRETRIAL PROCEEDINGS

A trial is preceded by pretrial proceedings. This includes "discovery," where one side may request documents, witness lists, and any other information from the other side that it may use in the trial (Kurland 1997:56–71). Pretrial discovery may include interrogatories, which are written lists of questions mailed to a witness on the opposing side, and the opposing side has a set period (for example, thirty days) to provide written answers, signed under oath. Depositions, where witnesses are required to appear at a specified location to answer questions posed by the opposing attorney, are also commonly used in pretrial discovery. Any notes or documentation made by the archaeologist on the case is subject to discovery and may be turned over to the defense at this point. The archaeologist may also be requested to give a deposition or answer an interrogatory.

Before the trial, the judge examines the evidence that each side wishes to present and decides what facts each side will be allowed to present and which witnesses each side will be allowed to call. Evidence that does not meet the rules of evidence, including the chain of custody discussed above, may not be allowed to be introduced into the trial. All evidence needs to be directly related to the case.

There may also be a series of motions and stipulations made by either or both sides. Stipulations are the facts that everyone agrees to at this point. This is where the court may decide that it does not need the archaeological evidence at trial (Kurland 1997:69). If everyone agrees that the deceased is, in fact, dead, and that he or she died of a gunshot wound, then the fact and cause of death will not be discussed in court. The trial will focus on who committed the crime, not whether a crime was committed.

Motions are requests filed by either side that may affect the judge's decisions (Kurland 1997:70). A motion may be filed requesting that certain evidence be allowed or not be allowed and stating why, or requesting a change in venue if there has been too much publicity in the locality about a case. There may even be a motion for a new judge, if one attorney feels that the judge cannot try the case fairly. Attorneys can present motions before the trial and throughout the trial.

Before the trial, a jury will also be selected. A jury consists of twelve citizens with two or more alternates. The only qualifications for jurors are that they must be U.S. citizens, nineteen years of age or older, and physically and mentally capable of serving. The jurors, usually selected randomly from the combined voter registration and driver's license lists, undergo a selection process where either side can strike a juror should it feel the person is prejudiced against its case. During the jury selection process, potential jurors will be questioned by the attorneys in voir dire ("speak the truth") examinations to see if they are fair and unbiased concerning the aspects of the case.

There are professional trial consultants who help lawyers with jury selection. These consultants devise questionnaires that help the lawyers determine whether it is likely the juror will vote for or against their clients. One professional trial consultant feels that about two-thirds of all people will vote for or against a defendant based on their own personal previous experiences with, for example, police, insurance companies, or large corporations. Less than one-third of individuals will vote based solely on the facts of the case (Martin Peterson, FAI, personal communication, 16 September 2006). The goal of the lawyers in jury selection is to find those people inherently prejudiced against their side and strike them from the jury; to find those people inherently prejudiced for their side and get them on the jury; and to fill the remaining spots with people who will listen to the case objectively.

THE TRIAL

In addition to the judge, the jury, the attorneys, and the defendant, there are several other important players in a trial. The clerk of the court takes care of all the court's business, including issuing subpoenas and summonses, and is responsible for court records, collection of fines, and other administrative matters. The court reporter is an employee of the court who transcribes a word-for-word record of all court testimony and proceedings. The bailiff is the court policeman and is responsible for maintaining courtroom order and assisting the jurors. Bailiffs also guard the defendant while he or she is in custody.

The witnesses give evidence to the court about the crime. Generally, there are three types of witnesses: (1) witnesses as to the events concerning the crime; (2) witnesses as to the character of the accused; and (3) expert witnesses who give opinions regarding medical, scientific, or other specialized evidence (Kurland 1997:7). The forensic scientist falls under the category of expert witness.

The trial, by law, consists of a sequence of events in a specific order. Each attorney makes an opening statement, where he or she states a claim and summarizes the evidence in support of the claim. The attorneys outline the evidence that will be presented during the trial and show how they will build their arguments.

In the direct examination, the prosecution presents the evidence against the defendant. In the cross-examination, the defense attorney can present questions about that evidence. The defense attorney then presents any evidence that he or she has and the prosecution (or plaintiff's attorney) can cross-examine the defense evidence. The prosecution can then present rebuttal evidence, which can be cross-examined by the defense attorney. This process frequently takes several weeks.

When the evidence has been presented, cross-examined, and rebutted, the attorneys present their closing arguments in which they argue their cases to the jury. The judge then instructs the jury about the law regarding the case and the jury retires to the jury room to deliberate. The climax of the trial occurs when the jury returns to the courtroom and presents its verdict.

EXPERT WITNESS TESTIMONY

Everyone who works on a forensic site needs to be prepared to testify in court as to what they did and how they did it. Any notes taken about the case can be requested by the defense during the discovery period of the trial. These will be examined by the defense lawyers minutely for inconsistencies and anything that can be used to create doubt that the defendant is tied to events at the grave site. The first important implication of this is that all notes should be solely about the single case. If the archaeologist is using a notebook, rather than forms, then that case should be all that is in that notebook. This will ensure that the lawyer does not obtain information that is irrelevant to the case, but that may be used to make the archaeologist look less than expert. Tearing pages out of a notebook will lead the defense attorneys to suspect that something incriminating was deleted before the material was handed over, so that is also not an option. Use forms on independent sheets of paper or a new notebook for each case.

Archaeologists need to learn the applicable rules for expert testimony in their jurisdiction. In the United States, the expert testimony criteria are decided by the state and fall under two criteria. The 1923 *Frye* criteria for expert testimony are based on Supreme Court decision *Frye v. United States* F 1013 at 1014 (D.C. Cir 1923). The *Frye* criteria allow expert testimony if there is proof the proposed testimony is generally accepted in scientific publications and by prior judicial decisions. The professional is usually accepted as an expert if he or she is generally accepted by his or her peers as an expert and has scientific publications based on the techniques used.

However, in 1993, the United States Supreme Court handed down an opinion in *Daubert v. Merrell Dow Pharmaceuticals, Inc.* (1993) that changed the way that courts look at expert testimony. The *Daubert* ruling has been accepted in many states, replacing the *Frye* criteria. *Daubert* requires judges to decide whether the reasoning or methodology underlying the proposed testimony is valid and can be applied to the facts of the case at hand. This shifts the focus of the legal decision from accepting the credentials of the expert to assessing the type of reasoning used in reaching the determination as given by the expert in testimony.

In the *Daubert* opinion, the court stated, "Ordinarily, a key question to be answered in determining whether a theory or technique is scientific knowledge that will assist the trier of fact will be whether it can be (and has been) tested. Scientific methodology today is based on generating hypotheses and testing them to see if they can be falsified; indeed, this methodology is what distinguishes science from other fields of human inquiry" (United States Supreme Count, *Daubert v. Merrell Dow Pharmaceuticals).*

The opinion then turns to four criteria for evaluating the admissibility of expert testimony:

1. whether the methods on which the testimony is based are centered on a testable hypothesis;
2. the known or potential rate of error associated with the method;
3. whether the method has been subject to peer review; and
4. whether the method is generally accepted in the relevant scientific community.

The *Daubert* criteria place a burden on all involved in forensic work—the burden of a sophisticated level of thinking. Investigations must be framed in scientific method. The forensic archaeologist must understand induction, deduction, and hypothesis testing. The forensic archaeologist is required to have the statistical sophistication to understand error rates and the difference between errors of false positives and false negatives. To use a particular method, the archaeologist must be familiar with the professional literature and know how that literature reflects on the methodology.

The archaeological methods presented in this volume are standard archaeological techniques applied to forensic cases. They are well documented in the literature and are accepted in the discipline. Depending on the jurisdiction, the court may use either the *Frye* criteria or the *Daubert* criteria to evaluate the testimony. The *Frye* criteria center on the methods being "generally accepted," as shown through peer-reviewed publications and acceptance by other experts. The *Daubert* criteria center on the use of the scientific method and an objective measure of the method's accuracy as well as general acceptance. These are criteria that the investigator needs to work with every step of the way. If the evidence is not admissible in court, it is useless.

The archaeologist may have to tell the law enforcement personnel that he or she needs more time, personnel, or equipment to meet professional standards. If such a request is made and denied, this needs to be clearly stated in the archaeologist's notes. In his memoirs, one forensic anthropologist (who will not be named here), describes a case where his team conducted the exhumation of what turned out to be a prehistoric burial site in the bank of a stream, after dark, excavating by the headlights of a car. Does this meet professional standards?

The job of the archaeologist includes conducting his or her work in as efficient a manner as possible. The archaeologist will testify in court as to whether the methods are professional. The defense may hire other archaeologists to evaluate those methods. The bottom line is that the archaeologist needs to feel that he or she can defend the methods used in court, and explain them to a jury of nonprofessionals.

If called on to testify, the archaeologist will undoubtedly receive advice on how to present him- or herself. However, honesty is the basic criterion. The archaeologist should report his or her findings accurately and never go beyond the limits of evidence or experience. The scientist represents the physical evidence and should not get drawn into testifying beyond the physical evidence. Another major criterion for an expert witness is to show respect for the court. This includes dressing appropriately and using proper language. It also includes addressing the evidence to the person or persons with the decision-making authority. In other words, if there is a jury, speak to the jury. If the judge will make the decisions, speak directly to the judge. If the expert witness does his or her best to be honest and respectful, that will show, and the judge and jury will see an honest, competent professional.

Being a successful expert witness does not begin during the trial preparation. It begins the moment the archaeologist receives a call about a case—and opens a new, clean notebook to write notes about that call. It continues as the archaeologist focuses on completing the job competently and using high professional standards throughout the exhumation and report writing. During the trial preparation, the archaeologist may receive advice on how to dress and present him- or herself during trial. But this is icing on the cake, and if the cake is sour, the icing won't save it.

SUMMARY

1. To make the transition to forensic work, an archaeologist needs to understand police protocols, particularly the chain of custody, and the basics of the legal system in which he or she will be working.
2. The goal of most forensic work is to be able to try the guilty person in a court of law. The forensic archaeologist must be familiar with the court system and what is expected of an expert witness.
3. The difference between murder and manslaughter is intent and premeditation. The difference between accidental death and murder and manslaughter is malice. The archaeologist needs to be sensitive to physical evidence that may show intent or malice.

GLOSSARY TERMS

Daubert v. Merrell Dow Pharmaceuticals, Inc.
deduction
discovery
Frye v. United States
hypothesis
indictment
induction
motion
scientific method
stipulation
theory
verification

SUGGESTED READING

Brodsky, Stanley L.
1991 *Testifying in Court: Guidelines and Maxims for the Expert Witness.* American Psychological Association, Washington, D.C.

Kurland, Michael

1997 *How to Try a Murder: The Handbook for Armchair Lawyers.* Macmillan, New York.

An engrossing and easy-to-read guide through the court system.

Osterburg, James W., and Richard H. Ward

2004 *Criminal Investigation: A Method for Reconstructing the Past.* Fourth Edition. Anderson Publishing, Cincinnati, Ohio.

A classic text covering all aspects of police investigation.

2

An Introduction to Archaeology for Forensic Scientists

ARCHAEOLOGISTS AS DETECTIVES

Forensic science is a historical science (Houck and Siegel 2006:53)—the time frame of the events that are reconstructed is simply usually shorter than the time frame of the events with which historians or archaeologists usually work. The forensic sciences have adopted some of the technological aspects of archaeology, such as the use of grids, trowels and square holes, in the recovery of buried remains. However, few forensic scientists have actually excavated an archaeological site, and fewer still have formally studied archaeology as a discipline.

What difference does this make? Archaeological techniques were developed for specific purposes, with specific ideas behind them. While archaeological techniques transferred into the forensic world, they transferred independently of the paradigms behind them. Also, for the most part, only the basic archaeological techniques learned in field school are used in forensic work (Hoshower 1998).

Archaeologists have theories, as well as methods, for reconstructing the past, whether recent or ancient. Precise labels define types of objects found on a site, and there are scholarly discussions on how to efficiently record a physical scene in a relatively short time period. Some of these concepts can beneficially be transferred to the forensic world.

ARCHAEOLOGICAL PARADIGMS

The underlying premises of archaeological work are that human behavior is patterned and that the artifacts left behind on a site reflect behavior. The relationship of objects to each other and their environment (their context) is of paramount importance; it is more important than the objects themselves. This is the reason archaeologists created detailed methods of documenting site excavations through photographs, maps, and notes.

Archaeologists, however, long ago realized that they could not record all attributes at a site. They had to think about the aspects that were important and document the relevant attributes. For instance, at the excavations at Little Bighorn Battlefield, the archaeologists decided that the depth of artifacts, for the most part, was not a relevant attribute. As the engagement on the main battlefield lasted only about sixty to ninety minutes, differing depths of battle-related artifacts reflected factors other than temporal differences (Scott et al. 1989). On other sites, recording the depth of artifacts and features is crucial to the interpretation of human activity.

Getting a body out of the ground should not be the only result of using archaeological techniques on a forensic site. The activities that occurred at the site should also be reconstructed. The archaeologist should be able to determine (independent of witness testimony) perimortem and postmortem activities at the site. This may include whether the location is an execution site, a burial site, or both. If the location is only a burial site, the investigator should be able to determine whether it is a primary burial or whether the remains were moved one or more times. If the location is also an execution site, the archaeologist should be able to reconstruct the relevant activities from the remaining artifacts and features. The archaeologist should also be able to determine whether the burial was affected by nonhuman factors, such as digging by dogs or coyotes or burrowing by mice.

The use of this contextual paradigm is the line between the exhumation of human remains and the excavation of human remains. The *exhumation* of human remains is simply the retrieval of the remains, whether archaeological techniques are used or not. The *excavation* of human remains results in the retrieval of the remains, but also the reconstruction of the human activity at the site and beyond. This brings the investigator beyond the use of trowels and grids, and into scene reconstruction.

ARCHAEOLOGICAL LANGUAGE

If we had no language by means of which to convey our thoughts and store our knowledge, we would be little different from the lower animals.

I would like to add to this, however, that if we had no language we would have no misunderstandings.

—*Kemeny, A Philosopher Looks at Science*

Rivers of ink have flowed, spilled by archaeologists trying to define terms useful to the reconstruction of past activities. Some of these terms have parallels in the forensic world; some do not. Table 2-1 includes a list of terms commonly used in archaeology that can usefully be included in forensic work.

The *crime scene* is roughly analogous to the *site*. In both worlds, the determination of site, or crime scene, boundaries depends on the spatial distribution of the remaining artifacts, or evidence. In archaeology, sites may be broken into *activity areas*, spatially discrete areas where the material remains show that specific activities were carried out.

After the sites have been created and before they are examined (or maybe even discovered), they are subject to a series of *formation processes*—those processes affecting the way in which archaeological material comes to be buried or distributed. This might include the activities of humans or animals, as well as natural or environmental phenomena or events. The study of the processes that affect material between deposition and documentation is called *taphonomy*. The concept of taphonomy has already made a successful transition into the forensic world, with emphasis in studies on the disposition of human remains (Haglund and Sorg 1997; 2002).

The concept of the artifact, analogous to the concept of evidence, is broken into subcategories by archaeologists. *Artifacts* are portable objects that are made, used, or modified by humans (figure 2-1). A *feature* is a non-portable result of human activity. Graves are features—they cannot be picked up and moved in the same sense that a cartridge case or a bullet can be moved. *Ecofacts* are non-artifactual organic and environmental remains that have cultural relevance. Ecofacts may include insects on a body or displaced soil. Each of these data sets has its own parameters, and is collected and recorded in a different way. Artifacts can be collected and studied in the lab. Features need to be recorded on-site; they cannot be collected and taken back to the laboratory. Frequently, their very investigation destroys them. When a grave is excavated, for example, it is destroyed. Tool marks or other attributes need to be documented as the grave is excavated. To the

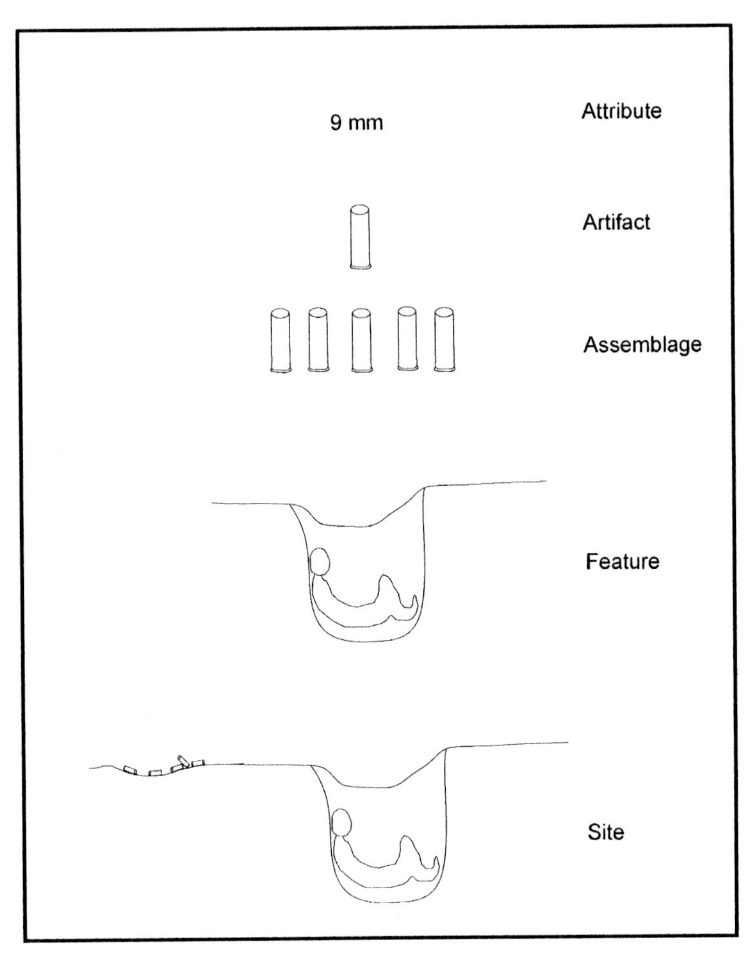

FIGURE 2-1
Relationship of an attribute to an artifact to an assemblage and their position on a site.

unsophisticated, ecofacts may not even register as material that can yield information. Methods of collection and study vary depending on the ecofact in question.

An *assemblage* is a group of artifacts which cluster together at the same time and place. A given assemblage of artifacts is frequently associated with a certain activity. For instance, an assemblage consisting of rags, an empty gas can, and a lighter could be associated with arson. Artifacts may be *associated* with features, ecofacts, or even characteristics of the landscape. Both the con-

Table 2-1. Archaeological vocabulary useful in forensics

Archaeological term	*Forensic equivalent*	*Definition*
absolute date		The determination of age with reference to a specific time scale, such as the calendar. For example, an event occurred at 5 p.m. 24 April 1989.
activity area	scene	An area within a larger site where a specific activity occurred.
artifact	evidence	Any portable object made, used, or modified by humans.
assemblage	evidence	A group of artifacts which cluster together at the same time and place.
association		The co-occurence of an artifact with other material.
attribute		A minimal characteristic of an artifact that cannot be further divided. An important attribute of a cartridge case is the caliber.
cognitive map		An interpretive framework of the world that exists in the mind of the person/people who created the site and affects actions and decisions.
context		The interrelated conditions in which an artifact occurs, for example, its association with its matrix, other artifacts, features, and the environment.
diachronic		Relating to phenomena as they change over time.
ecofacts	evidence	Non-artifactual organic and environmental remains that have cultural relevance.
feature		A non-portable artifact; something made or used by people that cannot be moved. A grave is a feature.
formation process		A process that affected the way in which archaeological material came to be buried or distributed. This might include the activities of humans or animals, as well as natural or environmental phenomena or events.
matrix		The physical material in which artifacts are embedded or supported.
relative dating		Determining a chronological framework without reference to a fixed time scale, but in a sequence. In other words, Action A happened before Action C, but after Action D.
site	crime scene	A distinct spatial clustering of a residue of human activity.
stratification		The physical placement of layers of material, such that the oldest is at the bottom and the youngest at the top.
synchronic		Phenomena occurring at a single point in time.
taphonomy	forensic taphonomy	The study of processes which affect organic material, such as corpses or bones, after death.

cepts of assemblage and association emphasize that the *context* of the artifact is more important than the artifact itself.

Artifacts, features, and ecofacts can have multiple *attributes;* an attribute is a characteristic of an artifact or feature that cannot be further divided. In fact, usually there are too many attributes on any given object to record or study. Attributes of a cartridge case may include the type of metal it is made from, the length, the circumference, the residue left on the inside, as well as markings on the case head. Most of these attributes are irrelevant and investigators are constantly making decisions on which attributes are worth notice. On a cartridge case, of all the possible attributes to record, usually the caliber and the firing-pin mark are the most commonly noted. This constant parsing of information causes much angst among archaeologists, as we can never be absolutely sure of which pieces of information will be relevant. Investigators frequently have a better perspective for parsing this information and can be more decisive.

Archaeologists have also developed concepts that deal with time and dating. A major distinction is between absolute and relative dating. An *absolute date* is tied into a specific time scale, usually the clock and the calendar. For instance, 4:30 p.m. on 1 March 2002 is an absolute date. A *relative date* is when the time is determined relative to something other than a specific time scale, usually another event. For instance, if there are two bullet holes in a piece of glass, then the fracture pattern can be used to determine which of the holes occurred first and which was second, yielding a relative date for each shot. However, without further information, the absolute time of when either shot occurred cannot be known, nor can the amount of time between shots. The distinction in types of data can have important ramifications when one is trying to reconstruct events. Relative times and dates usually need to be empirically tied to an absolute date to be useful in reconstructing events.

Events in time can also be examined diachronically or synchronically. *Diachronic* refers to examining phenomena through time, usually examining what happened with a single place or person through a defined time period. Constructing a timeline of what person X was doing for the days between 14 March and 17 March 2002 is a diachronic analysis. *Synchronic* refers to examining phenomena at a single point in time. Reconstructing what everyone in a group was doing at 4:30 p.m. on 14 March is a synchronic analysis.

Language gives us power to think more clearly about concepts. In reconstructing a time line of events around a death investigation, being able to differentiate, and give a name to, relative versus absolute dates may help the investigator differentiate incompatible data. Similarly, being able to name and define the difference between a synchronic look at events and a diachronic overview gives us the control to better differentiate between the two.

A DEATH IN DEALER PARK: USING ARCHAEOLOGICAL CONCEPTS

Jason Wunder had not been seen for three days by the time his mother and stepfather reported him missing. He frequently slept at friends' houses, and they assumed that he had done so the last couple of nights. However, after they got a call from one of Jason's teachers, they began to realize that it had been a while since they had seen him.

The parents gave investigators the names of some of his friends, but had no idea where he might be. His clothes, what money he had, and his belongings (as far as his parents recognized them) were still in his room. There was also a small bag of methamphetamine in his room.

The questioning of Jason's friends quickly brought the breakdown of a nervous sixteen-year-old, Trevor Read. Trevor was clearly stressed and with merely the appearance of the police, he began to babble. Trevor said that for his (Trevor's) birthday, Jason had offered to buy him some meth and introduce him to his dealer. Trevor had never bought drugs before and was nervous about the prospect. When they met at a picnic table at dusk in an isolated corner of a little-used state park, he brought his father's handgun with him.

The dealer, Ty, seemed a likable sort. In honor of Trevor's birthday, he brought out a bottle of whisky and some marijuana. After a little of both, Trevor started laughing about how nervous he had been, and even brought out the gun to show the others and make them laugh. Ty took the gun, stood a little way from the table, pointed the gun at Jason and said to empty his pockets. At first, Trevor thought Ty was joking, but then he got nervous again and reached for the gun to get it back. Ty resisted and the gun went off. A semiautomatic, it went off multiple times very quickly. At the end, Jason was lying on the ground bleeding from the head and abdomen. Both Ty and Trevor were sure Jason was dead.

Trevor's first instinct was to run, but Ty held him back. The boys took the cars down the road to a dirt cutoff and parked them out of sight. They waited about fifteen minutes to see if anyone would investigate the gunshots. When no one appeared, they took a folding shovel from Trevor's trunk and walked back to the picnic table where Jason lay on the ground. With one person acting as a lookout, they dug a hole in a weedy area next to the picnic bench and put Jason in it. Ty took Jason's wallet from his pocket. He told Trevor it was to hide Jason's identity if the body was found, but Trevor thought he wanted the money Jason had brought to buy the meth.

The officers took Trevor to Dealer Park and he showed them a disturbed area in the ground where he said the body was. The scene map is shown in figure 2-2. First, note that in making the map, the officer has already sorted the data into relevant and irrelevant categories. The first cut was made when the officers made the scene perimeter. In doing this they decided that the material inside the perimeter was relevant to their case and the material outside was not. This is defensible and is based on previous experience and department protocols, but the setting of a scene perimeter is the beginning of the constant sorting of information that happens continually while a scene is processed.

In making the map, the officer sorted other information. For instance, the distinction between mowed and unmowed grass (the area near the lilacs was left unmowed) was not put on the map, as the officer did not consider it relevant to the case. In archaeological terms, the grave pit itself and the picnic table (bolted to the ground) are features, or man-made objects that cannot be moved from the site. This class of evidence has to be documented in place. The hedge of lilacs is an ecofact; it is a natural object with cultural relevance. The hedge is also a type of feature, since it cannot easily be moved. Its relevance here is that it provides a screen, isolating this part of the park from other areas. Artifacts include the trash can, cartridge cases, jacket, and pistol.

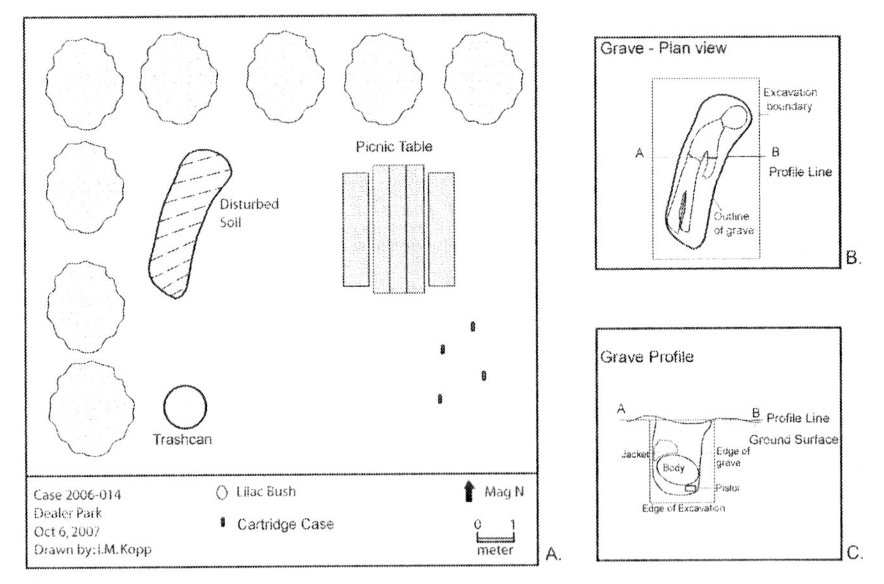

FIGURE 2-2
Scene map from Dealer Park.

All are movable, man-made objects. This class of evidence can be removed and analyzed in a lab.

Both the grave pit and the trash can provide evidence for the sequence of events. In the grave pit, the grave had to be dug before any material was placed into the grave. Then, stratification of material (see figure 2-2c) allows the officers to determine that what is at the bottom of the pit was probably placed there first, and what is at the top was placed last. So the sequence of events is:

1. The pit was dug.
2. The pistol was placed/thrown into the pit.
3. The body was placed in the pit.
4. The jacket was placed in the pit.
5. The grave was refilled.

This is a relative sequence of events, providing relative dates or times for each occurrence. There is nothing in this sequence itself to tie these events to the calendar or the clock. The testimony of a witness or other outside evidence will be needed to provide an absolute date for these events. Yet, the sequence, or relative dates, for these events can be useful in reconstructing the events at the scene.

Each cartridge case is an artifact. The cases can be picked up and analyzed in the lab. Each has a series of attributes, or minimal characteristics, which include material type, maker, and caliber. The entire group of cartridge cases is an assemblage, or a group of artifacts that occur together at the same time and place. It is the analysis of the assemblage, or comparing the attributes of each individual artifact, that will tell us information about the assemblage. In this case, the relevant information that will come from the assemblage will be whether more than one gun was used, and if there was more than one gun, what calibers they were.

The trash can also included an assemblage, and it too was stratified from top to bottom. The material from top to bottom included:

1. Two empty Budweiser aluminum cans
2. A cardboard Budweiser twelve-pack package
3. A plastic baggie containing dog feces

4. An empty Jim Beam bottle
5. A newspaper dated 15 March 2002
6. A crumpled, empty Marlboro box

As with the grave pit, this gives a relative sequence of events. We can suggest that the earliest user of the area represented in the trash can was a Marlboro smoker who reached the end of his or her pack here. On 15 March 2002, someone may have read and later discarded a paper here. The next users drank whisky nearby, after which a dog walker kindly picked up after his or her dog and deposited the remains in the trash. The last users of the area represented in the trash can were beer drinkers who finished the last of their twelve pack, possibly at the picnic table.

Looking at the material in the trash can in another light, it represents a diachronic view of events at this location. In other words, we can use the assemblage to look at changes in the use of the area over time and reconstruct activities before and after the event of interest.

There is an important difference between this sequence of events and the one in the grave pit. That is that the newspaper provides an absolute date, tying these events to the calendar. It is likely that the Marlboro box was deposited on or before 15 March. Since Trevor said that the boys drank from a bottle of whisky, it would be worth collecting the Jim Beam bottle to see if fingerprints or DNA evidence could confirm the witness statement. Finally, if the Jim Beam bottle is the one used by the boys, the material from the trash can strongly suggests use of the area after Jason's death. This use could potentially have changed the scene from the time of deposition to the time of recording. In archaeology, those changes are called the taphonomy of the site—what happens to the material between deposition and analysis.

Does the use of archaeological terms and concepts make a difference in the way the site is processed? No. But the thinking involved makes for a different understanding of why different material is processed in the way it is (as a single artifact, as a feature, or as part of an assemblage). Archaeological techniques were useful in the exhumation of the buried remains, and archaeologists have extensively studied site taphonomy—how cultural and natural events change sites, artifacts, and features. Most of all, looking at events using multiple paradigms (both criminalistic and archaeological) is like looking at different facets of diamonds: the same object is seen in different colors.

SUMMARY

1. Archaeological paradigms, as well as archaeological techniques, are useful in forensic work, particularly the contextual paradigm. This is the idea that there is more information in the context of any material object than in solely the object itself. The context may include other artifacts, features, and the natural environment.
2. Archaeologists have developed a specialized vocabulary to help them communicate about their findings of physical evidence. This vocabulary gives them the power to think more clearly about concepts.

GLOSSARY TERMS

absolute date
activity area
artifact
assemblage
association
attribute
cognitive map
context
diachronic
ecofacts
feature
formation process
matrix
paradigm
relative dating
site
stratification
synchronic
taphonomy

SUGGESTED READING

Crist, Thomas A. J.

2001 Bad to the Bone?: Historical Archaeologists in the Practice of Forensic Science. In Archaeologists as Forensic Investigators: Defining the Role, M.

Connor and D. D. Scott, editors, special issue, *Historical Archaeology* 35 (1): 39–56.

An overview of the history of the use of anthropology in forensic investigations and what the archaeologist brings to the investigation.

Stover, Eric, and Molly Ryan

2001 Breaking Bread with the Dead. In Archaeologists as Forensic Investigators: Defining the Role, M. Connor and D. D. Scott, editors, special issue, *Historical Archaeology* 35 (1): 7–25.

A history of archaeology in human rights and humanitarian forensic investigations.

3

Before Fieldwork

PROJECT PREPARATION

For many projects, there is little time to actually plan the exhumation. But if the team is prepared ahead of time, then it does not take much time to gather the equipment, personnel, and forms, and get to the site. Long before it is needed, equipment can be bought. Experts can be found who are willing to work at a scene when it would be useful. Are there entomologists at the local university who could be helpful? Where is the nearest anthropologist? Where is the nearest anthropologist who is a diplomate of the American Board of Forensic Anthropology (these individuals are the top in their field)? Where is the nearest professional forensic archaeologist? Periodic cross training with law enforcement and archaeologists forges a respect of each discipline for the other that cannot be gained otherwise.

Every case will be different. But there are some general stages of planning that are needed for every project (table 3-1). The first question is under whose jurisdiction the remains lie. In other words, who is in charge of the project overall? This is complicated by the fact that the remains may be recent, historic, or prehistoric. If there is the possibility that the remains are historic or prehistoric, then the appropriate authorities for those burials need to be contacted. Until shown to be otherwise, the remains need to be treated as recent and as a suspicious death.

A general assessment of the excavation is necessary. The goals of this assessment are to gain enough information to estimate the amount of time

Table 3-1. General project implementation outline

Define the Jurisdiction		
	Who is in charge of the project?	
	If the remains are shown to be historic or prehistoric, then who has jurisdiction?	
Project Assessment		
	Develop work plan, list of necessary personnel, equipment	
	Necessary information:	
		How many potential graves are there?
		How securely identified are the locations?
		How many people are suspected in each grave?
		Are the deceased likely to be skeletal, fleshed, or a combination?
		Where are the morgue facilities and how will the bodies be transported?
		Are there existing protocols and what are they?
Exhumations		
	Goals: Reconstruct activities at the scene, recover all pertinent evidence	
	Pre-Field Planning	List of personnel
		Forms: Excavation, photo, evidence collection logs
		Determine excavation, photo, and evidence protocols
		List equipment needed
		Determine reporting requirements and who is responsible
	Fieldwork	
	Post-Field	Clean equipment; repair and replace as necessary
		Process film and check against photo logs
		Complete final maps
		Evidence: stabilize, process, and check against logs
		Complete reports
Completion of Project		
	Organize notes and files	
	Turn in copies to project head, if requested	

necessary for the project, what equipment is necessary, what specialists may be necessary, and what logistical challenges may need to be met. Necessary information includes how many graves are involved, how many individual cases are involved, how securely identified the grave locations are, the probable condition of the remains, what field facilities are available, and the existing protocols. It may be necessary to contact utility companies before beginning an exhumation to determine if the team might hit underground electric, water, or sewage lines.

After this information is gathered, more detailed planning can start. Good people are the single most important resource. A list of personnel, including archaeologists, anthropologists, photographers, surveyors, evidence technicians, entomologists, investigators, and even a palynologist, can be developed well ahead of an actual exhumation. Developing a list ahead of time of people who are qualified and ready to assist will allow the team to contact the personnel quickly when they are needed. In large projects, personnel, travel, housing, and per diem may be the major portion of the budget.

A detailed list of equipment is also necessary. Tables 3-2 and 3-3 outline basic equipment useful for most excavations. These lists can be modified for different projects, and do not cover all the possibilities. For instance, work at a cave site may require climbing harnesses, pulleys, and rope in addition to the equipment listed. If personnel are committed to the project at this point, each specialist should review the equipment lists in his or her own specialty, to ensure that the materials he or she needs will be present.

One of the most important aspects of pre-field preparation is the discussion of protocols. These may be as formal or informal as the project demands, but they ensure that everyone on the project follows the same procedure.

When the remains are out of the ground and in the morgue, the field portion of the project is still not complete. Concerns include processing photographs, creating the maps, cleaning and repairing the field equipment, and writing the report. Proper maintenance of the field equipment will ensure that it is likely to be usable again, and this will save the next project a significant amount of funds. Also, without proper cleaning of the equipment,

Table 3-2. Items for individual tool kits

trowel, 4″ pointing
trowel, 6″ square
compass
line level
flagging tape
folding rule
3 m lockable tape measure
archaeological/geological pick
permanent markers
pencils with erasers
6″ ruler or straightedge
4″ and 6″ plastic ziplock bags
plastic vials with caps
rubber kitchen gloves
surgical rubber gloves
leather work gloves
2″ paintbrush
chopsticks or bamboo sticks
notebook
root clippers
sunscreen
insect repellant
hand sanitizer

Table 3-3. Team equipment

General Excavation Equipment
shovels
picks
large root clipper
saw
6″ nails
whisk brooms
screens
bastard file
plastic tarps
body bags
paper bags
buckets
permanent markers
plastic ziplock evidence bags
pin flags
flagging tape
surgical gloves
protective clothing
metal detector and batteries
tile probe
plastic numbers to number bodies or evidence
crime scene tape
evidence log
Photographic Equipment
35mm or digital camera with macro lens
camcorder
camera board
scales for photographs
video camera
film for cameras
batteries for cameras
photographic log books for still and video photography
Minimal Mapping Equipment
two 30 m tapes
compass
graph paper
6″ nails with flagging tape attached

there is a possibility of contamination of soils and other evidence between scenes. The maps from the project need to be completed and finalized. Any evidence not yet in a laboratory needs to be stabilized and processed so that when the investigators are ready to look at it, the material has not deteriorated beyond use.

After the final report is written, the disposition of the original notes and photographs needs to be decided. All notes from the project should be organized, as should photographs and copies of the maps. All computer files should be backed up and the original disks initialed, dated, and placed with the appropriate notes. Both should be provided to the investigating law enforcement agency as evidence. All material may be requested under discovery, and the more organized the documentation, the more professional it will look. Also, it will be easier to use the material to refresh the excavator's memory should the excavator need to testify.

If experts are used in the exhumation, such as forensic archaeologists, anthropologists, entomologists or palynologists, then each expert should have a chance to examine the other reports to cross-check the results.

PERSONNEL

The team needs personnel with specific skills, and these people need to be assigned duties in addition to excavation. Crime scene technicians involved in the excavation may complete some of these duties, and if the archaeologist is not a regular member of the investigative team, then the scene technicians and archaeologist(s) need to have a frank discussion on how these duties will be handled. These duties include photographing, mapping the excavation, and collecting, logging, and securing any evidence collected by the team. The people covering these duties should have proven skills for completing these assignments.

In addition, someone should be stationed at the entrance to the scene to log the entry and exit of every person who comes in or out and the time of the person's entry or exit. If possible, this individual should be not be part of the archaeological team, but a uniformed police person, with the authority to refuse entrance to individuals who are not working on the exhumation. If for some reason there is not a uniformed police person present, someone else needs to be assigned that duty. One team member also needs to be responsible for keeping the notes on the excavation, including times of starting and stopping and the time of major finds.

Each project will have a lead investigator, a lead archaeologist, and a lead pathologist or forensic anthropologist. The archaeologist, in addition to having forensic experience, should have credentials equivalent to those set out in the Register of Professional Archaeologists (www.rpanet.org). The final chapter discusses the credentials of archaeologists for forensic work in more detail.

EQUIPMENT

The equipment can be divided into two groups. The first is an individual dig kit (table 3-2). A convenient way to carry the equipment is in a small canvas tool bag, surplus ammunition box, or commercial tool or fishing tackle box. A pair of cotton overalls that can be slipped over street clothes is also handy.

Gloves are both a personal and professional choice. Many professionals do not wear any gloves working with skeletal material, as the gloves make it harder to feel bone when digging. In some cases, leather work gloves are appropriate as they offer protection against thorns, stickers, poison ivy, and blisters. If the remains are fleshed, the heavy excavation work can be done in a pair of rubber kitchen gloves and the fine work in a pair of rubber surgical gloves. The light rubber surgical gloves will tear, so wearing two pairs is practical. A small container of antibacterial hand sanitizer and some wet towels are useful for cleaning hands.

Boots or shoes are another important item. Depending on the hike into the site, the type of soil, and the size of the excavation it may be appropriate to use light hiking boots, sneakers, or rubber boots. If the remains are fleshed, or partially decomposed, then rubber boots are best as they can be hosed off and reused. The leather in sneakers or hiking boots will absorb the smell of the decomposing tissue and the smell will be difficult to remove. Fabric hiking boots or sneakers that can be thrown in the washing machine are good choices even for skeletal remains. However, another consideration is the tread of the shoe. An excavator should not wear shoes that will tear up the ground or leave a deep imprint. A smooth-soled work boot is ideal for many excavations.

If working with decomposing remains, then the excavator may wish to remove personal jewelry and other items. Leather and plastic will pick up the smell of decomposing tissue. A watch is almost always essential, and a good choice for a watch band is a cheap plastic band that can be disposed of easily, or a cloth watchband that can be washed.

The use of a biohazard suit depends on the grave. Many brands will tear if they get wet, as when the excavator is working outside in the rain or in damp soil. Sometimes, the suit will rip when the excavator is physically active. The suits are a good choice, though, when working on decomposed remains as removing the suit is the easiest way to remove most of the smell before entering a vehicle to leave the site. If the site area is damp, or the remains are truly gooey, wearing two layers of biohazard suits is an option. That way, if the exterior one tears, the second provides additional protection. A common choice among excavators is flexible exercise clothing with coveralls added on during the excavation. If necessary, a biohazard suit can be put over the exercise clothes and coveralls when working on decomposing remains.

The second group of equipment that should be ready before the excavation is the equipment for the team (table 3-3). This includes the large excavation gear, the documentation equipment, and the mapping gear.

The best shovels for the skim-shoveling method described below are flat (e.g., irrigation shovels), not rounded, and long handled. Shovels can be bought with a flat edge, so there should be no need to take a round or pointed shovel and cut the point off. Spades can also be bought with a flat or rounded edge, but spades tend to be narrower than shovels. Either spades or shovels can be bought with a long handle or a "D" handle, which is shorter and has a metal grip on the end. The long handle is better for maintaining control when skim-shoveling. In many places outside the United States, the handles are bought separately from the heads and the two are put together by the user. If this is the case, the heads need to be nailed securely on the handle to keep them from coming loose.

Skim-shoveling is a technique where the shovel is used to scrape only a few centimeters of soil off at a time, over a relatively wide area. It allows the person shoveling to see horizontal differences in soil as they work. In other words, if a grave pit outline shows up in the soil, skimming the soil with a shovel, rather than digging a hole, allows the investigator to see the soil difference clearly early in the excavation. Skimming the soil can be done with other implements as well. If using laborers, it is best to allow the laborers to use whatever implement they are familiar with to do the job (Bleed 2000). On a mission I was on in Sri Lanka, the Sri Lankan team used an implement called a *mamyte*, which looked like a large hoe. Using this, they were able to keep the soil even over a large area and exposed the grave pit perfectly (see implement used in figure 5-6).

The edge of the shovel should be sharpened on the front side with a power bench grinder (figure 3-1). Trowels can also have their edges sharpened with a grinder. Only the front side should be sharpened, creating a bevel on the edge that is flat on the back and slanted toward the tip on the front. The sharp edges are maintained in the field using a bastard file. The file should be used on the front of the implement only, so as not to create a bevel on the back, and should

FIGURE 3-1
Sharpening a shovel. Sharpen only the front of the implement; do not grind both the front and the back. This will result in a bevel on the front end of the shovel that is sharp and will slice through roots and clay rather than tear. A. Use a power grinder to put the initial edge on the implement. B. Keep the edges sharp in the field using a bastard file. The same method can be used with the working edges of a trowel.

only be run toward the edge, never back and forth; running the file from the edge of the implement toward the handle will dull the edge.

A sharp edge allows the shovel or the trowel to cut smoothly through soil and small roots without pulling and potentially dislodging subsurface material. Root clippers should be used to clip roots off at the ground surface, again so that roots don't pull when caught with the trowel. Dull instruments smear soil colors, pull on roots, and dislodge evidence.

A chaining pin (survey arrow) is a good choice to use to lay out the corners of the grid. It can often be pushed into the ground with the hand, and if something other than rock or soil is encountered, the person putting in the pin can feel it and investigate. On archaeological sites, wooden stakes or twelve-inch lengths of rebar are often used to mark the corners of the excavation. On forensic sites, these are often poor choices, as one can never be sure that evidence is not directly below the stake.

Screens are another important piece of equipment. Sifting through the dirt in a methodical manner allows the investigator to recover materials that might otherwise be overlooked. There are two main types of screening techniques: wet screening and dry screening. Wet screening uses water to carry the soil through the screen. A dry screen consists of a wooden box with an open top and wire mesh in the bottom. A quarter-inch mesh will catch most adult bones, bullets, and other evidence. If the investigator expects shot, children's bones, or other small items, the screen size can be adjusted accordingly. In fact, many archaeologists always screen a sample of the excavation with a very fine screen to ensure that they see at least a sample of items that may be missed with a coarser screen.

There are many types of screens. Two-legged screens, where the legs are placed at one end of the screen, and the screen is shaken by the person holding the other end of the screen box, are the most common (figure 3-2). In other types, the screen box is suspended from tripods or trees, where it can be shaken without the shaker ever having to support the weight. The screen box

FIGURE 3-2
Using a two-legged shaker screen. When the screen is shaken, the particles smaller than the mesh size fall through; the larger materials remain to be hand-sorted. The tarp below the screen is useful in separating the soil for backfill or to remove soil contaminated with decomposition fluids.

can also be simply placed on sawhorses and the dirt pushed through. Wheels can be placed on the screen box, and then the screen placed on a metal frame and shaken by wheeling it back and forth.

Wet screening is done by pouring water into the screen, to help break up the dirt and push it through. If there is a spigot nearby, this can be done using a hose. Otherwise, a small pump can be used to pump water out of a nearby creek or pond. If a water truck is available, a hose can be run from the truck to the screen area. The screen boxes are usually fixed on sawhorses or something to hold them in place and above the ground. In water screening, the investigator has to ensure that the water pressure applied to the screen is light enough that fragile bone will not be compromised. A second consideration is where the runoff water will go. Frequently, a drain will need to be dug from the screen area away from the work area (preferably downhill).

Heavy machinery, such as backhoes or front-end loaders, can move dirt quickly but their use must be properly monitored. Some machines come with a backhoe (the bucket used to scoop soil) on one end and a front-end loader (a wide metal bucket used to scrape and catch the soil) on the other. Both pieces of equipment come in varying sizes and the smallest possible one to do the job is the best. Both the backhoe bucket and the front-end loader's wider bucket also frequently come with large metal teeth—and these teeth are not appropriate for forensic work. If the machine finds the body before the investigator spots the soil changes that signal disturbed soil, the teeth can do a lot of damage to the evidence and the remains. So it is absolutely necessary to request a machine that does not have teeth on the bucket (called a "finishing" bucket).

OUTDOOR SAFETY

Exhumation projects often include people not accustomed to spending an eight-hour, or longer, day outside. Many searches include volunteers who may not be used to hours of physical activity. It's just good sense to be prepared for both the large and small injuries that may occur.

To deal with a major injury, all teams doing outdoor searches and excavations should have a well-equipped first aid kit, most of the team should have current first-aid and CPR training, and, whenever possible, they should have communication (cellular or satellite telephone or radio) and a plan to initiate a medical evacuation. These plans will differ depending on where the team is working, but the important thing is to talk about what to do if someone does get hurt and make sure everyone on the team knows (1) who on the team is qualified to deal with a medical emergency; (2) where the communication equipment is and how to use it; and (3) the location of the nearest emergency medical facility.

Many people have allergies that can be life threatening if they are not treated immediately (for example, severe allergic reactions to beestings or peanut oil). Such people should have with them medication (frequently a prescription kit) to counteract the allergy. They need to inform the team leader of the allergy and where they keep their medication. If they do not have their medication with them, they should not be allowed in the field.

Most health problems in the field are not immediately dangerous, but do detract from productivity. Dehydration is a common problem. People need to be provided and drink plenty of liquids. Blisters are another common problem, and one that can keep people from working to their full capacity if left untreated. A bandage or moleskin should be applied as soon as a blister appears. Likewise, small cuts should be cleaned and covered while working outdoors.

Outdoor plants that can cause problems for many people include poison ivy, poison oak, and poison sumac. Again, a patch of poison ivy is not a life-threatening illness, but it will keep people from working to their full capacity. Also, during exhumations people will encounter, and trowel through, the roots of these plants, which have a greater concentration of the allergen than the leaves. People who are allergic to these plants will tend to get an elevated allergic reaction if they encounter the roots when excavating or screening. The use of antihistamines and cortisone cream can help lessen the reaction.

The excavation site should be kept clean throughout the work. Tools should not be left where people can trip over them. Shovels and rakes should be turned working side down, so that if people step on them, the handle does not fly up and hit them. Small tools, such as trowels, measuring tapes, and picks, which are not being used, should be placed in a tool bag, to protect both the tools and the workers. Debris, such as used plastic gloves, should be placed in a designated disposal bag.

All injuries beyond a minor cut or bruise should be documented on official paperwork for the employer. Injuries that may appear minor in the field (for instance, a twisted knee) can later require extensive medical care or surgery (the twisted knee could mean a torn ligament). The documentation demonstrates to the insurance companies or workers' compensation that the injury occurred on work time as opposed to personal time. Poor documentation of the injury can be used to deny payment for work injuries. Therefore, it is well worth taking a few minutes to document an injury in a notebook or form.

PHYSICAL HEALTH CONCERNS

Archaeologists should be accustomed to many of the health concerns that an outdoor environment presents. Plants that cause allergic reactions, such as poison ivy or poison sumac, are probably already known to most archaeologists. Learning to avoid sunburn and dehydration and dressing for working in cold and wet weather are also part of learning field archaeology.

Working with nonskeletal remains, however, is new for most archaeologists. A decaying body is a high bacterial environment, and any open sores or cuts exposed to this environment are likely to become infected. Gloves and frequent hand washing are basic preventative measures to keeping infections away.

The chance of catching a virus from human remains varies with the state of the remains. A study in the Maryland State Medical Examiner's Office concludes that slightly over 32 percent of 414 bodies to be autopsied tested positive for viral infection, including hepatitis B, hepatitis C, and human immunodeficiency virus (HIV) (Li et al. 1993). Other diseases, such as tuberculosis and valley fever, survive as spores in the soil and can affect an excavator's lungs. Many of the dust masks available at hardware stores are inadequate protection. Tuberculosis bacteria are uncommonly small and only respirators with high-efficiency, particulate air (HEPA) filters will provide significant protection (Crist 2001:49).

All forensic scientists should be up-to-date on their vaccinations, understand how these diseases are transmitted, and be familiar with health regulations (Galloway and Snodgrass 1998).

DEALING WITH DEATH AND STRESS

The largest difference healthwise in moving into forensic work from traditional archaeology can be in the area of emotional health. Becoming a forensic archaeologist means dealing on a regular basis with violent death. Cases located near where we live can be troubling as they pierce the bubble of safety we have around our homes, reminding us that our own towns include killers. Cases involving abused or murdered children can be especially upsetting, especially if the archaeologist has children of about the same age.

Signs of being overly stressed by an event may include difficulty focusing on other aspects of life, being panicked or exhausted by feelings of fear or sadness, or extreme avoidance of dealing with or talking about the event. Character changes, where normally patient people are quick-tempered or normally sweet-tempered people make cutting remarks, can also indicate that a person is not dealing well with an event. A lack of enjoyment in the small things that normally bring pleasure—eating chocolate, reading, watching football, playing golf—can also indicate a need for a psychological realignment.

Most people can deal with trauma without outside help. If they are able to look back and understand what happened, if they are in a supportive environment where they can talk about what happened and have their feelings validated, people are usually able to cope. They need to work out an understanding of the event, and that may include a redefinition of their personal values, which may be the most difficult part of the process.

People can work in jobs where they repeatedly encounter traumatic experiences, but it helps if they generally attend to their personal and professional welfare. Physically, it helps to ensure that people get enough sleep and exercise and proper nutrition. Socially, people need support systems—friends they can talk with—and they need to care about the cause they work for. Psychologically, a balanced life, with forms of relaxation, forms of creative expression, and a sense of humor, are important.

People who regularly encounter stressful situations in their professional worlds need to set a balance between their personal and professional lives. They need to set professional boundaries and limits to their work. Being a professional forensic specialist means being committed to keeping yourself healthy enough, physically and mentally, to do your work well.

SUMMARY

1. A successful excavation starts long before a body is found. Protocols for buried bodies are established, personnel are trained, qualified experts are located, and equipment is bought.
2. Equipment should be bought before the excavation and personnel trained in its use.
3. Safety is not only a matter of planning for medical emergencies, but taking care of the small health problems immediately.

4

Maps and Site Layout

A map is a graphic representation of a portion of the earth's surface (Department of the Army 1993:2-1). Maps are basic to all archaeological and crime scene investigations. Investigators are usually trained in making sketch maps and experienced in indoor scenes. The outdoor scene presents several challenges. One is locating the scene in relation to the real world. This may mean using latitude and longitude or Universal Transverse Mercator (UTM) grid coordinates to specify the location of the area. Second, the investigator must create a scene map showing the location of the data that is relevant to the investigation.

REFERENCE SYSTEMS

Communicating to other people the location of the scene is extremely important. In rural areas it is sometimes difficult to tie the map into the real world. The map reader should be able to get to the scene and relocate the area exactly. In the United States, the common ways of doing this are through an address, through the legal description, through latitude and longitude, or through a reference to the UTM coordinate system. Of these, the UTM system is used worldwide.

Addresses

If the scene is within city or county boundaries and located on a developed street, it is likely that it has a street address. Frequently the county surveyor is responsible for assigning addresses to a location and is the person to contact for the proper address if it is not posted on the property.

Latitude and Longitude

The latitude and longitude system was used for centuries for navigation on both land and sea. For the purpose of the system, the poles of rotation of the earth are considered fixed, identifiable points. Arcs of circles (meridians) are drawn from pole to pole (figure 4-1). These are lines of longitude and run north and south. The meridian passing through Greenwich, England, is the first, or prime, meridian. Longitude is measured in degrees of arc, to 180 degrees east or west of the prime meridian. Each degree is divided into 60 minutes (′), which are each divided into 60 seconds (″). The direction east or west (E or W) must always be given.

A second set of lines running at right angles to the lines of longitude are the lines of latitude. A line running around the equator marks the zero degree of latitude. Starting with 0° at the equator, the extremities are the north pole at 90° north and the south pole at 90° south. Latitude can have the same numerical value north or south of the equator, so the direction N or S must always be given. These degrees are also divided into minutes and seconds.

Geographic coordinates are expressed in angles, degrees, and minutes. In this system, a location designation would look like 40°37′30″ North latitude and 96°37′30″ West longitude. This location is in southeast Nebraska. On a

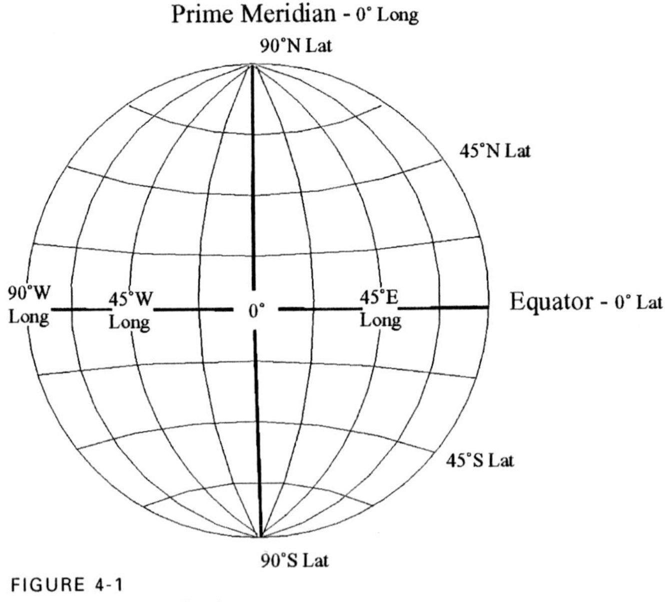

FIGURE 4-1
Latitude and longitude.

United States Geological Survey (USGS) topographic map, the degrees and minutes are written in the corner of the map (figure 4-2). Further along the sides of the map are designations abbreviated to the minutes and seconds.

Township and Range (Legal Description)

The U.S. system of public lands survey began in 1784, based on a system then in use in Europe and Great Britain (Brinker 1969). This is the system of land description currently used legally in the United States to describe the location of lands. The system subdivides the principal latitude/longitude lines into squares. The squares consist of townships, which are each six miles on a side. While each township usually has a name (e.g., Grant Township), townships are also numbered by their distance from a true north to south line called the principal meridian, and a base line that runs east to west. The north-south lines are called township lines and the east-west lines are called range lines.

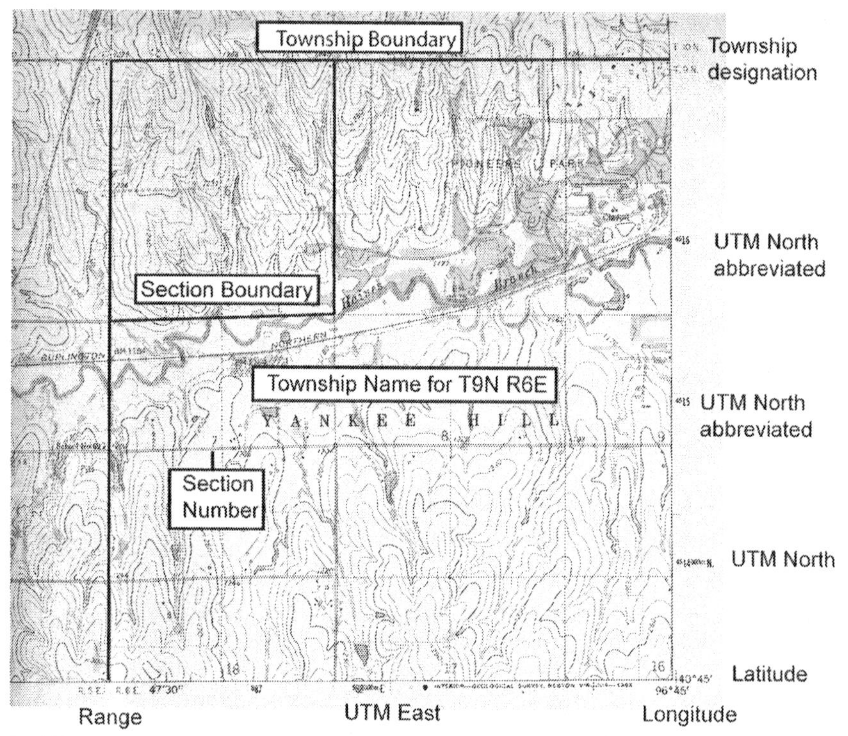

FIGURE 4-2
Portion of a topographic map showing how the township and range system, latitude and longitude, and UTM systems are designated on the map.

Thus, township numbers are such as Township 3 North and Range 4 West (abbreviated as T3N R4W). On a standard USGS map, the township and range lines are labeled on the map edges (figure 4-2).

The township is subdivided into thirty-six sections, each one mile on a side and comprising 640 acres. The sections are numbered, beginning with the number one in the northeast section, and proceeding west and east alternately through the township (figure 4-3). The sections are labeled by their township and numbers (e.g., Section 4, T3N R4W).

Sections are divided by half and quarter sections, and described from the smallest section of the area to the largest. The designation NE1/4 NE1/4 NE1/4 of Section 4 T3N R4W would refer to the 10 acres in the northeastern corner of the section. Describing a location by dividing sections is easiest using a standard template (figure 4-4). The template is made of clear plastic with lines dividing the sections already on it. The template is laid over the map with the location, and the location read from the template. The most common mistake is to write the section quarters backwards, from largest to smallest rather than smallest to largest. This can be avoided by reading the designation as a full sentence. The designation at the beginning of this paragraph would be the northeast quarter of the northeast quarter of the northeast quarter of Section 4.

Here are detailed instructions for designating the township/range location for an area on a USGS topographic map:

1. Determine the location you wish to designate on the map.
2. Find the section boundaries surrounding the location and the corresponding section number.
3. Look at the map edges to determine the township and range to which the section belongs.
4. Lay a template over the section dividing the section into quarter sections, or draw lines on the map doing the same. Starting with a 10-acre unit, determine which quarter-section of a 40-acre unit the location is in and write it down. Then determine which quarter-section of a 160-acre unit the 10-acre unit is in and write that down, after the previous designation. Finally, determine which quarter-section of the section the 160-acre unit is, and write that down. Next write down the section number, followed by the township and range designation.
5. Determine the designation a second time for accuracy.

STANDARD TOWNSHIP LAYOUT

6	5	4	3	2	1
7	8	9	10	11	12
18	17	16	15	14	13
19	20	21	22	23	24
30	29	28	27	26	25
31	32	33	34	35	36

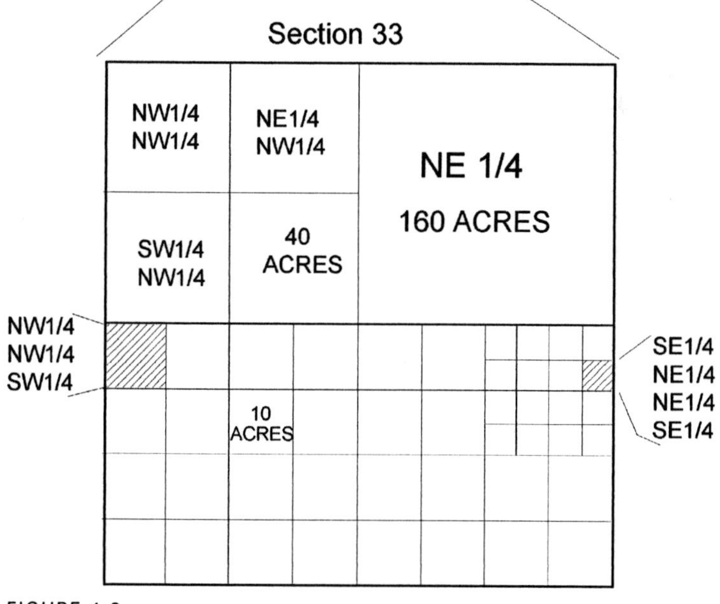

FIGURE 4-3
Standard township layout and designation of partial sections.

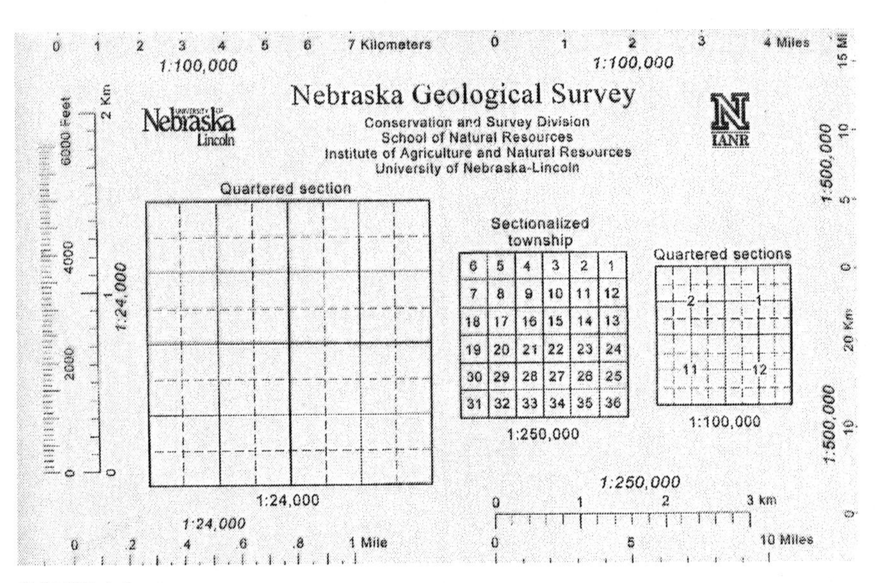

FIGURE 4-4
Laying a template like this over a map with the sections marked makes determining portions of a section much easier. Note that it can also be used to determine slope (percent grade) by matching the lines at the bottom of the template with the density of the contour lines on the map. The Topographic Map Helper's Friend, courtesy School of Natural Resources, University of Nebraska–Lincoln.

Universal Transverse Mercator

The UTM system is a metric location system used worldwide. The UTM is designed to cover the area between latitude 84° N and latitude 80° S. A separate grid, the Universal Polar Stereographic Grid (UPS), is used to represent the polar regions. The base of the grid is the location of the zero point, or the datum. The current widely accepted datum is the World Global System datum of 1984 (WGS 84). Other data exist and if the grid coordinate for the scene does not match the location on the map, the first potential source of error is the datum.

The initial grid lines are north-to-south lines that designate zones. On a topographic map, the zone designation is usually shown in the legend. There are sixty zones worldwide, each including six degrees of longitude. The continental United States includes Zones 10–21; Bosnia and Herzegovina are in Zones 33 and 34. Within the zones, the location is measured right and up (east and north) by meters (figure 4-5). Standard topographic maps frequently have UTM grids drawn over them. For maps at a scale of 1:24,000, the grid is in 1,000-meter increments. Near the corner of a map, the entire grid coordinate is written out (e.g., 4514000 m N or 688000 m E). Along the sides of the map, this is abbreviated by dropping the last three zeros (e.g., 4514 or 688). The user then employs a template to extend the ticks by the UTM designation across the map and then divide the grid into 1,000-meter-square units (figure 4-5). Theoretically, this system allows the description of the location of an item to the nearest millimeter. In reality, practiced use of topographic maps allows an error of approximately twenty meters on a scale of 1:24,000.

Here are detailed instructions for designating the UTM location of an area on a USGS topographic map:

1. Determine the location you wish to designate on the map.
2. Find the UTM designations on the top and side of the map designating the nearest north and east (or south and west) UTM ticks. Extend these lines

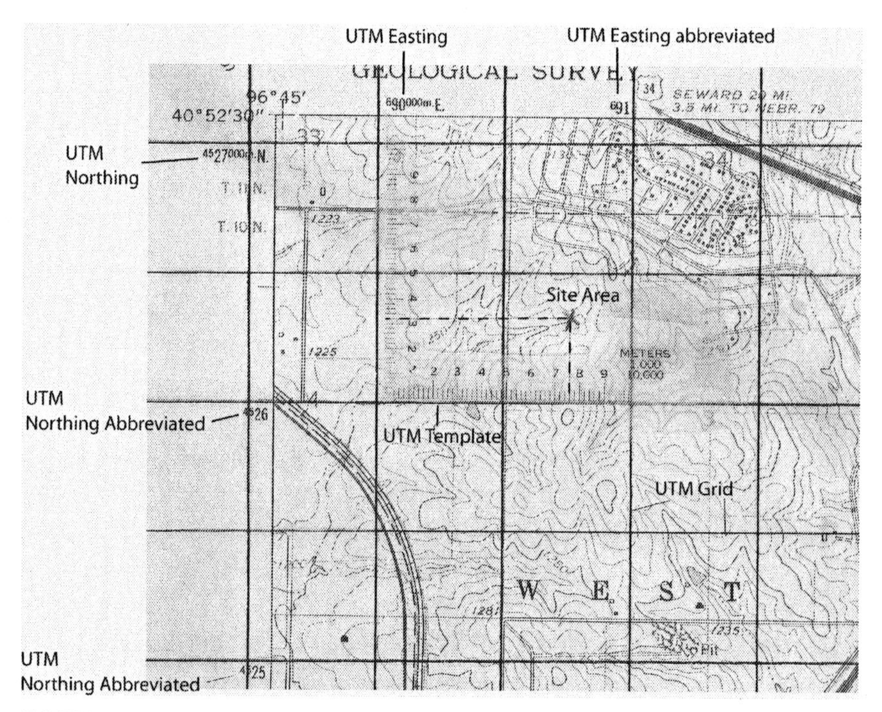

FIGURE 4-5
Determining UTM using a template. Find the northing ticks along the side of the map, the easting ticks along the top or bottom. Templates are used to measure between the ticks. The site area would be approximately at Zone X (read from the map legend) 4526300 m N 690760 m E.

across the map using either a pencil or a template. This will place your location in a unit that is a 1,000 meter square.
3. To determine the northing, measure up from the unit using a template that divides the unit into tens. From the template, read how many meters north of the UTM tick your object is. The last two digits will probably be estimates between the lines on the template. The northing is the digits on the side of the map and the number read from the template.
4. Repeat for the easting.
5. From the map legend, read the zone number.
6. The UTM is written Zone number XXXXXX m E XXXXXX m N.
7. Remeasure for accuracy.

Global Positioning System

The global positioning system (GPS) consists of a net of satellites over the surface of the earth that send signals with their positions to the earth. The entire system consists of twenty-four satellites and four spares. Usually, there will be eight satellites potentially in range at any one location. The GPS originated as a U.S. military system, and the commercial applications are a side product. The United States launched the first GPS satellites in 1978. In 1983, after Korean Air Lines Flight 007 was shot down by the Russian Air Force while passing over the Kamchatka Peninsula due to poor navigational tools, President Reagan made the system available without charge worldwide (Spector 2000:98). The satellite system is currently operated from Schriever Air Force Base, outside of Colorado Springs, Colorado.

Receivers on the earth's surface pick up the signals, take the location of multiple satellites, and triangulate the position of the receiver on the earth's surface. The more satellites the unit is receiving signals from, the more accurate the position calculated. Most receivers will tell the operator how many satellites they are receiving. The position of a single receiver, uncorrected, can have an accuracy ranging from ten to twenty meters. Once set, a receiver, like a radio, only needs to be turned on to pick up the satellite signals and read the position. Most receivers can be set to read in latitude/longitude, or in a UTM designation based on any number of different data.

The common models of handheld GPS receivers, available for about one hundred dollars, are programmed with over one hundred data. The user needs to match the datum on the GPS unit to the datum on the map used to locate the area. Usually, the datum is clearly printed in the map legend. The datum for USGS maps is usually either NAD 27 CONUS (North American Datum 1927 Continental United States) or NAD 83 (North American Datum 1983).

GPS receivers in the United States may be sold as "WAAS-enabled." WAAS stands for the Wide Area Augmentation System, a system of satellites and ground stations that provide GPS signal corrections and give greater accuracy. The system is being developed by the Department of Transportation and the Federal Aviation Administration for precision flight approaches. WAAS is only available in the United States and does not yet offer full coverage throughout the United States. The typical GPS unit without WAAS has an accuracy limited to about fifteen meters. With WAAS, the accuracy of the reading may be within three meters.

While WAAS is only available in the United States, other countries are developing their own systems. Europe is developing the Euro Geostationary Navigation Overlay Service (EGNOS) and Japan's system is the Multi-functional Satellite Augmentation System (MSAS). Eventually, there will probably be worldwide coverage of similar GPS signal corrections.

SITE MAPS

Map Basics

A map is actually the end product of two activities: surveying and cartography. Surveying consists of making the measurements for a scale map, and cartography is the science of drawing the map. The choices for surveying range from measuring one's pace and stepping out the distance, to using instruments that cost tens of thousands of dollars and that require years of experience to use proficiently.

Before a surveyor begins to measure a scene area, the boundaries of the scene need to be defined. The surveyor must have a clear idea of the boundaries, the features, and the objects to be included in the map. Always measure from the whole to the part. The outer scene perimeter should be measured first and the desired detail placed within this framework. If a survey begins at one place and is drawn to detail and then continued around the scene drawn to detail, errors will accumulate, rather than being immediately cross-checked.

All artifacts, evidence, and relevant features need to be clearly marked, so they will be included on the map. The surveyor needs to have a clear idea of the relevant natural or cultural features (streams, roads, buildings, cliffs) that need to be included, as well as an idea of which aspects of the features are relevant. It is impossible to decide on the appropriate techniques for measuring until an accurate mental picture of the scene exists. The surveyor needs to think about both aspects of making the map, the survey and the cartography, before actually beginning to collect data. He or she needs to have a mental picture of what the final map(s) should look like and what it (or they) will be used for (reports, court presentation, slide shows). This affects the entire map-making process.

In addition to evidence and natural features, the map should cite the location of photographs and any samples taken. The location of a photograph can be marked with a circle and then an arrow from the circle indicating the direction from which the photograph was taken. This should be labeled with the numbers of the photographs taken from this position, as logged by the photographer. The location of any samples taken need to be noted on the map also, along with the log numbers. All evidence on the map should include a symbol indicating the type of evidence and the log number should be next to it. The surveyor may also wish to include a symbol for material noted on the map, but not collected. This makes it explicit that this material was not collected, and that the surveyor did not omit a log number.

Before beginning the measurements, the surveyor

1. should know where most of the objects are that will appear on the map;
2. should know what the scene boundaries are and how the map can be tied into the real world;
3. needs to coordinate with the evidence technicians and photographer to ensure that the log numbers for the photographs and evidence will appear on the map correctly;
4. needs to know the range of objects that will be represented on the map in order to determine a legend; and
5. needs an idea of the uses the map will be put to and the media in which it will be presented.

When this information is clear, then the surveyor can determine the best methods for collecting the data that will be drawn on the final map.

An independent check of the measurements should be made whenever possible. Even if the investigator is not creating a sketch map, but taking measurements for a pace and compass or instrument map to be drawn later, he or she should keep a rough sketch as part of the notes. This will help ensure that the shape and relative positions of objects are correct in the final.

Before beginning the map:

1. Determine the boundaries of the scene.
2. Determine the major features that will be included.
3. Decide on the level of accuracy needed. (Is a scale map needed? If so, what scale?)

Determining Direction and Angle

All outdoor maps need a north arrow. This sounds simple, but there are actually three norths: magnetic north, true north, and grid north. The north that a compass points to is magnetic north. True north is the direction to the geographic poles. Magnetic north is affected by the fact that the earth is a sphere and the compass cannot point directly to the north pole, and by the variation in the earth's magnetic field. This difference between magnetic and true north is the declination. In part of the United States, the magnetic declination is almost nothing (in a line through Lake Michigan to eastern Florida), but on the coasts the declination is significant. For example, in Seattle, Washington, the declination of magnetic north is about 22 degrees. Local declination is found at the bottom of topographic survey maps and most compasses have instructions on how to set the compass to compensate for the declination.

The third north is grid north. On published maps, grid north refers to the north on the grid of the map. Otherwise, grid north may be a north set up by the surveyor to create the map. A search or excavation grid may be set up with regard to the terrain and the direction nearest north designated as grid north.

In addition to magnetic declination, compasses can be affected by large masses of metal or electricity. In other words, stand a few paces away from the car when reading the compass. In areas with metallic ores in the ground, such as northern Wisconsin, compass readings may bend due to the large amount of magnetic material in the soil.

There are two types of compasses. Some compasses read the azimuth, the direction as read clockwise from 0 to 360 degrees from a north base line. An azimuth is the direction from zero (north) to the east in degrees, such as 240 degrees or 80 degrees. Compasses that read in bearings are divided into four quarters, each labeled 0 to 90. Bearings are read as degrees from north or south to east or west (e.g., N70E, S22W). For most purposes, the azimuth is the simpler reading.

When at all possible the user should read the azimuth from point A to point B, then move to point B and check the azimuth to point A. Averaging the two readings will help to prevent error. Common mistakes in using a compass include reading the wrong end of the needle, setting the declination when reading magnetic bearings, parallax (reading while looking from the side of the needle, rather than along it), failing to check the forward and back bearings, and failing to make a sketch showing what is being measured (Brinker 1969:170).

Other problems occur when the compass is used badly out of level; if the needle cannot float freely, it will not give a true reading. In older, or less expensive compasses, the magnetism of the needle may be weak. This will make it more prone to pointing toward local magnetic attractions rather than the earth's magnetic field.

Types of Maps

The more accurate the map, the more sophisticated the equipment and personnel necessary to create it. Many times a quick sketch map is appropriate, but many police departments use a tape and compass for most crime scene maps. Many departments also now have electronic distance meters (EDMs) or total stations (see below) and personnel trained to use them. These are often used to quickly document large scenes or traffic accidents.

Sketch Maps

A sketch map consists of a drawing of an area as seen from above (a plan view). The minimum information necessary on all maps is a north arrow, an indication of the scale or lack of scale on the map, and a key as to what the symbols on the map refer (a legend). Without this information the map is simply not usable. On a sketch map not drawn to scale, the phrase "not to scale" should be included to make the degree of accuracy clear to the reader (figure 4-6).

Pace (or Tape) and Compass Maps

These are simple scale maps, usually completed without reference to elevation. The information needed is the direction and distance from one point to

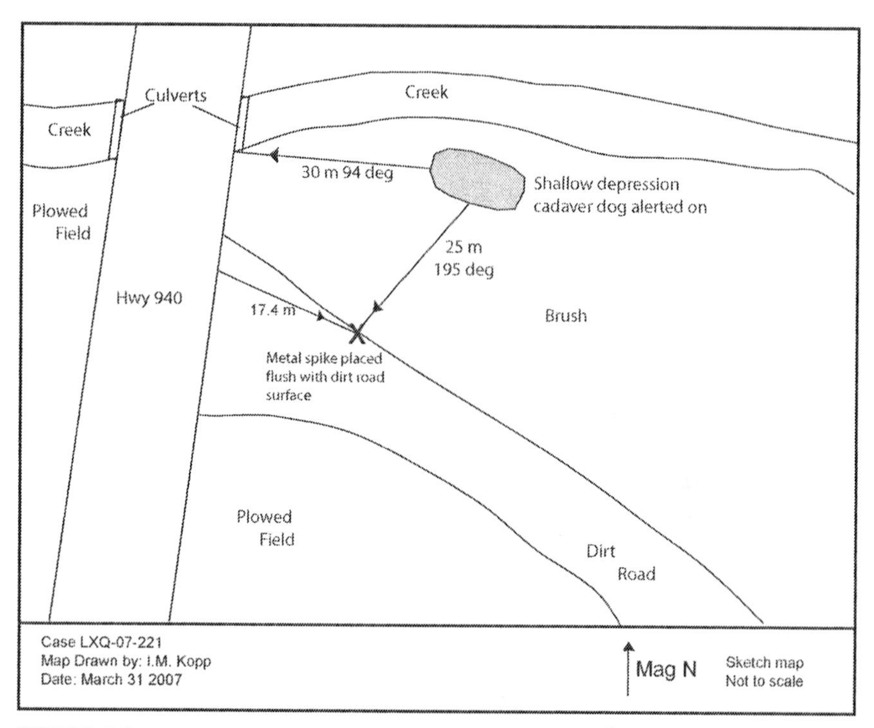

FIGURE 4-6

Sketch map of location of area on which a cadaver dog alerted. Measurements were taken so that the area could be relocated and these were taken as distance and angle measurements from relocatable points. One point was preexisting—the culvert. Lacking a second point, the team placed a metal spike flush with the road bed and measured from that. The metal spike can, if necessary, be relocated with a metal detector.

another, or from the datum point to all points. The direction is taken from a compass. The distance can be measured using your pace or with a tape.

Pacing requires prior measurement of paces and practice in the "mapping stride." However, given some practice, pacing yields a relatively accurate measure of distance without a tape. To practice pacing, lay a tape out on the floor for about ten meters and count the steps it takes to walk the distance. Keep doing that until you can complete the ten meters in a consistent number of paces. Divide the number of paces that it takes to complete the ten meters by ten and you have the average length of your stride in meters. The pace length will vary based on terrain, vegetation, and the experience of the pacer.

The basics of taping are simple. Take a tape of appropriate size (many scene maps are completed with 50m or 100m fiberglass tapes) and stretch the tape between two points. The most accurate distance measurement occurs when the tape is straight and level. When possible, objects that cause the tape to bend (e.g., plants) should be removed. When it's not possible to remove the object, two measurements may need to be taken, breaking the measurement at the obstructing object.

The tape may sag when held in the air between points. The sag adds to the length of the measurement and increases the distance being measured. This problem can be solved in two ways (Lufkin 1998:6): (1) Break the long distance into shorter distances, so that the sag for each increment is negligible; or (2) improvise supports at frequent intervals (about every 20 meters) to eliminate most of the sag.

Taping on a slope yields the distance on the slope, which is greater than the horizontal distance between the two points. The greater the slope and the distance, the greater the error will be. If the tape is sagging, the error is even greater. When measuring distances up to about 60 meters, use of a plumb bob and level will help reduce the error. One or both of the tape people can use a plumb bob to hold the tape above ground and level. Frequently, the person holding the tape on the downhill side does not hold the tape high enough and a third person can use a hand level to check that the tape is level. If possible, setting the downhill point as zero and reading the measurement from the uphill point is usually easier. It allows the downhill tape person to hold the tape solidly while the uphill tape person exerts a steady pull, gets the tape level, and makes his or her reading.

When the slope or the distance is great, then correcting the slope distance to a horizontal distance can be done mathematically. The slope angle can be determined with a transit. Given the slope distance and the slope angle, basic trigonometry is used to calculate the horizontal distance. The horizontal distance is the slope distance multiplied by the cosine of the slope angle. When the slope gradually changes, care must be used and it is usually better to use a number of small taping increments.

The easiest type of tape and compass map is a baseline map, the making of which is described below.

Instrument Maps

The most precise maps are made with surveying instruments. These measure the horizontal angle, the vertical angle, the horizontal distance, and the slope distance with a high degree of accuracy. The basic transit is a telescope mounted on a protractor (Hester, Shafer, and Feder 1997:217). Vertical angles are measured with another protractor clamped onto the telescope. Modern transits have electronic protractors and give the angle readings in an electronic readout.

The theodolite is an instrument designed for precision measurement of angles. On the mechanical models, the angles are read on a vernier; on the electronic models they are read on an electronic display. Distance-measuring devices tend to be built-in on the machine. Given the electronic nature of today's surveying instruments, the difference between the ways these tools are used is less than it used to be.

An electronic distance meter (EDM) is an instrument that sends a laser beam to a prism and measures the distance based on the time it takes the light to return to the instrument. The EDM may be separate from the instrument that measures angles (transit or theodolite), or it may be built into the same housing. An EDM with an electronic theodolite is called a total station. These are extremely popular instruments and gather the data for a map very quickly.

An additional piece of equipment is the electronic data collector. This is a small computer that can be used on any of the instruments above; it plugs into the instrument and electronically collects the angle and distance data. Usually, the instrument operator can key in a code to define the type of object just mapped.

A trained surveyor should be on surveying instruments. It is relatively easy on these machines to punch the buttons and have numbers displayed. Assessing the accuracy of these numbers and potential sources of error and doing the survey correctly, however, require more knowledge and experience. Some common sources of error include wind vibrating the machine; temperature changes during the day causing contraction and expansion of the metal and liquids in the leveling bubbles; settling of the tripod in soft ground; or kicking or stepping on the tripod legs during the work.

The use of an instrument to make the measurements for a map is the most expensive and complex of the options available. The high initial cost of instruments such as total stations is balanced by the cost savings realized by the lower number of people needed to complete the mapping and the time saved in completing the maps quickly and correctly.

SITE LAYOUT AND EXCAVATION GRIDS

Archaeologists owe their basic site layout philosophy to René Descartes, a seventeenth-century philosopher. Descartes first described the Cartesian plane, a geometrical abstraction. The Cartesian plane is a horizontal plane numbered by a coordinate system on two intersecting axes, usually labeled the *x* and the *y*. Imagine such a plane hovering over the crime scene, imagine labeling each item mapped with the *x* and *y* coordinates where the piece lay, and you have imagined the basic idea of an excavation grid. Elevations are taken by extending the grid system into three dimensions, labeling the third axis *z*.

Basic to the layout of any site is the establishment of a site datum, which is a location with a known grid coordinate. This should be a stable, physical object. A simple way to make a very stable datum is to pound an eighteen-inch length of rebar (reinforced steel bar) into the ground until it is flush or almost flush with the ground. Then tie colored plastic flagging tape to the top so that it can easily be seen. Clearly, this should be in an area where there is no possibility of buried material. A simple way to make a quick datum is to cut a tin or aluminum can open at one end and push the open end into the ground until the bottom is almost flush with the ground. Then hammer a nail into the center of the can, and use the head of the nail as the datum point. A second method is to use a unique, relocatable feature as a datum, such as a tree or fence post.

The datum should be in a place where it will not be disturbed during the work on the scene. If possible, the entire scene should be visible from the datum point. If the datum point can be at the highest point on the site, this will make drawing the contour lines on the map easier; the highest point may also be the best place from which to see the entire site.

Grids can be physical or theoretical. A string grid can be set up using nails or wooden stakes at the grid corners and using string (preferably nylon, as cotton stretches) to mark the grid lines. The electronic surveying equipment described earlier places a theoretical grid over the entire site, without anything being physically marked other than the datum point. If the grid coordinates (e.g., 0,0; 150,200) of the position that the machine is set on are keyed into the machine, and the machine oriented to grid north, then the readout can be set to give the grid coordinate of the point being read by the machine. With modern equipment it is not necessary to lay out a string grid to work within a grid system, although the strings are useful as a physical scale in the photographs.

Plan Maps

Baseline Maps

A simple, quick method of mapping the scene involves laying out only one baseline (figure 4-7). This can be string marked in meter increments, or simply a fifty-meter tape with the zero end attached to the ground with a nail or stake for stability. The zero end is the 0,0 point on the grid; the stable tape is the baseline. The distance between the piece to be collected and the baseline is measured with a second tape at a right angle to the first (the y measurement) and noted, and the distance along the baseline where the tapes intersect is noted (the x measurement). This method is not suitable where precise measurement is required, nor is it suitable if elevations are important. Since every piece is measured, it can be time-consuming in dense scenes, for instance, where there are large numbers of cartridge cases in one area. But it is useful in a number of outdoor crime scenes.

FIGURE 4-7
Making a baseline map. The team has flagged all bone and objects they found. The tape paralleling the hedge is the baseline. The team members are measuring from the baseline to each object while the woman with the clipboard writes down the measurements.

Grid Mapping

Grids are used in excavation. They can also be used to collect material on the surface when there are too many pieces to plot them using a baseline map. A simple string grid can be constructed with a quick reference to high school trigonometry. The Pythagorean theorem states that the sum of the squares of the two sides of a right triangle is equal to the square of the hypotenuse. This means that the line running diagonally across a 5 meter square will be 7.07 meters. Rather than calculating the hypotenuse each time, many archaeologists put a table with the common calculations in with their digging equipment (table 4-1).

To construct a 1-meter grid, lay one tape from the zero point (grid coordinate 0,0) to 1 meter and place a nail in the ground (figure 4-8A). This is one side of the grid. Now, take the first tape from the 0,0 point and lay it out 1.41 meters at a 45° angle from the baseline. Take a second tape to the 1-meter point on the baseline (grid coordinate 1,0) and run it out 1 meter perpendicular to the baseline. Where the two tapes meet is the grid coordinate 1,1 (figure 4-8B). To lay out the grid coordinate 0,1, at the 1-meter point on the baseline, lay out the tape 1.41 meters at a 45° angle from the baseline. At the 0,0 point on the baseline, lay out the tape 1 meter perpendicular to the baseline. The point where the two tapes meet is the 0,1 point (figure 4-8C). The result can be checked by running the tape between the 1,1 and the 0,1 point; this should be 1 meter (figure 4-8D).

Table 4-1. Common hypotenuse lengths for excavation or collection units with sides between one and ten units

Side length	1	2	3	4	5	6	7	8	9	10
1	1.41									
2	2.24	2.83								
3	3.16	3.61	4.24							
4	4.12	4.47	5.00	5.66						
5	5.10	5.39	5.83	6.40	7.07					
6	6.08	6.32	6.71	7.21	7.81	8.49				
7	7.07	7.28	7.62	8.06	8.60	9.22	9.90			
8	8.06	8.25	8.54	8.94	9.43	10.00	10.63	11.31		
9	9.06	9.22	9.49	9.85	10.30	10.82	11.40	12.04	12.73	
10	10.05	10.20	10.44	10.77	11.18	11.66	12.21	12.81	13.45	14.14

FIGURE 4-8

Triangulation of a square to create the corners of a grid. A. Laying out the first two corners of a 1-meter unit. B. The third corner of the square is 1 meter from one of the first two corners and 1.41 meters from the second. C. The fourth corner of the square is 1 meter from the first and third corners. D. The line between the second and fourth corner should be the same as between the first and third, 1.41 meters.

These units are traditionally labeled by the grid coordinates corresponding to the northeast corner of the unit. As the grid is laid out, it is useful to have a clipboard with a piece of graph paper nearby. Draw the grid and number the units on the paper as the grid is created. Also, take a piece of flagging tape, label the grid coordinates for each of the northeast corners on pieces of the tape and tie them to the appropriate corners. These measures will help you to number all material from the units consistently.

Polar Coordinate Mapping

The Cartesian grid systems described above are square grids. The polar coordinate system works on a circular grid system. A fixed datum is used as the center point and items are plotted based on their angle and distance from that point. Mapping using polar coordinates is especially useful in confined spaces (Hochrein 2002b).

A 360° circular protractor can be placed over the datum and the zero point oriented to north. Hochrein (2002b) outlines a system to suspend the protractor in place in wells, cisterns, and confined spaces that can be very difficult to map accurately. The angle and distance to each object can then be measured. This can be mapped onto grid paper with square grids using a protractor and ruler to measure the angle and distance from the datum on the paper. However, polar coordinate grid paper exists on which the grid radiates out from a central point. This makes polar coordinate scale mapping very quick and simple.

Elevation

Elevation, the third dimension, is called the *z* coordinate; it is measured in reference to a datum plane. This can be thought of as an invisible ceiling that extends over the entire scene. The depth of the evidence and features are measured from this invisible plane (Hester, Shafer, and Feder 1997:224). If a surveying instrument is used to measure elevation, the data collector attached to the instrument frequently completes all calculations for the excavator.

However, within the excavation, or when a surveying instrument is not used, it is useful to know how to measure the depth. Near the excavation, one sturdy point should be fixed with a known elevation. This should be related to the elevation of the site datum, either by instrument or by a modification of the technique described below:

1. Attach a nylon string to the known elevation. If using wooden stakes, it is useful to take a knife and make a notch at the correct elevation, so that the string will stay at the correct point. Alternatively, a nail can be pounded into the top of the stake and the nail used as the elevation marker.
2. Place a line level on the string, hold the string taut, and bring it to a level elevation by raising and lowering the string until the bubble is centered (figure 4-9).
3. A tape can be used to measure from the level line to the point being measured. The tape should be perpendicular to the level line. This can usually be checked by ensuring that the lines on the tape are parallel to the level line or by placing a string with an attached plumb bob next to the tape. The

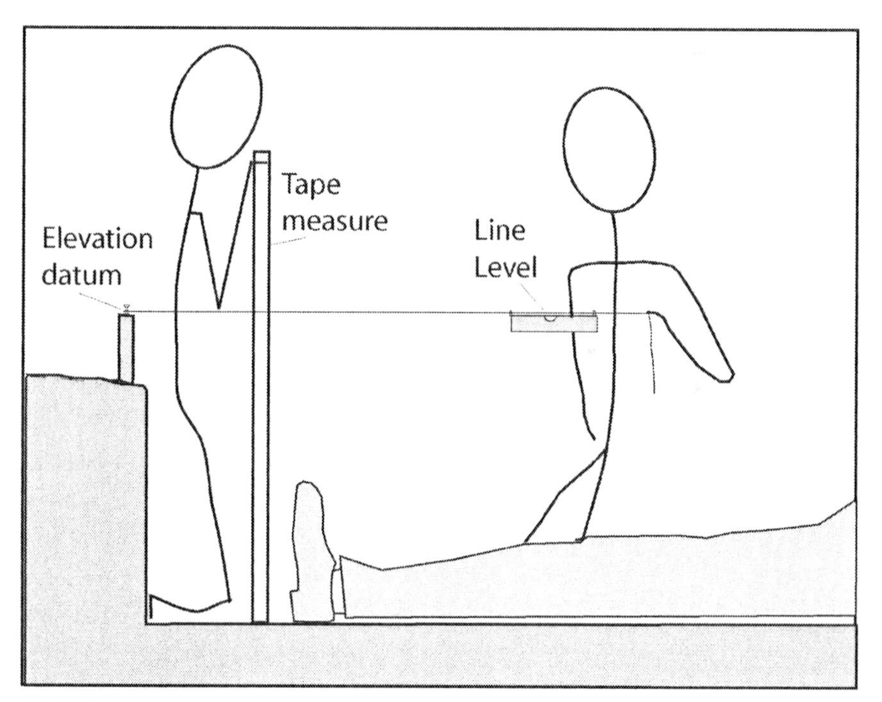

FIGURE 4-9
Measuring an elevation. A string should be attached to a point with a known elevation. A carpenter's line level should be placed on the string and the string held taut and level. A tape measure or folding ruler can be used to measure from this line with a known elevation to the unknown elevation. Usually, one person will be needed to hold the line level and a second to read the tape measure and ensure it is perpendicular to the level line. This drawing is also an example of a profile drawing, showing elevation differences from the side, or profile.

most meaningful measurement is at the bottom of the evidence, as the top of the material is a result of the elevation that the piece was placed at plus the thickness of the evidence. If a number of pieces of evidence are at the same depth below the surface, they will have the same bottom depth, but different top depths.

Drawing profiles of graves is different than drawing standard archaeological profiles of features. In drawing archaeological profiles, half of the feature is generally excavated so that the profile can be clearly seen, photographed, and drawn. However, in a grave, this would mean that the body would need to be cut in half, so it could clearly show in the profile. This is clearly not acceptable.

Instead, the information is collected on a series of plan maps showing the topographic information at different depths, a series rather like that shown in figure 4-10. A line can be drawn through each of the plan maps at the same location and the information from each level placed onto a profile drawing. Thus the surface elevations from the top of a grave will be one layer, the elevations from the top of the body a second layer, the elevations from the bottom of the body a third layer, and the elevations from the bottom of the grave a fourth layer. The information from these layers can then be put together to create the profile.

This method yields data for drawing a map in three dimensions. The problem, as the investigator will quickly find out, is that the paper to draw the map on is in two dimensions. Computer mapping programs actually work in three dimensions. Using the *x*, *y*, and *z* measurements in such a program can yield a drawing that can be viewed in three dimensions and rotated to show all sides.

Showing the three dimensions of the real world on two-dimensional paper is commonly done in one of three ways: (1) a profile (figure 4-9); (2) a drawing with an isometric projection, which shows three faces of the objects in two dimensions (figure 4-11); or (3) a series of plan maps showing different depths (figure 4-10). The choice depends mainly on the complexity of the objects being drawn and the media in which the cartographer works. Simple changes in elevation can frequently be seen easily in profile. When there are many objects and the changes are complex, then a series of plan maps may communicate more effectively. Isometric drawings are easiest when working with a computer,

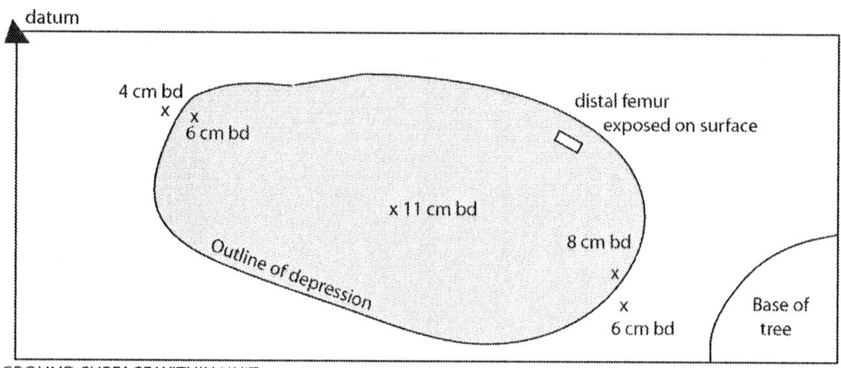

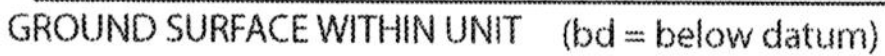

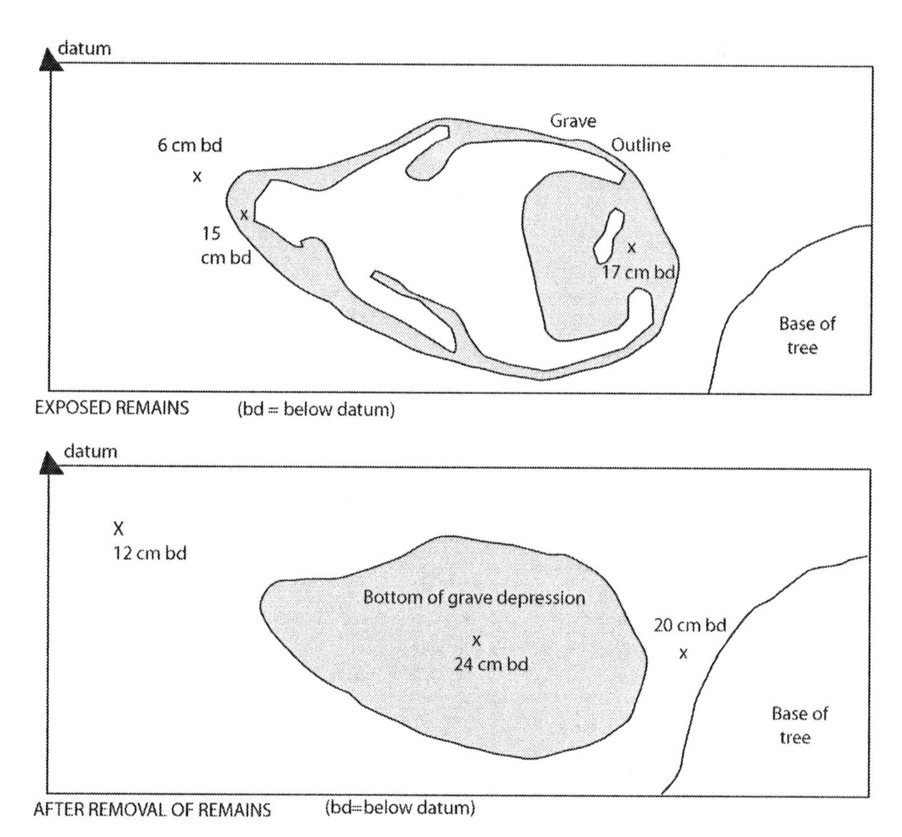

FIGURE 4-10

Showing the changes in elevation as a series of plan maps at different elevations.

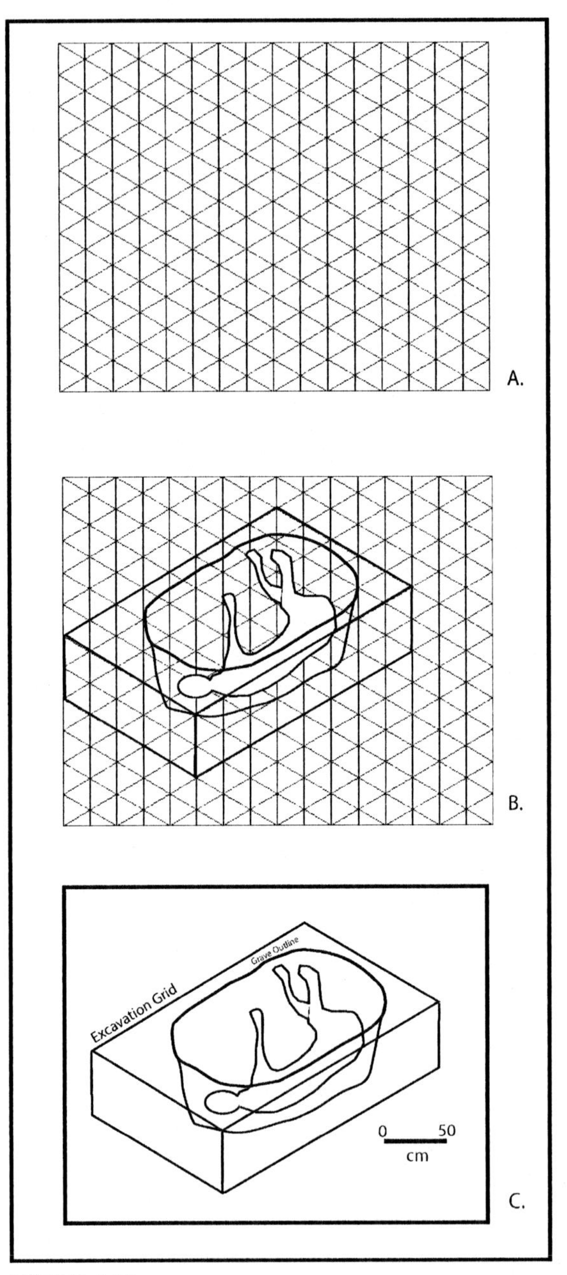

FIGURE 4-11

Isometric projection. A. An isometric grid. B. Drawing the map using an isometric grid. C. The finished drawing.

where the *x,y,* and *z* coordinates can be entered into the computer and the drawing can be rotated to view the top and one side of the object. This view can then be printed out onto a two-dimensional piece of paper.

SUMMARY

1. Locate the scene in the real world by obtaining an address, the township and range location, or a UTM designation.
2. Decide on the scene boundaries and the objects to include in a map.
3. Decide on the accuracy and precision necessary for the map. This will determine whether to use a sketch map, tape and compass, or instrument map.
4. Gather the data and create the map.

GLOSSARY TERMS

azimuth
cartography
GPS (global positioning system)
latitude
longitude
surveying
township
triangulation
Universal Transverse Mercator (UTM)

SUGGESTED READING

Hochrein, Michael J.
2002b Polar Coordinate Mapping and Forensic Archaeology within Confined Spaces. *Journal of Forensic Identification* 52 (6):733–49.

Lufkin
1998 Taping Techniques for Engineers and Surveyors. Cooper Tools, Apex, North Carolina.
A short booklet on using tapes correctly and accurately for measuring distance.

Spector, Michael
2000 No Place to Hide. *The New Yorker*. 27 November, pp. 96–105.

A well-written explanation of the global positioning satellite system and GPS receivers.

United States Department of the Army

1993 *Map Reading and Land Navigation.* Field Manual 21-26. Headquarters, Department of the Army, Washington, D.C.

Very clear, basic introduction to latitude and longitude, the UTM system, and basic map reading.

5

Soils

A basic awareness of soil is necessary to body recovery as soil is much more than simply dirt; it is a product of its environment and reflects the history of change in that environment. The knowledgeable observer of soil has the opportunity to read that history, which helps to locate disturbances, like graves, and reconstruct the events that created them. A basic knowledge of soil formation helps to determine whether the natural soil has been disturbed—and burying a body always disturbs the soil.

Also, the characteristics of soils affect both the preservation of the remains and evidence and excavation techniques. An understanding of soil chemistry, moisture, and temperature helps the investigator to understand what may have decayed in the grave. In a later chapter, remote sensing techniques for locating graves are discussed, and these techniques differ in their effectiveness in different soil types. In deep graves, the consolidation of the soil may affect how large the excavation needs to be so that the walls do not collapse. The information presented in this chapter forms a basis for a discussion of grave location techniques as well as excavation techniques, but there is much more to understanding soils and site formation processes than can be presented in this basic introduction.

The U.S. Department of Agriculture's Natural Resources Conservation Service (NRCS) publishes official soil descriptions for every county in the United States (and they're free!). These are very detailed and they are useful descriptions of the natural soils.

SOIL FORMATION

A soil is the result of the interaction of a variety of physical, chemical, and biological processes acting on rock or sediment over time. A particular type of soil is a result of the parent materials, climate, organisms, topographic relief, and time (Jenny 1941).

The parent material is the original substance before any soil development begins. It may consist of disintegrated rock, water- or wind-deposited sediments, glacial materials, or decaying plant materials. The parent material influences the texture and mineral composition of the soil. Glacial and water-laid deposits tend to range from sands to silty clays. Sandstones high in quartz tend to weather to produce sandy soils.

Temperature and precipitation are the most important climatic factors in soil formation. They affect the types and intensity of the weathering processes, the amount and type of soil organisms, soil temperature and moisture, and the rate of decay of organic material (Foth and Turk 1972:212). A low rate of decay may lead to the accumulation of leaf litter, rather than its decomposition. In forensic situations, climate will affect the decay of organic matter in the soil.

The topographic relief of the area refers to the configuration of the surface of the earth. It affects soil drainage and the amount of water running through the soil. Topography also affects the amount of soil removed through erosion. On steep slopes, erosion may prevent the soil from developing, as the soil may erode as quickly as it forms. Depressions and the bottom of hills will fill with soil eroded from higher areas. Minor variations in topography may determine significant differences in soils.

Soil organisms refer to both the organisms in the soil and the vegetation supported by the soil. Some soil scientists suggest the effects of the biota are so great that soil is really a biological phenomenon (Thornbury 1969:72). The microfaunal species that contribute to soil formation include soil bacteria, algae, and fungi. The soil fauna include protozoa, nematodes, mites, and insects. All, of course, also play a role in the decomposition of human remains.

The final factor in soil development is the amount of time it has to develop. Geologic age affects the thickness and maturity of the soil profile. Immature soils may have an accumulation of organic matter on the surface and little weathering or leaching. These soil profiles will consist of a highly organic layer (humus) overlaying the parent material. As the soil ages, the actual size of the particles that make up the soil become smaller through weathering, formation of pedological structures, and other processes that create layers intermediate between the parent material and the humus.

SOIL DESCRIPTION

Soil scientists use a standardized method of describing soils. This is superior to the personal system often used by both archaeologists and crime scene investigators (frequently using words like gummy, dusty, or sticky) as it allows comparison between sites and investigators.

Color

The standard method of measuring soil color is to reference a commercial soil color chart. The Munsell color book is the most widely accepted color chart. The book includes a systematic numerical and letter designation of the hue, value, and chroma of the color. Hue refers to the dominant wavelength or color of the light. Value refers to the total quantity of light (brightness), and chroma refers to the relative purity of the dominant wavelength. The values are always given in the order hue, value, and chroma.

Munsell charts are notebooks with color chips mounted on the pages (figure 5-1). The colors are arranged by hue, value, and chroma. Each page shows color chips for a hue, designated by a numerical value (10, 7.5, 5, or 2.5) and a letter (R for red, Y for yellow, G for green, and B for blue). Value units range between 0 (darkest) and 10 (lightest) and are arranged vertically on the page. Chroma units also range from 0 (increase in grayness) to 10 (pure color); they are arranged horizontally on the page. Thus, a typical Munsell designation may be 5YR4/3, with 5YR designating the hue, 4 the value, and 3 the chroma.

In the color charts, there are usually clear plastic pages between the pages with the color chips and a small hole under each color chip. A small quantity of the soil can be placed on a trowel and held under the holes to compare the soil to the color chips. The plastic page prevents the page below from being dirtied by the soil.

The color of soil changes with moisture. To be accurate, the color should be taken with the soil both wet and dry. If the soil is wet in the field, it can be dried in the lab and the color measured there. If the soil is dry in the field, water can be added, and the wet color matched to the Munsell chart. Soil color

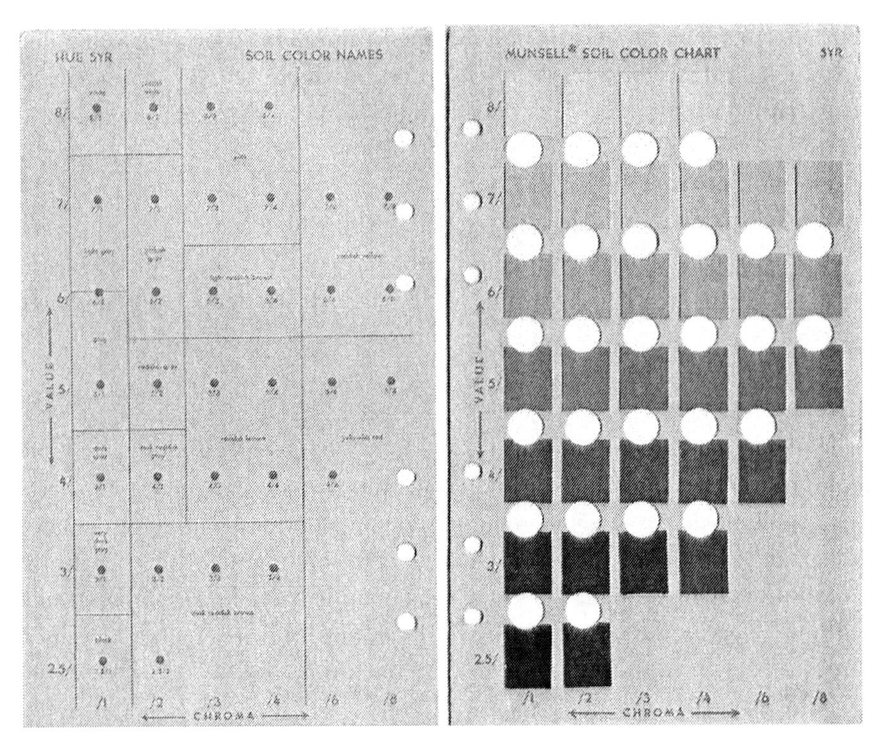

FIGURE 5-1
Page from a Munsell soil color chart. Courtesy of GretagMacbeth.

should be measured at a standardized moistness. If the deposits are dry, they can be moistened with a fine spray of water.

Many soils have more than one color in them. They will have a dominant background color and then be mottled with other colors. The dominant color can be described by the Munsell designation. The mottled areas should be described by the relative amount of mottling, the size of the average mottle, and the contrast in color between the matrix and mottle (Reed, Bailey, and Onokpise 2000:14), and by Munsell if the mottled areas are large enough to determine the color.

To estimate the relative amount of mottling, draw a 10 cm square on the soil profile and estimate the amount of space taken up by the mottles. Mottles that occupy less than 2 percent of the horizon are classified as *few*; 2 to 20 percent as *common*; and more than 20 percent as *many*. Mottles less than 5 mm in diameter are classified as *fine*; 5 to 15 mm as *medium*; and greater than

15 mm as *coarse.* If the contrast in color between the matrix and the mottles are recognizable only after close examination, it is classified as *faint.* When the mottles are the prominent feature of the horizon they are considered *predominant.*

A Munsell color chart for soil comes with about seven pages and sells for about two hundred dollars. It can be purchased from many major bookstore chains.

Texture

Soil texture refers to the relative proportions of sand, silt, and clay in the soil, which are precisely defined according to the size of soil grains. The soil texture is the physical property that most influences the soil characteristics. It influences permeability, water infiltration rate, porosity, and fertility. Experienced soil scientists can determine the soil texture by rubbing the soil between their thumbs and fingers (see flow chart in figure 5-2).

The U.S. Department of Agriculture defines twelve different textural classes of soil based on the proportion of sand, silt, and clay in the soil (figure 5-3). Many universities have departments of agronomy or soils, with laboratories that accurately determine soil texture for a minimal fee. For the analysis, the lab would need about a cup of soil placed in a clean, plastic ziplock bag. The bag can be left open until the soil dries. It is wise to clearly label the bag, and then place it upside down into a second ziplock plastic bag, in case the first bag opens. Samples should be dried or stored in a refrigerator to retard the growth of mold until sent to the lab for analysis.

Sand grains are mineral particles 0.06 to 2.00 mm in diameter. Sand can be divided into very fine, fine, medium, coarse, and very coarse. Sand particles are visible to the naked eye and feel gritty when the soil is moistened and rubbed between the fingers. Sand-sized particles are chemically inert, as are silt-sized particles. Sand differs from silt in being large enough to resist wind erosion. Sandy soils are dominated by the properties of sand: weak structure, rapid infiltration rate, slight erosion potential, loose consistency, and low fertility.

Silt grains are mineral particles between 0.002 and 0.060 mm in diameter. Particles cannot be seen with the eye. Soils with a large silt fraction will have a "soapy" or "silky" feel and are only slightly sticky. Silt soils are highly erodible and relatively infertile soils. A field test for a silt soil is that it will form a ball that keeps its shape under gentle pressure.

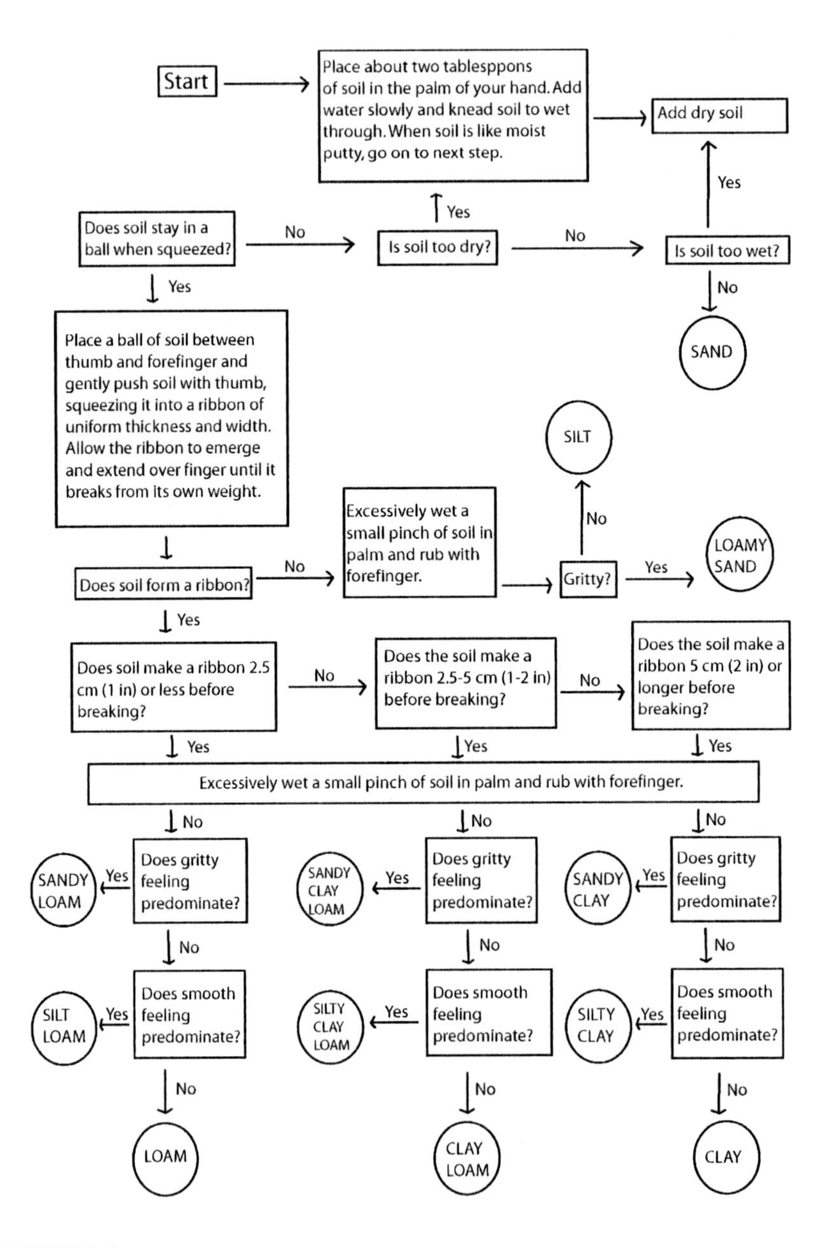

FIGURE 5-2

Flow chart for determining soil texture by feel. After Reed, Bailey, and Onokpise (2000, figure 6).

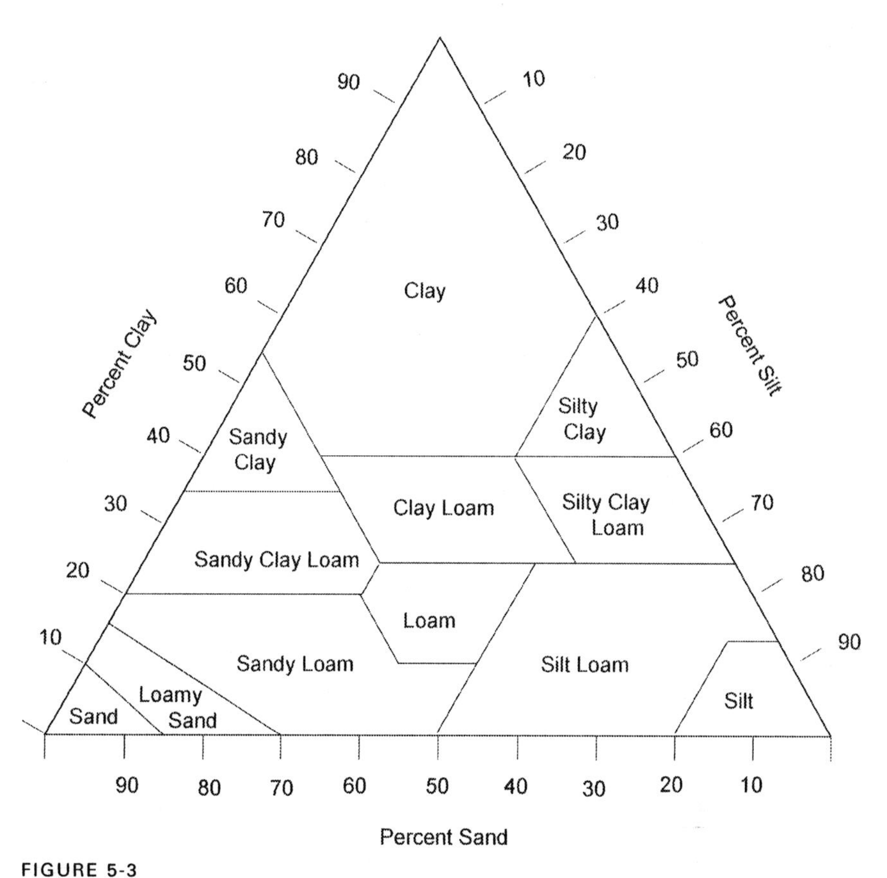

FIGURE 5-3
U.S. Department of Agriculture soil triangle. The soil type is determined by the percent of different sized soil grains.

Clay grains are less than 0.002 mm in diameter. Clay gives a sticky feel when wet and may be shaped into a ribbon when pressed between the fingers. Clay particles are chemically active and stick together in aggregates that resist wind erosion and increase soil porosity (Reed, Bailey, and Onokpise 2000:16). Clay soils have a slow infiltration rate, drain slowly, are very sticky and plastic when wet, and form hard clods when dry. Wet, or dry, they are hard soils to work through a screen.

Coarse Components

Frequently larger particles are present in the soil. They are described by the size of the particle and the approximate frequency (e.g., soil includes 10 percent gravel). To estimate the frequency, delimit a 10 cm square on the soil profile and estimate the area taken up by the larger particles. The terms used to describe the particles are precisely defined:

very small, 2–6 mm
small, 6 mm–2cm (gravel)
medium, 2–6 cm (pebbles)
large, 6–20 cm (pebbles)
very large, 20–60 cm (cobbles)
boulders > 60 cm

Structure

Soil structure is the aggregation of primary particles into secondary shapes called *peds*. If soil is allowed to fall naturally out of the exposed horizon, the shape of the ped may be seen in the remaining horizon. The soil structure can be further divided into grade, class, and type. But for the purposes of this volume, it is sufficient to note that disturbed soils have no soil structure and undisturbed soils may have a soil structure. If a clear soil structure is seen, then it is a sign that the soil has not been disturbed.

STRATIGRAPHY

Stratigraphy is the layering of soils. Soils can be layered by natural events, such as the soil formation processes described above. They can also be layered by cultural events, such as when a developer adds fill on top of the natural soil. Stratigraphy conforms to a law of superposition that states that in undisturbed soils the older soil layers are below younger soil layers.

Large road cuts and backhoe trenches open up the soil profile so that it can be readily studied. Figure 5-4 shows a soil profile as revealed at an archaeological site. Only by knowing what the natural soil profile is in a given area will the investigator recognize what is not natural, or what may be the result of a man-made feature such as a grave.

SOIL PROFILES AND GRAVES

In creating a grave, a hole is made in the soil (figure 5-5). When the soil is replaced in the hole, the soil from different soil layers is mixed and no longer occurs in the natural soil horizons. In areas with well-developed soil horizons,

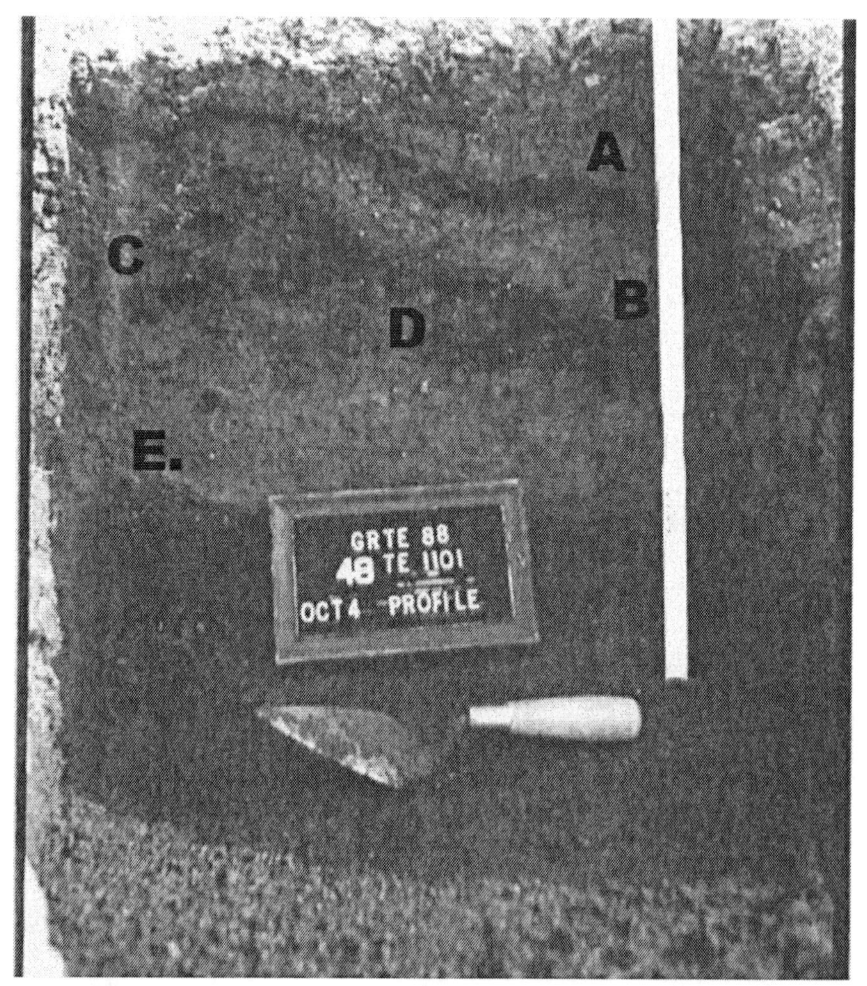

FIGURE 5-4
Reading a soil profile. This is a soil profile at an archaeological site in Grand Teton National Park. The layers seen in the soil are due to a combination of cultural and natural factors. The lighter layer at the bottom (E) was sharply truncated by the beach sands above it, and is the oldest soil horizon in the picture. Layer D was laid down earlier than layer C, and both were eroded before layer B was deposited. Layer A is the youngest of the dark soil horizons.

the mixture will be lighter than the soil near the surface and darker than the deeper soil. These are locations where it is beneficial to use backhoes or front-end loaders to locate graves, as the color difference can outline the grave pit (although as discussed later, heavy machinery is a last resort in locating remains). (See figures 5-6; figure 5-7A, 5-7C.)

FIGURE 5-5
The soil change at the right side of the soil profile in the trench is where a grave was dug through the natural soil profile. Excavations conducted by Physicians for Human Rights.

FIGURE 5-6
Grave exposed in subsoil. The color differentiation is due to organic material in the upper soil horizons being mixed with the grave backfill and contrasting with the deeper, lighter colored soil. Excavations conducted by Sri Lankan forensic experts.

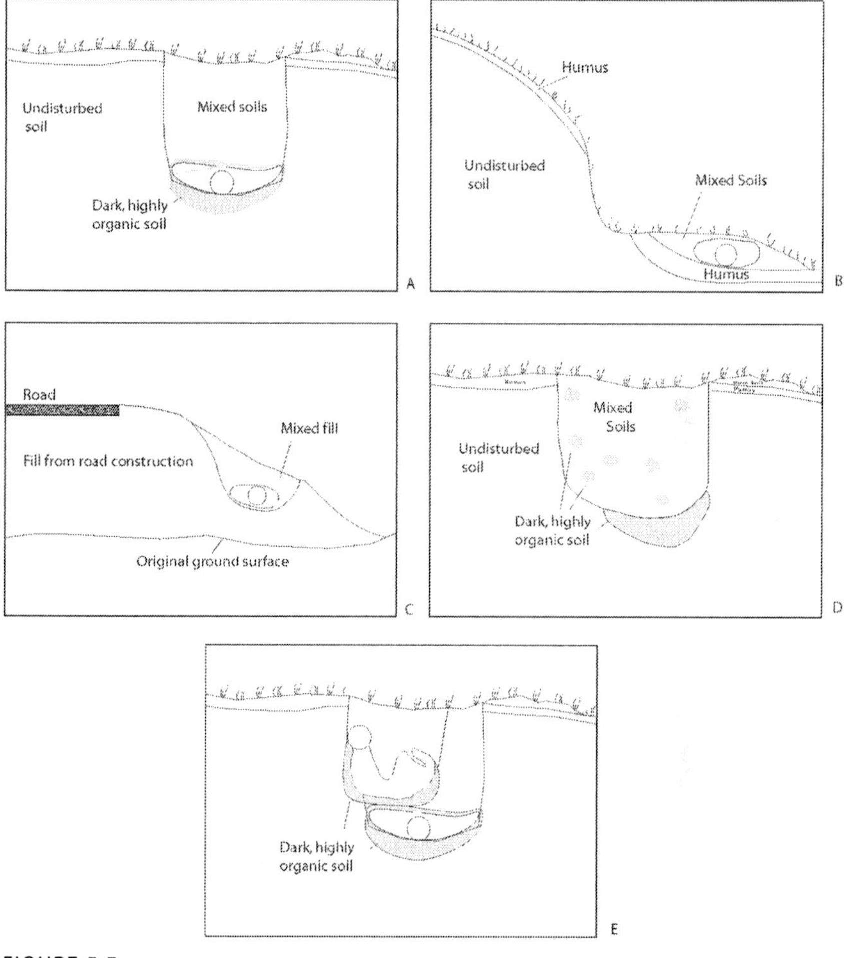

FIGURE 5-7

Model graves showing changes in soil horizons. A. Grave cut through natural soil profile and filled with mixed soils. Depending on the stage of decomposition of the remains, there will be an area of soil around the body where the soil is saturated with fluids from the decomposing remains. B. Grave dug into a hillside where the cut is actually mainly on the hillside above the remains. C. Grave dug into fill where there may be no soil differentiation between the mixed soils of the fill and the mixed soils of the grave fill. D. Grave where body was removed, leaving soil clumps saturated with decomposition fluids. E. Grave area used twice, showing multiple cuts into the natural soil horizons.

In areas where the soil is already disturbed, such as areas filled with soil for the construction of buildings or roads, there may be no color differentiation with the grave pit, as the soil is homogenous (figure 5-7C). The same may be true where the darker, organically rich soil has been removed either purposely or through erosion. In some housing subdivisions in the United States, developers sell the organically rich soil as topsoil and then put sod over the organically poor, deeper soil. Here, again, there may be no soil color differentiation. These are very poor areas to use backhoes to look for burials as it is likely the first indication of the grave will be finding the burial itself—with the backhoe bucket.

Figure 5-7B shows a situation applicable to steep terrain. Here, shoveling soil over a body can be much easier than digging a hole. This type of feature should be visible from the surface as a cut into the side of the hill exposing soil layers normally below the surface. The humus layer below the body delineates the area that was not disturbed.

Body preservation depends to some degree on where in the soil profile the body is placed. The greater the depth of the body, the greater the preservation (Mant 1950:31). In a shallow grave, the body is subject to the effects of animals and insects. In addition, shallow soil tends to be better aerated, and rainwater can percolate better, hastening decomposition. Also, the soil and body will be more subject to temperature changes and become warmer in summer, also increasing decomposition. In any soil type, any covering over the body slows decomposition. Clothing, a body bag, or a tarp retard decomposition significantly.

Frequently there is a layer of highly organic material around the remains (figure 5-7). This is a result of decomposing body fluids. Depending on the state of decomposition of the remains, and the drainage of the soil, it could show around any of the remains in the model graves. The decomposing body fluids leach mainly downward, more deeply into the soil, although some will percolate some distance up. The fluids turn the soil darker than the matrix soil and they have the unmistakable smell of decomposition.

Even if the body was removed from a grave, soil saturated with this fluid will most likely remain (figure 5-7D). If a body has been removed, particularly before skeletal elements were exposed, such soil may be the only remaining indication that a body was there. As it is difficult to dig a hole exactly the same way twice, there may be indications in the soil profile of two cut lines on one side or the other, but in mixed soils, these can be difficult to discern. If a body was removed from a grave, then the soil profile, any tool marks seen on the side of the grave, and the recognition of decomposition fluid–saturated soil can be extremely important in documentation.

If more than one body is located in the area, then the soil profile may be one way to determine whether the remains were buried in the same event or separate events. Since disturbed soil can be much softer and easier to dig than undisturbed soil, it makes sense that if a person knows where there is a previous grave, he or she will partially dig it out to deposit a second body as an easier alternative to digging a new grave. Again, it is difficult to dig a hole in exactly the same space twice and the soil profile should show overlapping cuts (figure 5-7E). Also the remains may show differing states of decomposition.

BODY SILHOUETTES AND SOIL CHEMISTRY

In forensic situations, there are two ways that soil chemistry impacts investigations. First, the decomposing remains impact the soil chemistry. Second, soils impact the preservation of bodies, clothing, and any associated materials.

As bodies decay, elements leach into the soils. After the remains decay, a careful excavator may still see what archaeologists refer to as a body "ghost" or body silhouette. This is where there has been complete skeletal destruction, but a stain in the soil remains, indicating where the remains had lain (Beard, Hilliard, and Akridge 2000; Bethell 1989; Biek 1970; Haughton and Powlesland 1999:19–20). Usually, they are found by archaeologists excavating in graveyards where this type of stain can be anticipated and found before the team excavates through it.

To confirm that these are body silhouettes, a chemical analysis of the soil can be completed; the analysis will reveal if there are elements in the sample that have a higher concentration in the body than in soil. The inorganic portion of bone is hydroxyapatite, which contains calcium, phosphorus, oxygen, and hydrogen. Zinc and strontium are trace elements that find their way into bone in amounts dependent on the amounts in the diet. Heavier concentrations of calcium, phosphorus, sodium, and zinc in the feature as compared to the surrounding soil may be indicators that the feature is a body stain (Bethell 1989; Solecki 1951).

Calcium and sodium are easily leached from soil, and if the area is subject to heavy rainfall or flooding, it is less likely that these elements will remain in the soil. Farmers and gardeners add nutrients to crops and one of these is phosphorus, so there are reasons for localized high concentrations of phosphorus in the soil aside from it being the past location of human remains.

Studies of body decomposition have found that there is a large rapid release of elements (Na^+, Cl^-, NH_4^+, K^+, Ca^{2+}, MG^{2+}, SO_4^{2-}) as a body initially decays (Vass et al. 1992). A second, smaller peak may occur when bone decays (Vass 1991). Volatile fatty acids (VFAs) also are released during decomposition. They are the product of the breakdown of both muscle and fat. The VFAs are released into the soil in a temperature-dependent pattern and can be used in determining time since death (Vass 1991; Vass et al. 1992; Vass et al. 2002).

Several studies have used the zinc/copper ratio in the soil to identify burial areas as old as the Paleo-Indian period (about ten thousand years ago) (Akridge 1994:5–9; Morse 1997:93–95). Zinc is not as soluble as the major elements in bone, and copper has about the same solubility as zinc. Under most conditions, both will precipitate as minerals, rather than combine with other elements. Chemically, copper in soil acts much as zinc does, but it is much less concentrated in bone than zinc is. Thus, a high zinc/copper ratio should be expected in burial locations. The ratio is used because a number of factors (e.g., pH changes, groundwater movement) could change the overall abundance figures, but the ratio should stay similar.

One relevant factor in preservation of remains is the pH of the soil. The pH notation indicates the degree of acidity or alkalinity of the soil. Low pH numbers indicate acidity, high numbers indicate alkalinity. Technically, pH is the common logarithm of the reciprocal of the hydrogen-ion concentration (grams per liter) of the soil system. A neutral soil has a pH of 7. Because pH is a logarithmic measure, each unit change in pH represents a tenfold change of acidity or alkalinity.

A soil pH reflects a particular set of chemical conditions. Usually, soils of humid regions are acidic and soils of arid regions are alkaline, or basic. (Foth and Turk 1972:179). Most soils have a pH from about 4 to 10. The pH of the soil is an indicator of what minerals may be free for specific plants (e.g., pin oaks are subject to iron deficiency when grown on neutral or alkaline soils). Thus, people change the pH of the soil by adding acidic (such as sulfur) or basic (such as lime) components to the soil. Particularly in farm fields or flowerbeds, the pH may be different than the surrounding soil.

Acidic soils generally tend towards poor preservation of most materials. Metals corrode in acidic soils, the acids break down the proteins in organic materials, and most fabrics preserve poorly. On the other hand, other things being equal, alkaline soils tend toward better preservation of metals, organic materials, and fabrics (Sease 1987:2).

Many investigators have wished for a fundamental soil characteristic that would differentiate an area with a decomposing body from surrounding areas. Unfortunately, the major constituents of the decomposing remains tend to leach down into the soil below, rather than percolate to the surface, so that the soil below the remains, rather than the soil above them, would need to be tested.

The interaction of soil and bone chemical constituents is a process called diagenesis. The chemical composition of bone reflects the diet of the individual, thus archeologists are interested in bone chemistry and diagenesis. Much of this body of literature is summarized by Whitmore and others who include a summary table of postmortem impact on bone by various elements (Whitmore et al. 1989:220–39, table 5.2).

For forensic purposes, it is sufficient to note that given a generally basic soil pH, bone can be found in soil after tens of thousands of years. Should the investigator wish to complete any chemical testing on the remains, samples of the soil adjacent to the body should be taken. These will give the chemists an idea of the post-depositional environment of the remains and potential diagenetic impacts on the test results.

SUMMARY

1. Investigators need to be familiar with their local soils in order to determine what is abnormal.
2. Soil formation is determined by the parent material, climate, topography, soil biota, and time.
3. Soils are described by their color, texture, coarse components, and structure.
4. Changes in soil profiles due to digging through, and disturbing, the natural soil profile are very useful in grave location and determining whether the grave was tampered with.
5. There are changes in soil chemistry due to body decomposition, but to date they have not been useful in grave location.

GLOSSARY TERMS

clay

law of superposition

Munsell chart

ped

pedology

pH

sand

silt

SUGGESTED READING

Beard, Lorna, Jerry Hilliard, Glen Akridge

2000 Historical and Chemical Traces of an Ozark Cemetery for Enslaved African-Americans: A Study of Silhouette Burials in Benton Country, Arkansas. *North American Archaeologist* 21 (4): 323–49.
An interesting study where the remains in a historic cemetery were degraded to the point that only stains in the soil where bodies used to be could be seen.

Murray, Raymond C.

2004 *Evidence from the Earth: Forensic Geology and Criminal Investigation.* Mountain Press Publishing, Missoula, Montana.
A discussion of the use of soils and other geological evidence in the forensic context.

Reed, Stewart, Nathan Bailey, and Oghenekome Onokpise

2000 *Soil Science for Archaeologists.* Florida Agricultural and Mechanical University and Southeast Archaeological Center, National Park Service.
A nicely illustrated and clearly written guide to soil description. Available through National Technical Information Service (www.ntis.gov).

6

Surface Remains

Surface remains result from either (1) a body that was never buried; (2) a body that was buried and then brought to the surface, either in whole or in part; or (3) a secondary deposit, such as ashes from a cremation (which may actually contain many bone and tooth fragments). Factors that can bring buried human remains to the surface and scatter the remains include erosion, agriculture, and removal of the remains by either humans or animals. An understanding of these taphonomic factors can help the investigator determine whether, or where, to look for missing skeletal elements or additional evidence.

Many outdoor burned-bodies sites are also surface-remains sites, and are included in this chapter. Also briefly discussed is the dispersal of cremated remains by relatives in lieu of burial, as these can initially be mistaken for forensic or historic cases. The fragility and fragmentation of burned bone necessitates great care in recovery. Finally, a general strategy for dealing with surface remains is presented, with a decision tree for the investigator.

Part of the fascination of forensic science, of course, is that every case is unique. For instance, bodies have been deposited on the surface rolled in carpet, initiating studies on how this affects skeletal decomposition and dispersal (Mondero 2005; Morton and Lord 2002). The strategies presented here will need to be modified for almost every individual case. Nevertheless, having a basic mental template of how the investigation should proceed is useful.

TAPHONOMIC FACTORS AFFECTING REMAINS ON THE GROUND SURFACE

Once on the ground surface, a number of factors affect the body and associated evidence. Skeletal elements become scattered by agents such as animals, gravity, plowing, humans, fluvial action, or trampling. The amount of scattering is monitored from the original position of the complete skeleton (Lyman 1994:162). If the remains are not found in anatomical position, the investigator should determine the reason. The remains can be modified through weathering, abrasion, or chewing by a variety of scavengers.

Scavengers

As much as humans like to think that we are at the top of the food chain, once we're dead, we're just another link in the food chain. Carnivores, omnivores, rodents, and insects all feed on human remains, and their effects on surface scatters are widely documented (Haglund 1992; Haglund, Reay, and Swindler 1989; Willey and Snyder 1989). These creatures can damage and modify bone, but this section will emphasize their effect on the recovery of surface remains, rather than their potential to modify the skeletal elements.

Rodents feed on human corpses and bone and impact recovery and analysis. Rats have been observed nesting in the thoracic cavity of a partially skeletonized body (Haglund 1992). Mouse fur was found with the remains of a decomposing surface pig in Nebraska (Mondero 2005), probably the result of a nest. Rodent gnawing, however, is more common than nesting, and in documented cases rodents have gnawed on bodies ranging from fresh (Haglund 1992) to ancient proto-human (Brain 1981). This gnawing can be extensive enough to affect the identification and the interpretation of injury and cause of death.

The significant factor in terms of recovery, however, is that these ubiquitous rodents move bones. The most noted accumulators of bones are porcupines (Brain 1981), although most rodents will move smaller bones. If all of the skeletal elements are not present during the inventory, and if the missing bones are the small bones of the hand and feet, then rodents may well be the cause. Finding rodent tooth marks on the remaining bones will provide a clue that the pests have been at work (figure 6-1). Excavating the area under and around the body may locate rodent tunnels (krotovina), where the elements were dragged.

Carnivores and omnivores can include dogs, coyotes, wolves, bobcats, raccoons, opossums, and/or bears. They feed on remains, chew on bones, and

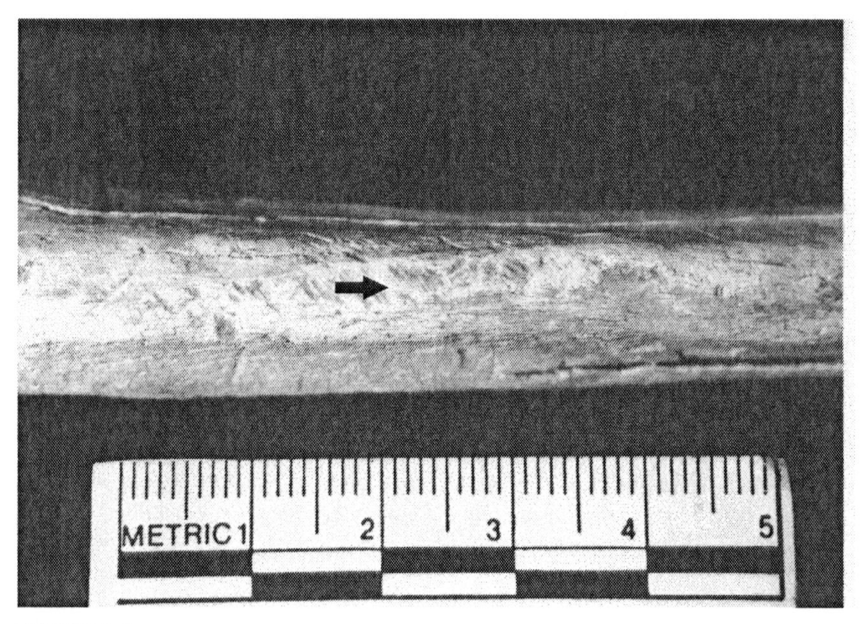

FIGURE 6-1
Tooth marks from rodent gnawing on bone. The arrow points to parallel striations on the bone which are tooth marks.

displace portions of skeletons, causing immense amounts of damage to the original scene. Each animal has its own distinctive manner of feeding and corpse dispersal, and the species that may be in the specific geographical locale need to be identified when dealing with the possibility of carnivore-ravaged remains.

Dogs and coyotes are the most common carnivores in nearly all areas in the United States. Studies on canid scavenging in most areas of the United States have been completed and are available to the researcher (Blumenschine 1986; Haglund, Reay, and Swindler 1989; Haynes 1981; Willey and Snyder 1989). Willey and Synder (1989:896) observed the following sequence of disarticulation of deer remains by wolves:

> Initially, the meaty sections such as the hindquarters are consumed, the thoracic cavity is opened, and the ribs are eaten. Often the throat is torn open, and the nose is eaten, disarticulation of one or more limbs commonly occurs within 24 to 48 hours, usually the forelimb before the hind limb. Following consumption of meaty parts, there is extensive destruction of limb bone ends, the vertebral

> column, and the associated rib heads. Remnants of the vertebral column and hide are the last portions consumed, usually in four to seven days. The consumption sequence may take as little as 24 hours for six-month-old fawns (16 to 24 kg) to four to seven days for fully mature deer (55 to 73 kg).
>
> In addition to the general disarticulation pattern outlined above, individual deer elements and element portions are heavily damaged or completely destroyed and consumed by the wolves. The more porous long bone ends, such as the proximal humerus and both ends of the femur, are often destroyed as the wolves chew through the thin bone cortex and consume the spongier cancellous tissue inside the bone. In contrast, compact bone ends, such as the distal humerus and distal tibia, usually survive, although bearing tooth scoring and puncture marks. The harder, thick-walled shafts of humeri, femora, tibiae, and metapodials are likely to survive. . . .Ribs and vertebrae are almost always destroyed. . . .Smaller elements, such as carpals, tarsals, and phalanges are invariably swallowed, often whole. These elements reemerge heavily gnawed and eroded, but often identifiable, in the wolves' scats.

Willey and Snyder also point out that wolves may move the carcasses. Dismembered parts may be moved freely and repeatedly. This results in groups of bones that are separated from the remainder of the body and moved together as a unit. With a human body, the hands and arms, including the scapula, tend to be removed before the legs (Haglund, Reay, and Swindler 1989:601). The lower limbs are then disarticulated, often in association with the pelvic girdle. The segments of the axial skeleton may still be articulated, but moved away from the remainder of the body. In the final stage of scavenging, all bones are disarticulated and scattered.

If the remains were scavenged (seeing tooth marks on the bones would be an indication of scavenging), then it is necessary to determine how close the elements are to the original site of the remains. Drag marks or disturbed ground cover may indicate the direction from which the remains were moved. Previous places where the body has lain may be indicated by discolorations due to body fluid leakage, insect larvae, pupae casings or a strong odor (Haglund, Reay, and Swindler 1989:602). The immediate area and trails that provide access to the area should first be searched for disarticulated elements. Isolated teeth may be recovered from the original resting place of the crania or the area between the original resting place and where the cranium was found (Haglund, Reay, and Swindler 1989:603).

Some research suggests it may be possible to distinguish bear scavenging from canine scavenging based on the representation of elements (Carson, Stefan, and Powell 2000). Bears may be more likely to consume, remove or damage the vertebrae, ribs, and sterna, while canids are more likely to scavenge the extremities and organ cavities. A single case of reported pig scavenging (Berryman 2002) suggests that the pig focused on the viscera, throat, and face as opposed to the meaty areas of the appendages. The other indicator of pig scavenging was the difference in tooth marks on the bones. However, a carcass can be scavenged by more than one species of animal. Over time as the animals chew or eat less-favored parts of the skeleton, the assemblages may come to resemble each other.

If the remains have been scavenged, then there may be a need to search for and collect animal feces found near the scene. These may include bits of bone or small items of jewelry.

Weathering

When an animal dies, and the soft tissue over the bone decays, the bone is exposed to the elements and begins to weather. Weathering consists of the effects on bone of saturation, desiccation, and temperature changes (G. Miller 1975:217). The deterioration of bone passes through predictable stages. The surface of the bone deteriorates at the same time that its organic content is lost. First the bone displays a network of fine, usually parallel lines. These cracks progressively deepen and widen and over time the bone surface deteriorates (Behrensmeyer 1978; White and Folkens 2005: 52–54). The amount of weathering has been used to examine the age of the assemblage and the post-depositional environment of the assemblage, but the weathering varies greatly depending on the environment in which the remains were deposited.

Figure 6-2 shows an assemblage of horse bones at the Little Bighorn Battlefield. The battle occurred in 1876 and the photograph was taken in 1879; the remains lay on the surface over the intervening years. In 1881, the skeletal elements were gathered together and placed in a mass grave on the battlefield. They were exhumed in 2002 as part of a National Park Service compliance project.

Figure 6-3 shows the weathering on the surface of the horse bones as a result of their laying on the surface in arid eastern Montana for five years. The weathering demonstrates that the remains were once surface remains, despite the fact that they were subsequently buried for over a century.

FIGURE 6-2
Surface scatter of horse bone, Last Stand Hill, Little Bighorn National Battlefield Monument. The battle was in 1876, and the photograph taken in 1879 by Stanley R. Morrow. Note the disarticulation of remains, and the downhill displacement. These bones were gathered in a mass grave in 1881 and exhumed in 2002 (Scott 2002). Courtesy Little Bighorn Battlefield National Monument, U.S. National Park Service.

Figure 6-4 shows extreme weathering on human bone from the Custer National Cemetery at the Little Bighorn National Monument. These elements were probably initially shallowly buried after the battle in 1876, then eroded to the surface at some later point. They were collected from the surface and reburied in the Custer National Cemetery, which is the final resting place of many of the soldiers who died in the Battle of Little Bighorn, as well as veterans of America's later wars. Finding this type of weathering on buried bone is an indication that the remains lay on the surface for some period of time after the flesh had decayed.

Factors that affect weathering on the bone include the skeletal element involved (the specific bone), taxon, microenvironment, duration of exposure of the elements, and the overall history of the assemblage (Lyman and Fox 1997).

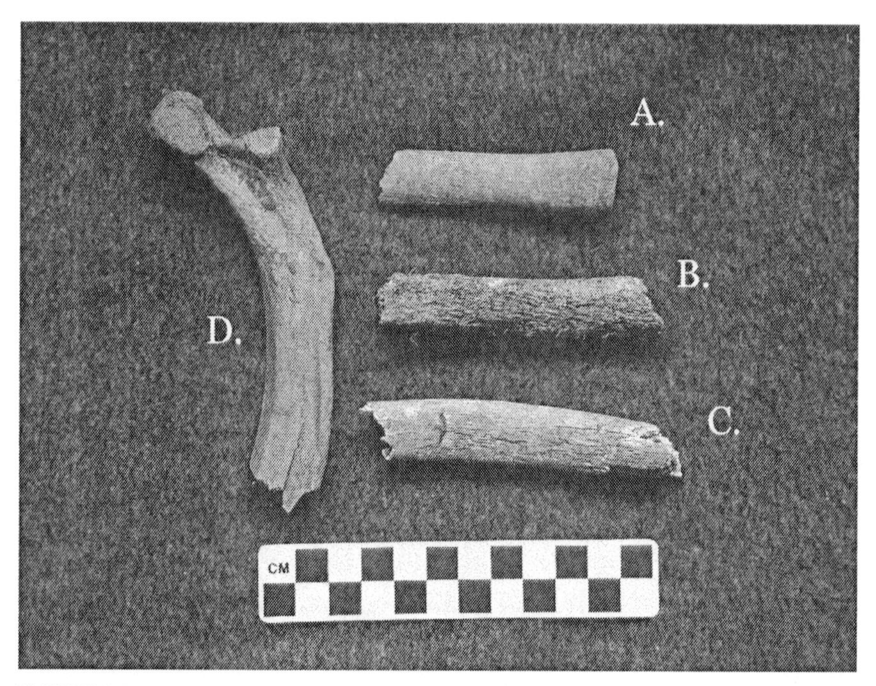

FIGURE 6-3
Weathering on horse ribs from Last Stand Hill, Little Bighorn Battlefield National Monument. Note the differences in the amount of weathering on the bones, despite the similar taphonomic history. Sample A shows little cracking, although it does not show the grease seen on fresh bone. Sample B shows a great deal of exfoliation and deterioration. Samples C and D are in-between. Photograph courtesy of Douglas D. Scott.

Behrensmeyer (1978) suggests that different bones from the same skeleton may weather at different rates.

In a single bone, there may be different weathering stages seen on different parts of the element. If a bone has not been moved much since deposition, then the bone should be more weathered on the exposed surface than on the ground surface. If the bone is more weathered on the surface next to the ground, then it is likely that it was moved.

The microenvironment is probably one of the most important factors in determining the amount of weathering on the bone. Local vegetation, shade, and moisture are the most important characteristics. The magnitude of seasonal changes in weather and durations of the seasons are also important (Brain 1967; Cook 1986; G. Miller 1975).

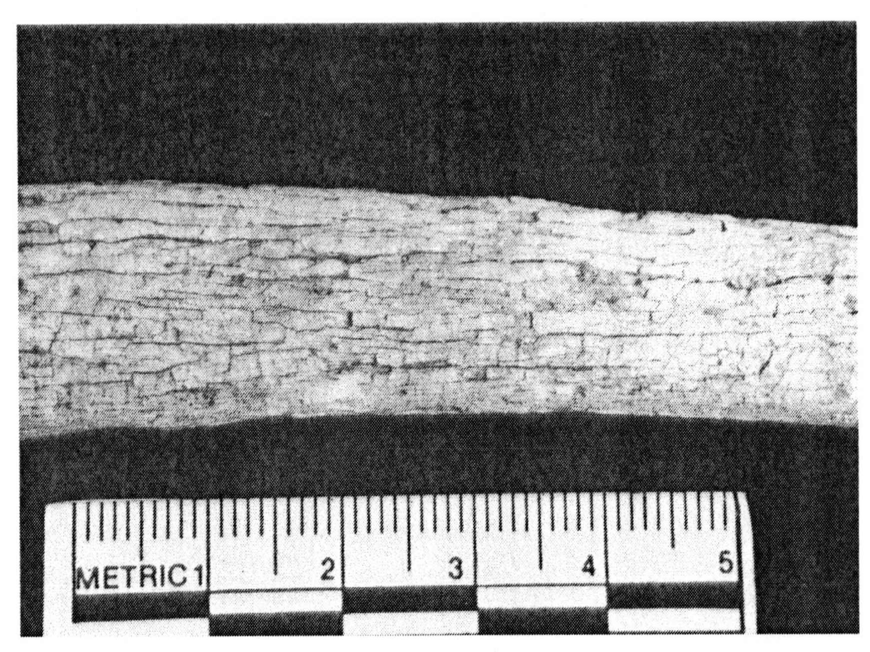

FIGURE 6-4
Detail of deterioration of the bones caused by their exposure to the elements. These were later buried at Custer National Cemetery. Photograph courtesy Douglas D. Scott.

As the examples from the Little Bighorn Battlefield show, the length of time that the remains have been exposed to the surface is not necessarily the interval since death. If the remains have eroded since burial, differences in the weathering among the elements relate to the time since the bone was exposed to the surface. In fact, different elements from the same individual may show vastly different weathering based on the duration of the exposure of that element.

Bone weathering does not reflect time in a direct manner (Lyman and Fox 1997: 242). However, observations on the degree and type of weathering can yield relative information on the length of time the element was exposed and may yield information on other taphonomic considerations, such as movement of the remains.

Slope Wash and Water Transportation

As remains disarticulate, they are more vulnerable to movement by gravity or water, or a combination termed "slope wash." Fluvial transport of animal bone has been studied extensively (Behrensmeyer 1975; Boaz 1982; Voorhies 1969) and tends to preferentially sort and transport remains. Less structurally dense bones are more likely to be moved by fluvial transport than more structurally dense bones. The shape of a bone influences whether it is transported and how far. In strong currents, long bones tend to orient with the current with the heavier end upstream, while in weak currents elongate bones may orient perpendicular to the current (Behrensmeyer 1990:234).

When bones are moved in fluvial transport, the most likely places for their final burial are in areas where the coarse fraction of a sediment load is transported, such as the actively aggrading parts of a channel (such as point bars and sand or gravel bars) (Lyman 1994:174).

Trampling

Surface remains in pasture or wilderness areas may be subject to trampling by livestock, wild game, or humans. The major documented effects include substantial downward migration of material, fracturing of bones, and the creation of marks on bones (Lyman 1994:377). In harder soils, there is evidence that material disperses more horizontally than vertically. Variations in the substrate, in the intensity of activity, and in the interactions of objects, both with each other and with the soil, can affect the distribution and damage on the material (Gifford-Gonzalez et al. 1985:817). Also, the entire site can be much less visible and more difficult to locate because the evidence is pushed into the ground.

Experiments have been conducted to determine the effect of trampling on surface archaeological materials. In one such experiment, five one-meter squares were set up with eight stone flakes in each (Van Vuren 1982). All were in pinion-juniper woodland and grassland near Ash Fork, Arizona. Three of the units were in areas of high feral sheep density, and two were in areas of low sheep density. After six months the area was raked to expose the buried flakes. In the areas of high sheep density, two-thirds (ca. 66 percent) of the flakes were lost and the rest were no longer in their original positions. In the area of low sheep density, only 6 percent of the flakes were lost. This suggests that the longer surface remains lay in a pasture area, or an area with wild animal grazing, the more difficult the recovery.

Trampling can reduce bone to fragments, especially bones that are weathered and easily broken (Haynes 1981:253). Trampling also produces marks on bone. Prehistoric archaeologists doing studies on bone trampling found that the marks were similar to cut marks made by stone tools, although relatively shallow. Trampling marks tend to be random and multidirectional (Olsen and Shipman 1988).

Agricultural Activities

Agricultural activities may bring buried human remains to the surface. Soil in a cultivated field is plowed, pulverized, crushed, fertilized, aerated, compacted, burned, and thrown into a harvester (Haglund, Connor, and Scott 2001). If the bones are in, or on, the edge of a plowed field, then the search should continue throughout the field. Farm technology is continually improving, and farmers are plowing, disking, and fertilizing ever deeper. Combined with the erosion of topsoil from the fields, graves can be plowed to the surface. This is especially possible if the body was buried on the edge of a field that has since been expanded, so that the plow caught one edge of the burial (figure 6-5).

A grave may initially be on the edge of a field, or in a field, and over time the plow will catch a portion of the body. As it does, bone will be distributed through the field in the direction of the plowing. Over time, all the skeletal elements may be distributed throughout the field and subject to being broken through tilling activities and weathering. The burial of human remains within the depth of soil disturbed by a plow and other agricultural activities is not conducive to the long-term preservation of the remains, or to the preservation of evidence to determine cause of death and identification.

Human Movement of Remains

The intentional moving of remains may also create a scatter of bone at the site of the original burial. A body may be moved from one area to another for many reasons. Many cultures bury their dead for a given period, then exhume the (by then) skeletal remains and store them above ground (e.g., Vietnam; see Holland, Anderson, and Mann 1997:267). In Greek Orthodox Catholic graveyards, a family may own a single plot. When it is time to bury a member of the family, the bones of the previous family member buried in the plot are gathered in a cloth bag and placed under, in, or near the coffin of the recently deceased family member. In clandestine burials, the people who buried the remains may become uncomfortable with the original location and move the remains, or part of them, to what they consider a less obvious area.

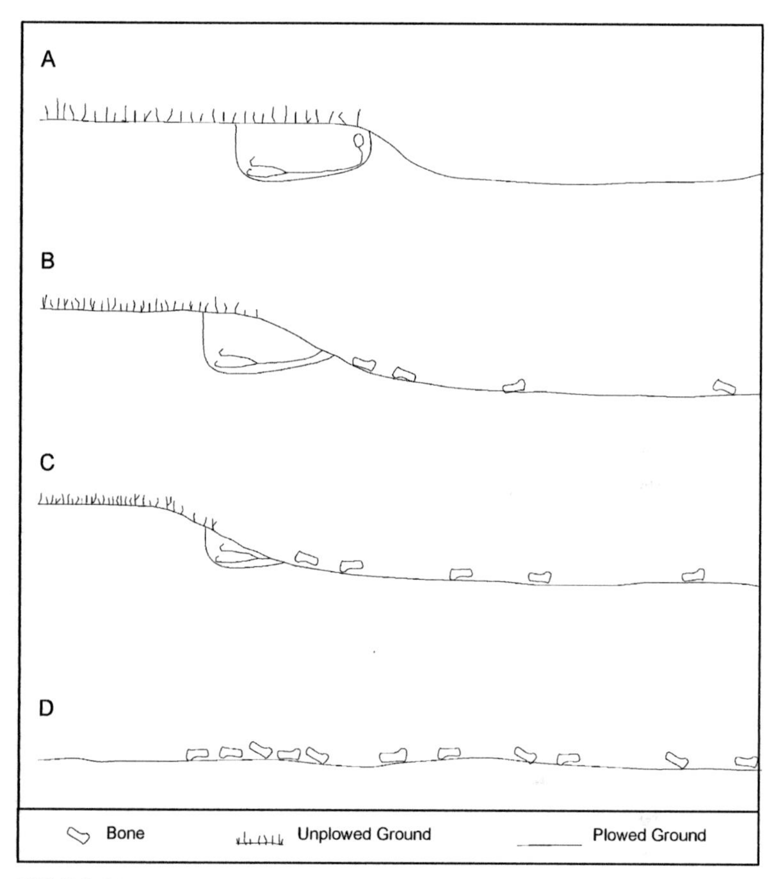

FIGURE 6-5
Model of a grave destroyed through agricultural activities. Redrawn from Haglund, Connor, and Scott (2002).

Frequently, where bodies were removed from the ground, human bone will be found on the surface and mixed in the grave fill. The small bones of the hands and feet, as well as the patellae, are frequently lost during recovery by nonprofessionals. At disturbed sites in Bosnia and Herzegovina, Skinner, York, and Connor (2002) found that incomplete remains, either fleshed or skeletal, occurred at all of the disturbed sites examined. Clothing fragments also occurred at all sites. Body containers (such as blankets, plastic, wood, and body bag fragments), without the remains, were observed at three of the four sites examined. At all the sites they examined, there were artifacts that supported the suggestion of the prior presence of human remains. Fragments of bone and other artifacts were scattered on the surface. In sum, there was plenty of evidence remaining on the ground surface that a body had been buried and exhumed.

GENERAL PROCEDURES FOR COLLECTING SURFACE REMAINS

Throughout the investigation there are a series of questions to be answered regarding the remains (figure 6-6):

1. Are the remains human?
2. Are they relatively modern?
3. How many people are represented by the skeletal elements found?
4. Are the remains complete?
5. If the remains are not complete, where is the rest of the body, and why is it not there? (Is it still buried? Was it moved by a scavenger, water, gravity?)

If suspected human remains are found in an outdoor setting, then it is important not to destroy evidence while determining whether or not the remains are human. If the remains are fleshed or partially fleshed, the investigators should park either on a hard-surfaced road or at a distance from the remains, so as not to destroy any prints or tire tracks that may be near the remains themselves—bodies are heavy to carry and it is likely the body was either driven to the place where it was deposited or the person walked there before being killed. The investigator should also examine the obvious paths to the remains for impression evidence, such as footprints. If the remains are skeletal, it is likely that it has been long enough that such evidence has washed away or otherwise been destroyed.

A decision tree for the collection of surface remains is shown in figure 6-6. The search for surface remains usually starts with a pedestrian inventory. Even when the first human skeletal element is located, an inventory of the general area should be completed, to ensure that all the areas containing bone concentrations are found. All finds should be marked as they are located, to guarantee that they can be found again. The team will then want to search the area near the bone more thoroughly.

If the ground cover is thick, the searchers will want to use root clippers to cut the grass, or other cover, off at the ground surface. Pulling the vegetation out by the roots may dislodge subsurface material that is better uncovered

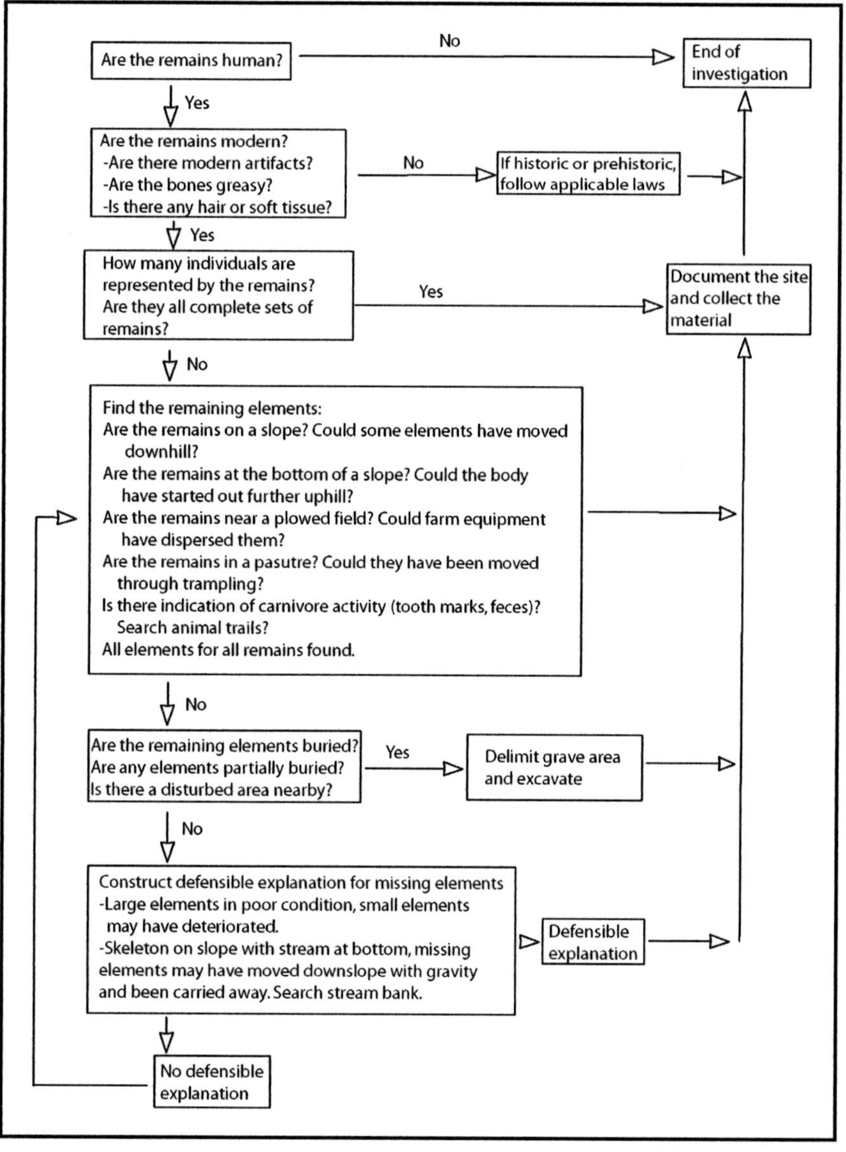

FIGURE 6-6
Decision tree for surface remains protocol.

through excavation. Each searcher needs first to check that they are not standing on a bone; they can then squat to remove enough vegetation so they can work on their hands and knees without kneeling on a skeletal element. Once the searchers know they are near the body, but may not be sure where each element is, they should never put their hands or feet where they cannot see the ground, so that they do not unknowingly step on, and break, a bone.

From a clear space, the searchers can work out from the remains located. Standard survey pin flags (available in surveying equipment stores) can be placed next to each element and piece of evidence located to clearly mark the location of the material. Using one color of flag to mark evidence and another color to mark the skeletal elements is useful. If the evidence is dense, rather than pin flags it is frequently more convenient to use nails or brads and flagging tape (also available in surveying equipment stores); tie the tape around the nail and place the nail in the ground.

If there are elements from multiple bodies it is helpful to mark each case number with a separate color of flags; unassociated elements with a separate color; and unknowns in their own color. It is important to try and associate each element with a case as much as possible in the field. Reassociating commingled skeletal elements with partial bodies in the lab is time-consuming and is usually only partially successful. In the field, the spatial arrangement of the remains and the topography of the scene can be grasped instantly, and both of these are pertinent in determining to which set of remains an element is most likely to belong.

The intense search should go five or ten meters from the farthest skeletal element, or to a topographically logical conclusion. In other words, if there is a cliff, the initial intense search can stop at the cliff edge. A less intense search (not on the hands and knees) should continue for a greater perimeter from the remains—the size of the entire search area, depending on the ground cover and topography. The intense search ends when the skeletal inventory is complete or there is good reason to suspect what happened to the missing elements. If all the elements are not accounted for, the search is not complete.

The team should search a larger area around the remains until they are sure that all pertinent evidence has been found. If the area is covered by leaves or other debris, team members can rake the area to be sure that they are seeing all the material in or below the leaf litter. At one case worked by the Lancaster County Sheriff's Office (Lancaster County, Nebraska), the police team raking the surface found a jacket. Inside the jacket was an identification card. Hoping the card identified the deceased, who was covered with a shallow layer of soil a short distance away, the police ran the name through their computer system and found that the individual had been arrested within the past year. The body was totally skeletal. Disappointed that it was unlikely that the remains were those of the individual on the identification card, they nevertheless followed up on the lead. The investigation found that the card identified the killer. While it is unusual for a killer to leave a picture identification card at the scene, it would be sad to miss it because the search was not thorough enough.

As the elements are located, the team can evaluate the potential reasons for disarticulation, if indeed, the elements are disarticulated. The investigator should be aware that the remains could be scavenged, weathered, trampled, plowed, eroded, or moved by humans—or affected by any number of other taphonomic factors. The preceding pages should give the investigator some idea of strategies to use in these cases.

The searchers should be able to create some testable hypotheses as to why the remains may be disarticulated and deduce predictions as to where the remaining elements may be located. If the remains are on a slope, the searchers may hypothesize that the missing elements eroded down the slope. They might predict that the elements would be at the base of the hill, and can search further based on that prediction. If the searchers hypothesize that a carnivore might have fed on the remains and disarticulated a portion of them, they should predict that they might then see carnivore tooth marks on the remaining skeletal elements, and disarticulation in the groups of bones as described by Haglund, Reay, and Swindler (1989), and the pattern of gnawing described by Willey and Snyder (1989). These predictions can be tested, and the hypotheses verified or rejected. As this is done, it should be included in the notes to document why the team's search took a certain direction or why the search was completed without finding all the skeletal elements.

If any of the bones are only partially on the surface, but still partially in the ground, then the team needs to set up an excavation grid, and excavate the skeletal elements still in the ground. A partially exposed skeletal element should never be pulled out of the ground. It can easily be broken this way. Also, if the bone is lying adjacent to anything else that is also buried, that association is lost when the bone is pulled to the surface. The bone could be lying next to the articulating element, or next to a bullet, or a piece of jewelry.

The detailed mapping of surface remains is useful. The position and orientation of the remains often show a well-defined pattern that reveals the taphonomic factors that resulted in the condition of the remains.

During the excavation, the team needs to look carefully at the soil around the remains to determine whether any evidence remains of a grave pit. Figure 6-5 shows one scenario of how a skeleton may be partially exposed and partially buried. However, sometimes soil can be deposited over unburied remains. The excavators can dig a small hole away from the remains to find out what the undisturbed soil in the immediate location should look like. They can then compare the color, texture, and structure (see chapter 5) of the soil next to the remains to the soil away from the remains to determine whether a grave pit can be identified.

Insects in and around the remains may be an important source of evidence. The information contained in these annoying life-forms may be important in correctly determining time of death, location of death, and other factors important to the investigation (Goff 2000). During the recovery of remains, the entomological evidence needs to be collected and preserved. Haskell and others (1997:439–40) give a detailed description of how to collect useful samples.

Haskell and others (1997) suggest collecting eggs and a mixed-size sample of several hundred larvae from the remains and placing them in vials of solution for preservation. A second sample of larvae should be collected alive for rearing, so the species can be identified. Samples of the leaf litter under the body and the surrounding soil should also be collected and labeled. Clearly, collecting entomological data is more complicated than including maggots with the corpse in the body bag. If possible, a forensic entomologist should be included in the body recovery team. If this is not possible, then an entomologist can be consulted on-site using a wireless telephone.

The surface scatter should be fully documented before removal. This includes photographs and a detailed map. Some kind of base point, or baseline, should be included on the map as well, so that when the body is removed, the team still knows exactly where it was located. Elements for each individual should be removed to separate body bags. If appropriate, entomological and soil samples should be taken. When all the surface material is removed, the team should search the vegetation below the body and the soil to at least 10 cm below surface. This will ensure that any items that fell below the body are recovered. Finally, before completing the post-investigation photographs, a metal detector should be used in the immediate area to ensure that no metal objects, carried further into the soil by their own velocity, or by rodents or insects, are left behind. If any material is located, it needs to be photographed and added to the scene map, as well as to the evidence log.

OUTDOOR BURNED AND CREMATED REMAINS

This text uses the term *cremation* to refer to an intentional mortuary practice. Cremation is a common mortuary practice, not only currently, but also historically and prehistorically. In prehistoric North America, cremated bone was gathered and placed in a pouch, basket, or pottery jar (Heye 1919) and the container buried in a pit. Today, cremation is a relatively inexpensive burial alternative; it is becoming increasingly popular in the United States.

Modern crematory furnaces can reach temperatures over 1500°C (Kennedy 1999:142), but there still frequently remains an amount of ash, bone, and dental fragments in most cremation urns, unless the crematorium pulverizes the residue. The cremated remains, referred to as *cremains*, may also contain small pieces of bone, whole teeth, or pieces of teeth, or implants that may survive a fire. Due to commingling of cremains in the crematorium, some mortuary establishments are now pulverizing the remaining bone and teeth before returning the "ashes" to the family (Kennedy 1999).

Cremated remains can become forensic cases. People often have a romantic notion of the disposal of their cremated remains. Friends or relatives may scatter the ashes of their loved ones in their favorite spots—creating a forensic case. National parks and recreational areas tend to be a favorite place to scatter the remains of a dear one who favored the area. Willey and Scott (1999) discuss the recovery of the cremains of a descendent of a soldier who fought with General George Custer and had asked that his remains be scattered at the Little Bighorn Battlefield. There are seven known sets of recent cremains at the Little Bighorn Battlefield (Scott personal communication 2006). Indications that the bone fragments may have come from a modern crematorium include consistent indications of exposure to very high heat (very white or blue bone), and the occasional inclusion of a metal crematory tag. Willey and Scott (1999) note that all these modern bone scatters are usually a short walk from the parking area, but off established asphalt and dirt paths. The particular areas are thought to have had personal significance to either the deceased or the people that scattered the cremains, but they may also simply be out of the way places to quickly dispose of the cremains without being seen by authorities.

Most open fires produce less heat than cremation kilns. Burning of bone tissue at lower temperatures may closely mimic bone-weathering processes, and microscopic analysis may be necessary to distinguish between the two (T. White 1991:361). One clue that the bone was burned may be in the soil beneath. A fire in an outdoor area creates a recognizable archaeological feature in the soil. Soil will oxidize at about 500°C to 750°C. When soil is burned, the clays in the soil fire, hardening the soil next to the surrounding dirt. The fire also oxidizes the minerals in the soil, turning the irons red or the manganese black. In areas of a natural forest fire, half-moon shaped areas of blackened and reddened soil consistently occurred under areas where logs had fallen on the forest floor (Connor and Cannon 1991; Connor, Cannon, and Carlevato 1989). In an intense fire, these effects will be seen several centimeters below the surface of the fire, the limit appearing to be about 7–10 cm in a natural forest fire (Chandler et al. 1983:173). Exceptions include where tree roots spread the fire deeper into the soil profile or where the fire follows rodent runs, burning nest materials and rodents (Connor, Cannon, and Carlevato 1989; Wettstead 1988). Shallowly buried bone can be burned post-depositionally through such a surface fire (Bennett 1999).

Effects of burning on the remains themselves vary with the intensity of the fire and the amount of flesh remaining on the bones. Bodies burned in the flesh in an open fire show transverse cracks oriented at right angles to the axes of the diaphyses of the long bones, while fat-free dry bones show longitudinal cracks (Baby 1954; Kennedy 1999; Trotter and Peterson 1955). Greater warping occurs in bone encased in muscle and fat exposed to heat than in burnt dry bones. At temperatures above 700°C, bone begins to shrink; at over 1100°C, it begins to split. The degree of heat intensity, length of exposure, and location relative to direct or indirect burning affect the color, weight, and surface texture of the remaining burned bone. Yellow or brown bone results from the retention of body oils during exposure to relatively low temperatures. White or blue bone indicates very high and prolonged temperature.

Investigative Strategy

These are difficult scenes to work, as many untrained investigators have trouble distinguishing burned insulation, whitewash or plaster, and bone. This is where having a trained archaeologist or archaeologically trained anthropologist working with the recovery crews from the beginning can be critical.

Once the remains have been located, the investigator needs to determine the extent of the remains. Careful examination over a wide area can determine the extent of the bone scatter and the remnants of the fire. If the bone is lying in soil, and was burned in place, then the soil under the fire may well be a different color and slightly harder. Clays in the soil will have fired, creating a harder surface than the surrounding soil. Minerals in the soil will oxidize due to the fire, turning iron a pink to red color and manganese to black. In an intense fire, the soil may heat enough to change color and harden several centimeters below ground surface. There may also be remnants of whatever was used as fuel for the fire. If the fuel was a liquid, such as gasoline, it may have soaked into the soil and the investigator may be able to smell it. Soil samples may be necessary to help the laboratory determine the accelerant. If there is burned bone and no indication of a fire, the remains may have been moved (Owsley 1993).

Once the investigator has determined the extent of the scatter of remains, he or she should also have an idea of the condition of the remains, whether they have been reduced to small pieces of white bone, or are only partially charred possibly leaving soft tissue on portions of the remains. Excavation can continue around the remains, leaving them in place on a soil pedestal by removing all soil from around the fired area or from around the remains. This is what is referred to as "pedestaling" the bone. The dirt in areas where small pieces of bone have been located can be taken back to the lab and sifted through a fine screen, such as a flour screen.

Any larger pieces of remains that can be lifted as a whole should be pedestaled and collected. If the soil and bone is placed into a container to be examined in detail later, it is still important to be aware of the spatial arrangements of recognizable fragments of bone. This may indicate body position and the number of bodies found. If the remains are badly burned, it will be much more difficult, if not impossible, to determine the number of individuals represented.

The methods used in the recovery of burned and cremated remains can vary greatly, depending on the needs of the individual case (Correia and Beattie 2002). Burned remains tend to be extremely fragile and friable. Photographing any large pieces of bones before they are removed from the soil can be critical in case the bone crumbles when it is lifted from the soil or in transport. Close-ups should be taken of any defects in the bone for the same reason. Placing friable bone in a bag sometimes causes it to crumble from the pressure from the side of the bag. Packing it carefully in a small box with a little crumpled, smooth tissue paper (not newspaper or toilet paper) to keep the bone from moving within the box may be the best method to transport the bone to the lab.

The discussion above emphasizes techniques for dealing with burned remains found outdoors. Unfortunately, many scenes also occur in burned structures or vehicles. These scenes also benefit from detailed archaeological-type investigation (Dirkmaat 2002), but are beyond the scope of this volume.

SUMMARY

The general procedure for working on an area with surface remains is as follows:

1. Ensure the remains are human and constitute a forensic case.
2. Examine the remains and determine the number of individuals that the remains represent.
3. If the remains are burned or not in anatomical position, it may be useful to create a grid to collect the material. Otherwise, all material should be piece-plotted.
4. Systematically search the area until all elements of all individuals are found. Use pin flags or flagging tape to mark each element and piece of evidence located. This may include soil stained by decomposition fluids of the remains. Use a metal detector to find bullets, casings, or other objects that may have been pressed into the soil.
5. Inventory the skeletal elements or body parts. If all the elements are not present then either continue the search or use your knowledge of site taphonomy to determine what happened to the missing elements.
6. Create a site map showing the site boundaries, location of each body part or skeletal element, each piece of evidence, and where the photographs were taken.
7. Take overall photographs of the site from multiple directions, close-ups of each piece of evidence and body part. Take close-up photographs of any signs of perimortem trauma on the body parts. If any of the skeletal elements are shattered, photograph them and take any applicable anthropological measurements before collection.

8. Collect the material, carefully logging the artifacts as evidence and filling out a case form for each body.
9. When the material is collected, use a metal detector over the site area to ensure there are no signals for objects that were obscured by material on the surface.

GLOSSARY TERMS

cremains
pedestal
taphonomy
weathering

SUGGESTED READING

Dirkmaat, Dennis

2002 Recovery and Interpretation of the Fatal Fire Victim: The Role of Forensic Anthropology. In *Advances in Forensic Taphonomy: Method, Theory, and Archaeological Perspectives*, William D. Haglund, and Marcella H. Sorg, editors, pp. 451–72. CRC Press, Boca Raton, Florida.

Lyman, R. Lee

1994 *Vertebrate Taphonomy*. Cambridge Manuals in Archaeology, Cambridge University Press, Cambridge.

7

Locating Buried Remains

THE GRAVE AS AN ARCHAEOLOGICAL FEATURE

"One can never dig in the ground and put dirt back exactly as nature had put it there originally" (Bass and Birkby 1978:6). Most methods used to locate graves rest on this simple axiom. Archaeology considers features immovable objects resulting from human activity (see chapter 2). Graves are a type of feature with a specific function. Most of the methods used to locate graves actually locate a feature with an unknown function. Often, only excavation will show that the feature is a grave.

This chapter reviews a number of techniques used to find graves that rely on little or no technology. These should almost always be exhausted before using remote sensing techniques. The hi-tech methods tend to be expensive with ambiguous results. But another basic axiom of grave location is that the use of several complementary search methods is more effective than the use of a single search method (France et al. 1992).

DIRECT METHODS OF GRAVE LOCATION

Finding the Grave Using a Witness

A witness who saw the burial, or who did the burial, is a great help in locating the grave. But a witness does not guarantee a good location on the burial. The day that a person has a need to dispose of a human body usually qualifies as a stressful day. The witness may have blanked portions of the day out of his or her memory. He or she may have been in an unfamiliar area and not remember any landmarks. It may have been a very long time since the person last was in the area. The investigator needs to understand what physical aspects of the landscape the witness is using as landmarks in order to understand the accuracy of the location.

Taking the person to the area of the alleged grave, rather than trying to locate the grave based on the witness' description of the area, lets the investigator see how sure the witness is of the location. The group with the witness should be a small group, to keep the person from being too intimidated; this will allow the person to take the time needed to be sure of the location. For this, and security reasons, the archaeologist is often left out of the group and must rely on location information from others. The location information given by the witness must be recorded in such a manner that it can be exactly conveyed to others at a later date. Even if the interview is videotaped, it may be difficult to place in context the area the witness points to, if it is out of the view of the camera.

When the witness has pointed to a location, the location needs to be securely marked, so it can be relocated when the time comes to exhume the body. A global positioning system (GPS) unit is useful to record the place. The position can also be marked using flagging tape or pin flags, but these may draw unwanted attention to the area or may disappear over time. Many animals (deer, antelope, and elk) eat flagging tape and the flags on pin flags. So it is best not to leave the flagging for an extended period. In addition to obtaining UTM coordinates on the location, a sketch map is useful in relocating the site later (see chapter 4).

The team will often return to the site without the witness and with the equipment for the excavation. Usually, the team will start at the exact spot the witness indicated and look for the grave. How far from the exact area the witness pointed to should the search continue? This depends on how featureless the area is. The search should legitimately continue until it reaches the next landmark that a witness could have used as a reference. If the alleged location is in the middle of a broad, flat cornfield, then the search should continue throughout the field, unless there is another reference point that the witness remembers. If the location is an urban area, perhaps a small yard, then the search may involve only the yard. If the witness remembers a tree next to a well, and there are no remains at the initial location, the investigators should look for nearby areas also containing a tree and a well. The less familiar the witness is with the area or the longer it has been since the witness saw the grave, then the broader the search area should be.

Broadening the search area is always a good idea. At one location in Bosnia and Herzegovina (Zecovi, near Priador) where the author worked, the Bosnia and Herzegovina Federation Commission on Missing Persons investigated a grave of five individuals. There were two witnesses who each told of seeing people from a local detention camp bury a group of five people in the end of a field. The team located a grave of five in the approximate location indicated by the witnesses. While the team was excavating around the grave in order to pedestal the bodies, a second grave containing five individuals was found (Connor field notes, 12 August 1998). Each witness had actually seen a different grave created. Without broadening the excavation to create room to work around the remains, the team would have missed the second grave.

Soil, Topography, and Vegetation Changes

When a grave is dug, soil is taken from one area and piled in another. A body or bodies are placed in the grave and the soil is placed back in the grave. Frequently, not all the soil is placed back in the grave and there is still a small mound of soil on the side of the grave. Both the lack of compact fill and the decay of the remains create a depression marking the grave. In many soils, the loose grave fill falls away from the compact, undisturbed soil profile, leaving a crack in the surface outlining one or more sides of the grave.

Reading these signs may not be as simple as it sounds. At the Little Bighorn Battlefield, an 1890 army detail was given the job of placing marble markers at the locations where the bodies lay on the battlefield (Scott et al. 1998:103–5). The head of the detail remarked, "All parts of the field show evidence of a large number of men who fell by two's or as comrades in battle" (official report of O. J. Sweet, 1890, Little Bighorn Battlefield National Monument files). Sweet's party placed forty-three pairs of markers over the battlefield, based on shallow depressions in the soil that they interpreted as indicating graves. For decades, explanations like Sweet's were proffered, that is, that the pairs represent where "bunkies," men who bunked together, fought and died together.

During archaeological projects at the park during the 1980s, the area around many of these marker pairs was excavated. The remains collected at each marker pair represented only a single individual (except in one case, where the remains of one human and one horse were found [Scott, Willey, and Connor 1998:156]). The soil in this area is very hard and it is likely that in order to cover the remains, the dirt was scooped up from either side of the deceased and piled on top. This left a mound and two shallow indentations on the ground surface. Sweet's party took the depressions, rather than the mounds, as indicators of graves, thus mistaking the number of graves and the actual locations (Scott, Willey, and Connor 1998).

The low mounds and depressions sometimes associated with graves can be seen by their shadows when the angle of the light is low, or when a light snow cover blows over the area (Hunter 1996; France et al. 1992). These topographically induced shadows can be spotted through pedestrian inventory (discussed below) at the right time of day, or under the right climatic conditions (figure 7-1). Searchers should be briefed to watch for them.

Typically, disturbed soil is less compact and looser than undisturbed soil (chapter 5). Below the surface, a disturbed area may contain surface material like vegetation, leaves, road gravel, or garbage like cigarette butts. The color

FIGURE 7-1
A pig grave that can be delimited by the shallow depression, pointed to by the arrow. The unconsolidated soil also holds moisture better than the harder packed soil and the difference in color on the photograph is the difference in soil moisture.

of undisturbed soil tends to grade from darkest at the surface, where organic matter decomposes, to lighter the further below the surface the profile extends. The dark color in soil results from the decay of the organic material on the ground surface. Generally, just below the plants and leaf litter on the surface of the soil is a rich, dark, loose soil called humus. This contains the decaying plant material. Deeper in the ground, the soil takes on the characteristics of its parent material, usually the bedrock below. In the soil used to fill a hole that has been dug, the organic-rich surface soil is mixed with the less organic subsurface material, creating a color difference between the soil in the disturbed area and the soil in the undisturbed area (see chapter 5, figures 5-5, 5-6). When a backhoe or a front-end loader is used to clear the soil to the lighter subsoil, the color difference in the disturbed soil is sometimes clearly visible.

When a grave is dug, not only is the soil disturbed, but so is the vegetation on the surface. In all regions, there is a vegetation sequence leading to the "climax" vegetation, which is a relatively stable vegetation community for that environment. The first plants to grow on disturbed soil are species frequently considered weeds. In the temperate regions of the United States, dandelions, chenopod, nettles, and poison ivy may be some of the first growth on disturbed soils. In time, these will be replaced or joined by young members of the climax community. An investigator familiar with the vegetation sequence of the local region will be able to spot a small area where the vegetation community is younger, or at least different, than the surrounding growth. A "weedy" area is a good indication of recent disturbance.

Soil testing has also been used to locate graves (see "Body Silhouettes and Soil Chemistry," in chapter 5). As bodies decay, elements leach into the soils. Heavier concentrations of calcium, phosphorus, sodium, and zinc in an area as compared to the surrounding soil may be indicators that the feature is a body stain. However, as elements tend to leach down into the soil profile, rather than percolate to the top, it takes a very heavy concentration of the element to indicate a grave.

Calcium and sodium are easily leached from soil, and if the area is subject to heavy rainfall or flooding, it is less likely that these elements will remain in the soil. Farmers and gardeners add nutrients to crops, including phosphorus, so there are reasons for localized high concentrations of phosphorus in the soil aside from it being the past location of human remains.

As discussed in chapter 5, several studies have used the zinc/copper ratio in the soil to identify prehistoric burial areas (Akridge 1994:5–9; Morse 1997:93–95). Zinc is not as soluble as the major elements in bone, and copper has about the same solubility as zinc. Both copper and zinc will usually precipitate as minerals, rather than combine with other elements. Copper in soil acts chemically much as zinc does, but it is much less concentrated in bone. Thus, a high zinc/copper ratio should be expected in burial locations. The ratio is used because a number of factors, (e.g., pH changes, groundwater movement) could change the overall abundance figures, but the ratio should stay similar.

Pedestrian Survey

If the witness indicated a broad area or if there is another reason to suspect that there is a grave in a larger area, it is necessary to search the area in a systemic manner. This consists of people walking the ground in an organized manner looking for disturbed soil, skeletal elements, clothing, or other indications of the goal. There are different ways of conducting such a survey depending on terrain and vegetation.

On flat ground with short vegetation, the simplest method is to walk shoulder to shoulder in a straight line across the area in question. The row of people walking is often referred to as "the line"; the column that they walk is "the transect." The person on either end of the line should have a landmark to walk toward in order to keep the entire survey line straight. The person on the outside end of the line can place pin flags so that when the line returns, walking in the other direction, they know exactly where they walked on their previous pass.

If the survey team finishes transects in one direction, say north to south, without finding anything, then walking transects in the other direction, say east to west, will put a different perspective on the ground (figures 7-2A). Changes in lighting, vegetation, and small differences in terrain can all help in spotting an object. If the team has a distinct reason for starting in one spot (e.g., an object of clothing was located), then walking in ever-wider circles around the spot may be the fastest method of finding related objects (figure 7-2B).

When the terrain is steep, walking with the contour is the easiest and most effective method of survey (figure 7-2C). This keeps each individual on one level, rather than continuously walking uphill or downhill. Walking transects continuously uphill and downhill will tire the searchers very quickly. The team needs

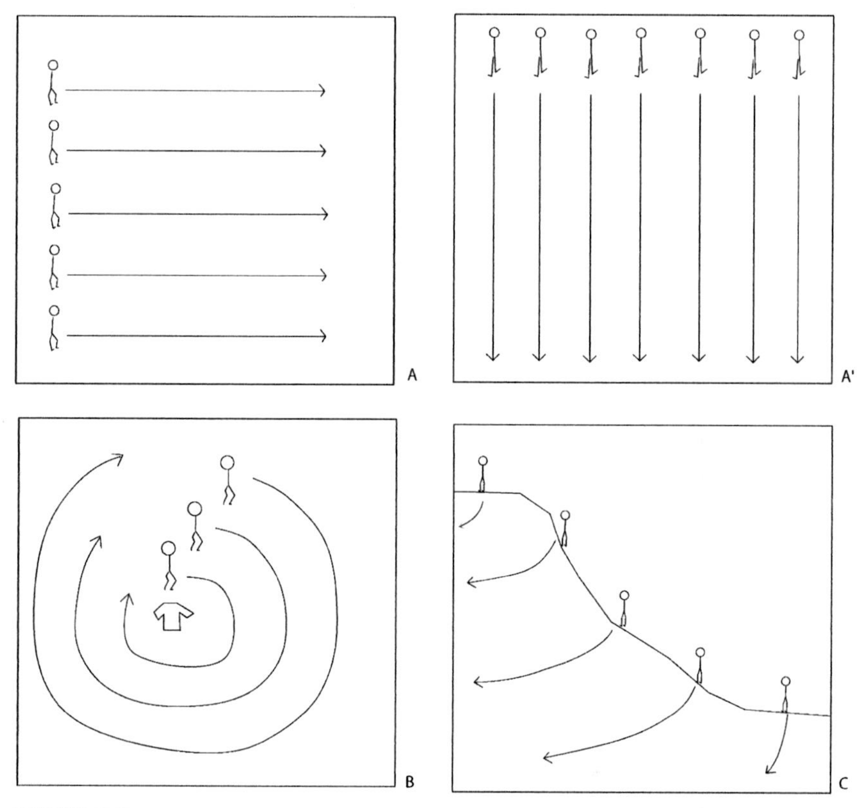

FIGURE 7-2
Methods of pedestrian survey. A. Straight transects across level terrain. A' If the initial transects do not uncover evidence, then walking the same area in a different direction may allow something new to be seen. B. Walking increasingly large circles around a piece of evidence already located. C. On steep terrain, walkers should keep to the same contour.

to stay together in the line. If one person walks faster and gets ahead of everyone else, or one person lags behind, it is more difficult for the person on either side to stay in their transect. Thus, the entire line can only go as fast as the slowest individual.

When a potentially relevant item is found, the senior member of the team will break the line to examine the object. Everyone else should stay in place until the senior team member decides whether or not to concentrate the search around the object. When this person leaves his or her place in the survey line, everyone else needs to stop. The person breaking the line should mark his or her position, with anything from a pack or a jacket to a pin flag. This way, he or she can return to that exact spot.

It can be difficult to return to an area at a later date and remember exactly where the team searched the first time. So documenting the area the team searched and did not find anything is important. A sketch map of the area searched, in combination with taking UTM coordinates with a GPS unit, is valuable.

Probes

Probes are effective in looking for graves (Morse, Duncan, and Stoutamire 1983:56), particularly when the area is small and the soils are not rocky. The recommended type of probe is called a *tile probe*. It is a metal stick about 1.5 m long with a blunt end and a solid "T" handle (figure 7-3). The probe can be lengthened or shortened with the use of extensions, but the 1.5 m length is most convenient for the broadest range of situations. The end of the probe is pressed into the ground. Disturbed soil is much softer and looser than undisturbed soil, and with a little practice, this difference can be felt with the probe (figure 7-4). If the remains are still decomposing, then the end of the probe will smell like decomposing remains when pulled out of a grave (figure 7-5). The soil may become more compact over time, but burials as old as 150 years have been detected using a probe (Owsley 1995:737).

Hollow soil probes are also used. These are similar to the tile probes, except they have a hollow core for about 30 cm at the end. They are designed to bring a sample of the soil to the surface, and in doing so have the potential to damage remains and evidence. The soil core allows the investigator to see changes in the soil, rather than simply feel them. However, if the investigator can't feel the difference in the soil when it hits the grave, the soil core may include decomposing flesh and clothing. Most investigators have the sense not to push the probe hard enough to go through bone, but the probe has the capability of doing so. Owsley (1995:737) suggests the use of the soil-coring tool after a potential grave has been located with the tile probe in order to validate the find. Experienced archaeologists use the soil probe to look for the disturbed soil indicative of a feature. However, less experienced personnel run the risk of damaging material with a soil probe.

There are a number of additional types of probes, most designed for sampling soil. There are corkscrew probes, and varying sizes of augers. All have

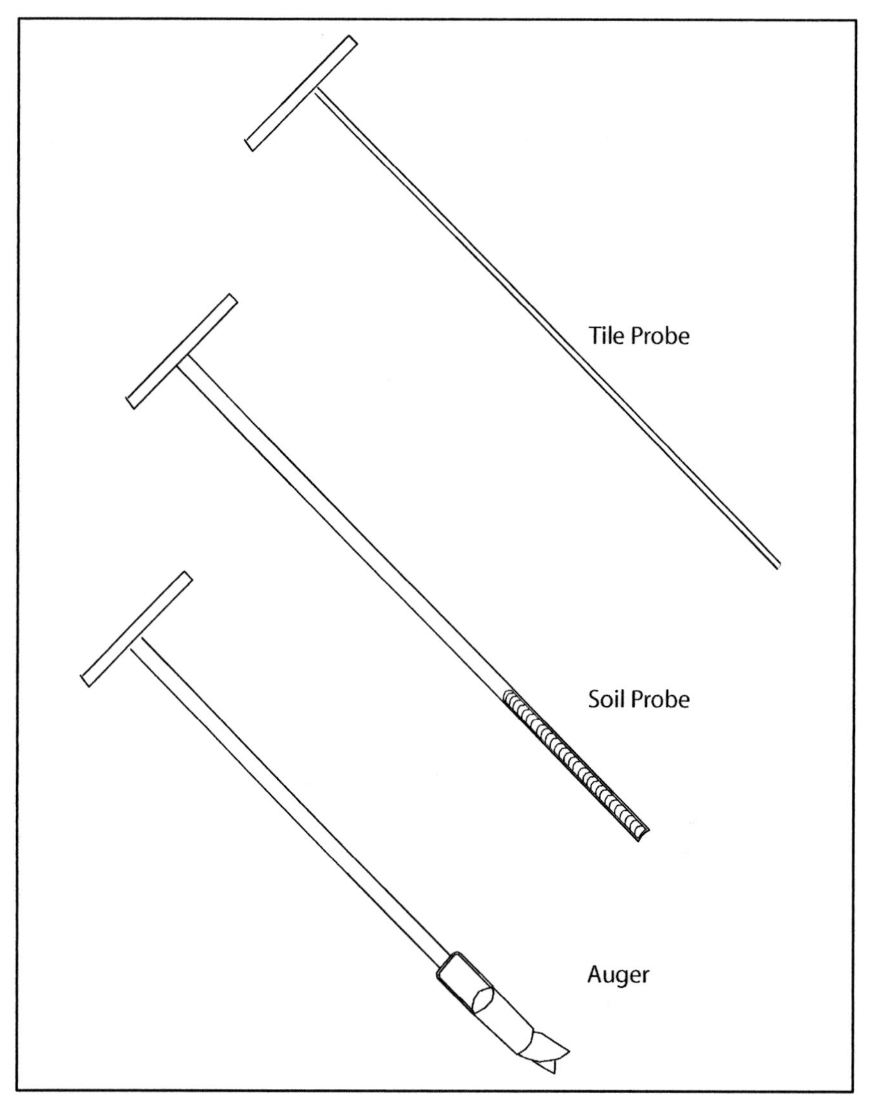

FIGURE 7-3
Types of probes and soil sampling equipment. The tile probe is recommended as it causes least damage to the remains and to evidence. An auger can go through hard soil more easily, but may cause a great deal of damage to clothing and remains.

the potential to do enormous damage to the remains and evidence. The tile probe is definitely the most effective and least damaging type of probe to use. However, if the investigator has to choose between damaging the remains with

FIGURE 7-4
Tile probe in use. User pushes the probe into the ground, searching for an area that feels softer than the surrounding ground.

FIGURE 7-5
If the probe is near the decomposing remains, the odor of the decomposition fluids will adhere to the soil and to the end of the probe.

a probe, overlooking the grave, or using a backhoe or other heavy equipment and potentially damaging the remains, then damaging the remains with the probe is the least destructive choice. Mapping the location of the probe holes as they are placed in and around the burial allows a hole to be matched to potential damage of material in the grave.

Cadaver Dogs

Cadaver dogs are search dogs that are specially trained to smell decomposing human tissue. A well-trained dog should be able to separate human remains from animal remains. The biggest factor in the success of the use of the dog is the skill of the dog and the dog-handler team, and this can vary widely.

When looking for buried remains with a dog, it can help to use a probe to aerate the soil and bring up odors from below the ground. Dogs have also been useful in locating scattered surface remains, significantly increasing the number of elements located (Komar 1999). Additional information on the use and training of dogs can be found in Rebmann, Koenig, David, and Sorg (2000).

Cadaver-dog handlers should be able to provide references, which the investigator should take the time to confirm. The investigator should look at the certifications that the handler and dog have earned, as well as previous successful finds. If the dogs and law enforcement can train together before being needed in the field, then poor dog/handler teams may be spotted during exercises.

Test Trenches

Sooner or later, in order to confirm the presence of a grave the ground will need to be disturbed. The first choice then is whether to use a shovel or heavy machinery. If the remains were buried with mechanized equipment, they will probably have to be uncovered using mechanized equipment. A backhoe or front-end loader can dig a hole too large and deep for the remains to then be relocated manually.

If the team is looking for a single individual in a grave that was initially dug with a shovel, then the use of shovels to exhume the body is appropriate. A *slit trench* is a narrow trench across the area in question, extending beyond the potentially disturbed area. It is a good method with which to start. The soil profile of the trench should allow someone who can read the soils to determine whether the soil has been disturbed in this area. If it has, then a perpendicular trench will help determine the size of the disturbance in that direction. In a best-case scenario, the grave size and location is then known before the body is exposed. The soil from the test trenches should be placed aside in a specific location. If a grave is located, then these soils should be placed through a screen so small pieces of evidence are not overlooked.

Heavy machinery may be necessary if the area to be searched is large or the grave may be deep. Either a grader or backhoe may be appropriate depending on the terrain and search area. In either case, neither the blade nor bucket should have teeth. The large teeth common on earth-moving equipment can do a lot of damage to bodies and evidence. Either piece of machinery should be a small to medium-sized four-wheel-drive model. Although it is sensible to start with a small backhoe, if the remains were put in the ground with a large backhoe, then the depth of the grave may exceed the reach of the small backhoe, and the team will need to use a larger machine.

A front-end loader may be more useful in large, open areas. The front-end loader will take off soil in small increments until disturbed soil can be seen; the disturbed soil can then be delimited using hand tools. The soil outline in figure 5-6 was initially found using a front-end loader and then cleaned using hand tools. The advantage of a backhoe over a front-end loader is that it can stand in one place, off the area of interest, and extend the arm of the backhoe onto the possible grave site. This keeps the machine from repeatedly rolling over the potential grave area and keeps the weight of the machine off the body.

When using heavy machinery to look for a grave, the witness' landmarks should be kept intact. Until the grave is located, the trees, boulders, or other features that the witness used as landmarks need to stay intact, so the witness can come back if the team does not locate the body.

The use of heavy machinery requires skill and monitoring or the remains will be damaged. A skilled machine operator can remove the soil in 10 cm increments. At least one team member should be designated to work directly with the backhoe operator at all times. The backhoe monitor should have previous experience in working with heavy machinery, so that he or she knows the capabilities of the machine. The monitor also needs to be able to recognize all forms of decomposing remains in the ground in order to halt the machine immediately if a body is hit by the backhoe. Finally, the monitor needs to be able to read the soil so that he or she can tell when the machine is working in a disturbed area.

The monitor will also need to explain exactly what is needed to the operator. The monitor needs to watch the bucket from the front—the direction from which the driver cannot see (figure 7-6). If bone or clothing, or anything unusual, is pulled from the soil, the monitor needs to stop the backhoe immediately. A second person needs to stand where the backhoe is depositing the soil and watch that for bone or clothing. *But the goal is to find the grave before the body.* Changes in soil color, composition, and color should let the investigators know they have found disturbed soil. Then the grave can be delimited, an excavation grid set up, and the body excavated with hand tools.

REMOTE SENSING

Remote sensing techniques are those techniques that investigate and define an object without direct contact with the object. Remote sensing has many advantages: it is nondestructive and noninvasive, and it may pick up disturbances below the surface when there is no indication of disturbance on the ground

FIGURE 7-6
Backhoe being used outside of Sarajevo to locate graves. Note the individuals crouched, watching the soil removed by the backhoe. The individual in the black shirt is also carefully watching. Using a backhoe to find graves should always include monitors who watch the removal of the soil from different angles, as well as people who look through the soil removed. Excavations conducted by the Bosnia and Herzegovina Federation Commission on Missing Persons.

or when the surface is covered in asphalt or cement. However, remote sensing is not a panacea. Some techniques do not work in areas close to electric lines, cars, or other magnetic sources. Other techniques may give false readings in clay soils or rocky areas. In no case does any technique show definitely that an area below ground is a grave. In addition, these remote sensing techniques are equipment intensive and usually require trained technicians to operate the equipment and interpret the results. The remote sensing technologies discussed here are aerial photographs and a variety of geophysical techniques.

Aerial Photographs

Disturbances in the ground can sometimes be spotted more easily from above the ground and aerial photographs may be the best method to see them. Photos taken from the air work best when the vegetation is low, such as in agricultural areas, pastures, or cropland. Aerial photographs come in all scales and are taken at different altitudes. Generally, they fall into the categories of high altitude, low altitude, or satellite photographs. The USGS's National Aerial Photography Program coordinates the collection of aerial photographs of the forty-eight conterminous states every five years. Flights are flown at 20,000 feet above mean terrain and photos are taken at a 1:40,000 scale. This is too large a scale to see an individual grave, but the photos can be used to organize searches and other ground reconnaissance activities.

As graves are usually rather small disturbances, it is unusual for the satellite images or high-level aerial reconnaissance photos to have the resolution to show them. Rather than looking for a grave, aerial photographs may show newly constructed features such as gardens, pools, or decks over a burial. To search for new construction, the investigator needs aerial photographs from both before and after the time of an individual's disappearance.

Mass graves may, however, show up in aerial photography (figure 7-7).

A model plane with a camera fixed to it can provide an inexpensive aerial view (figure 7-8). Walker (1993) describes the design of such a device and fitting a remote-controlled model airplane with a camera attachment for low-level aerial photographs. Other models of remote-controlled model planes with cameras already fitted onto them are available commercially. Crashes of these aircraft are frequent and the controller needs to have skill in both flying and repairing the models. Despite this, model aircraft are ideal for obtaining low-cost, low-level aerial photographs.

FIGURE 7-7

Aerial photographs showing mass grave burial activity at Branjevo Farm, Donje Pilica, in the Srebrenica area of Bosnia-Herzegovina. A. The grave shown was dug in 1995 and does not appear disturbed on 21 September 1995. B. This aerial photograph shows that the grave is disturbed on 27 September 1995. This brackets the time of the disturbance between 21 and 27 September 1995.

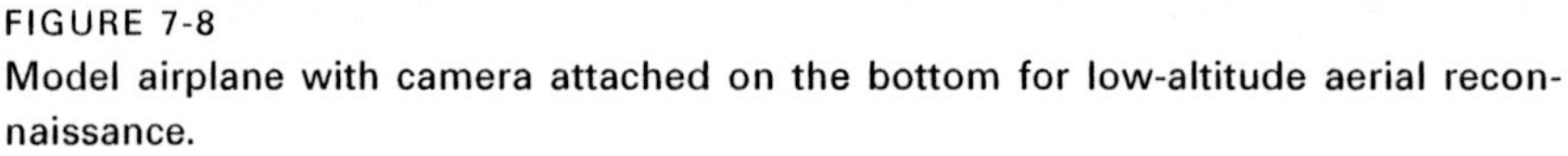

FIGURE 7-8
Model airplane with camera attached on the bottom for low-altitude aerial reconnaissance.

Geophysical Techniques

The basic premise when using remote sensing techniques is similar to the basic premise used with other grave location techniques: the ground was disturbed and it cannot be put back as it was originally. In the disturbance, the soil becomes less compact and there are inclusions not natural to the area. The geophysical data determine that there is a subsurface anomaly, an area different than the surrounding material. Interpreting the anomaly requires experience on the part of the technician running the equipment. The only way to actually determine that an anomaly represents a grave is to excavate it.

All geophysical methods have problems in some site conditions. The choice of geophysical method may rest on local conditions. Anything in the ground that the investigator does not wish to detect may cause problems by obscuring the features that the investigator does want to detect. Bevan (1996, table 2) summarizes some of the factors that make geophysical survey difficult, and these are shown in table 7-1. Unless noted by the technician, these factors will make almost all geophysical surveys difficult. Bevan (1998) provides a good general overview of geophysical methods, and Davenport (2001a, b) provides

Table 7-1. Difficult conditions for geophysical surveys and the problems that may result. After Bevan (1996, table 2)

	False Anomalies	*Interference*	*Access*	*No data*
Steep slopes			x	
Brush			x	
Large trees	x		x	
Flower beds or crops			x	
Multiple landscaping	x			
Rocky soil	x			
Clayey or saline soil				x (GPR)
Fences	x		x	
Brick walls	x		x	
Near buildings	x			
Prior or current excavations	x		x	
Surficial trash	x			
Pavement (metal reinforced)				x
Buried pipes or wires	x			
Power lines		x		
Nearby trains		x		
Radio transmitters		x		
Passing vehicles		x		

an overview of techniques used to locate graves. Other summaries include Heimmer (1992) and Clark (1990).

For most of the geophysical methods discussed here, particularly the magnetometers and the electromagnetic induction meters, the standard method involves setting up a grid, frequently twenty meters on a side. The instrument is then run up and down the lines; the technician takes readings at specified intervals (e.g., at one meter or every fifty centimeters), or some instruments sample continuously. This produces a set of data representing the twenty meters square with data points for every square meter. If the feature being searched for is smaller than a square meter, the sampling interval needs to be reduced or the feature may be missed. On the other hand, if the feature being searched for is significantly larger than a square meter, then the sampling interval may be enlarged to cover additional ground more quickly.

Metal Detectors

Metal detectors are a relatively simple, inexpensive remote sensing technique, readily available to most archaeologists and law enforcement agencies. Metal detectors, of course, do not detect buried bodies, but they will detect metal objects buried on or with a body. This could include the nails in shoes, rivets and zippers on pants, rings, or even dental fillings. They can also be used in a grave to search for cartridges, bullets, or personal items.

The depth of penetration is less than that of other geophysical techniques outlined here, but for many shallowly buried graves, a metal detector's depth is sufficient. The depth actually depends on the size of the coil, and most eight-inch coils will penetrate about one foot into the ground (Connor and Scott 1998). Metal detectors also have the advantage that should the site be the execution area, as well as the burial area, additional material relevant to the investigation, such as cartridges cases and cartridges, may be uncovered.

Another advantage of a metal detector is the relative ease of use. In about ten minutes most people can be trained to use a standard detector, though continued use increases a person's skill. Most detectors come apart and can be packed in a suitcase or placed in a backpack. In many situations, the ease of use and transportation makes up for the limitations of the machine.

Ground-penetrating Radar (GPR)

Ground-penetrating radar transmits short wavelength electromagnetic waves into the ground and records the energy scattered back by the reflecting materials. Ground-penetrating radar detects differences in moisture content between materials, material composition, and/or material texture. This creates approximate soil profiles, with reflections caused by contrasts in dielectric constant and electrical resistivity (Bevan 1991:1311). The data is usually displayed on a monitor or a strip chart. Single graves produce anomalies of an elongated object at about one to two meters underground (DeVore and Bevan 1995:21). Ground-penetrating radar works well when the natural soil has a regular, planar profile, and then the disturbed soil that fills the grave—and has no regular planar profile—has a recognizable signature. Problems occur with GPR in stony soils, such as in formerly glaciated areas, where the radar bounces off the rocks and may make the profile of the grave difficult to recognize. The worst conditions for GPR are clay soils or areas with complex soil profiles, which may obscure the anomaly caused by a grave.

Ground-penetrating radar units include some sort of box or cart containing the antennae (figure 7-9). The need to push or drag a unit like this over the ground limits the terrain and topography that can be covered. Steep hillsides or places with lots of bushes or crops are a few of the areas where accessibility prohibits GPR use. The sled in the unit shown in the photograph is molded into a single piece, and transporting the unit to the site can also be a problem. The standard GPR output is a series of lines incomprehensible to the untrained, so that the unit needs a specialized operator who has had both training and previous experience.

Electromagnetic (EM) Induction Meters

Electromagnetic induction meters provide a measurement of the electrical conductivity of the soil by sending a low-frequency electromagnetic field into the earth. They propagate waves that are reflected back to the surface changed in frequencies and characteristics based on the chemical composition of the subsurface materials and differences in moisture content (DeVore and Bevan 1995:19). Again, because the soil in the grave was disturbed, the conductivity may be different than that of the surrounding soil. Electromagnetic induction meter readings also react to other changes in the electrical conductivity of the soil, which include burned areas, buried brick, or metal.

Many units cannot be used around large metal objects, which produce read-

FIGURE 7-9
The Noggins system, a ground-penetrating radar unit.

ings so high that they obscure the readings produced by a grave. The Geonics EM38 (figure 7-10) is a model designed for use around larger metal objects, although power lines may interfere with the readings. The EM38 is also relatively small and transportation issues are less of a problem than with some other models. Compare this to the EM31 (figure 7-11) which has much greater depth

FIGURE 7-10
Geonics EM38 in use. One of the advantages of this machine is that it can be used near metal objects, such as the fence in the background. The depth penetration of this model is about 1.5 meters.

FIGURE 7-11
EM31 in use by its inventor, Duncan McDonald. The large area between the sensors allows for greater depth penetration (ca. 5–6 meters), although there is loss in resolution. Accessibility and terrain are factors in determining the usefulness of this model.

penetration, but whose length presents logistical difficulties. The output of the EM survey is a series of numbers usually reflecting readings from a grid. Specialized software is used to plot these onto a map in isobars. This allows anomalies and the shape of the anomalies to be seen and pinpointed on the map. Only actually excavating the anomaly, however, will tell whether it represents a grave.

Electrical Resistivity

Electrical resistivity surveys use probes in the ground to send an electrical current into the ground. Probes at a different location measure the voltage loss to variations in the subsurface materials (figure 7-12). Like the EM surveys, resistivity surveys detect changes in the chemical composition and the moisture content of the soil. They are less sensitive than the EM surveys to aboveground metal objects and power lines, and may be useful where the EM surveys cannot be used.

A survey in Saipan looking for a mass burial from World War II used both EM and GPR and had very positive results from the EM survey. The GPR sur-

FIGURE 7-12
Electrical resistivity unit in use. Both probes are pushed into the ground. One probe sends the electrical impulse and the other records the amount of electricity it receives through the ground.

vey helped to define the boundaries of the site, but the EM survey, Doolittle and Kaschko believe, located and defined the boundaries of the mass grave (Doolittle and Kaschko 1990).

Magnetometers

Magnetometers (models include the proton-free percussion magnetometer, the fluxgate [figure 7-13], and the proton magnetometer) measure variations in the magnetic properties of subsurface material (Weymouth and Huggins 1985:192). Magnetometers are not suitable for areas where large amounts of metal occur on the surface as they will overwhelm the subsurface readings. This includes overhead electric lines, automobiles, wire fences, and other such objects. Also, the operator (unlike the demonstrator pictured in the photo) will need to remove all clothing with metal, including pants with metal zippers, and wear rubber boots instead of shoes or boots that would have metal eyelets or nails.

Magnetometers may be built with one or two sensors. The machines built with two sensors are called *gradiometers*. If the machine has only one sensor, two magnetometers are used. One is used outside the grid as a base reading. The second machine is walked over the area from which data is needed. The first machine acts as a control on the second. When the operator of the roving machine is over a marked point to take a reading, he or she will press a switch so that both machines will take a reading at that point. Subtracting the base reading from the rover reading accounts for fluctuations in the earth's magnetic fields that may occur during the work. These readings are usually fed into a computer and specialized software is used to make the calculations and print a map of the magnetic anomalies in the grid area. Again, these must actually be excavated to determine what they represent.

Geophysics Case Study

The National Park Service (NPS) was asked to assist Scott Air Force Base in Illinois in locating graves in areas historically known as pioneer family cemeteries (DeVore and Bevan 1995). The NPS used magnetics, EM, GPR, and electrical resistivity over the cemetery areas, providing a study that allowed comparison of the output from the different geophysical methods over the same area. This case study is reported in DeVore and Bevan (1995) and the illustrations were generously provided by Steven DeVore, National Park Service.

FIGURE 7-13
Fluxgate magnetometer in use. The operator, unlike the demonstrator pictured, should be wearing no metal, and the machine is not useful near large metal objects.

DeVore and Bevan (1995) looked at two family cemeteries; the findings at one will be presented here, the Perschbacher Cemetery. At the time of the study, the cemetery boundary was marked with a wooden picket fence, which was removed to aid the survey, although the posts remained (figure 7-14). The

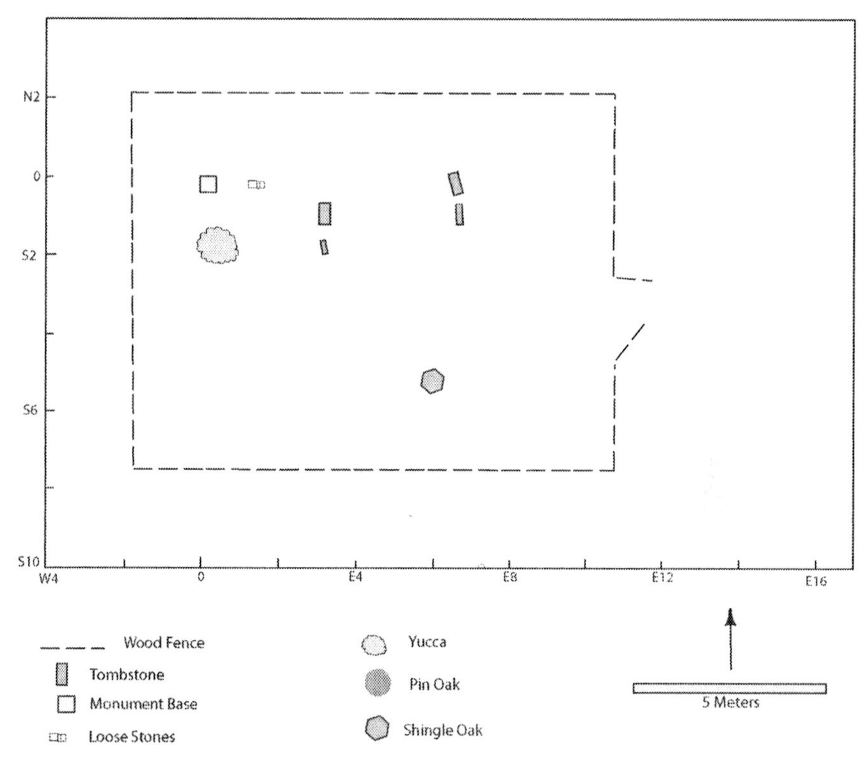

FIGURE 7-14
Map of the Perschbacher Cemetery, Scott Air Force Base. Redrawn from DeVore and Bevan (1995, figure 21).

vegetation consisted of cut grass and scattered trees and bushes. The survey lines had to deviate around the two oak trees. The cemetery is in a relatively remote area on the air force base, with the nearest passing traffic about eight meters away. A potential source of interference was heavy earth-moving machinery operating adjacent to the cemetery, so the magnetic survey was completed after the heavy equipment crew quit for the day and moved the machines away from the cemetery.

The GPR system was run over the cemetery on the grid both east to west and north to south (figure 7-15). The scans shown in the figure represent profiles along the grid from S10 to N4, the horizontal depth of the slice represented by the scale on the left. The lines represent changes in the soil seen by the GPR. Straight, or roughly straight, lines are probably natural changes in the earth's strata. In both these scans, the lines change at about

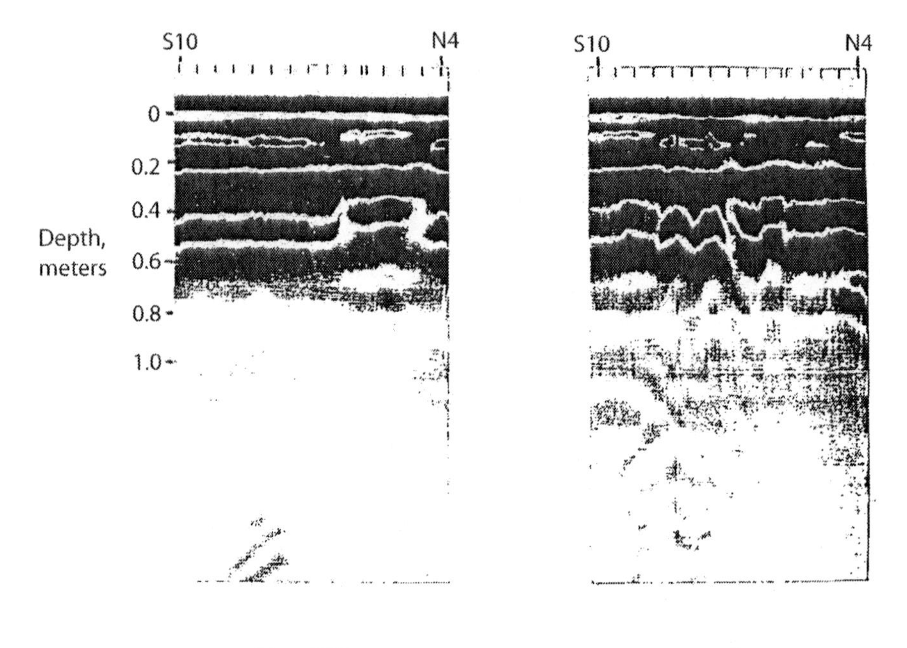

FIGURE 7-15
Raw scans by GPR unit.

0.4 m below the ground surface, suggesting a subsurface object. As with any GPR unit, the depth scale needed to be calculated by estimating the velocity of the radar pulse and calibrating the depth scales accordingly. DeVore and Bevan (1995:21) were not confident in their calibration of the depth at this cemetery and feel that the depth estimate may be overestimated. The data were plotted into the map in figure 7-16. The strong anomalies shown by the stars are probably metal objects such as tin cans. Anomalies that appear in the soil strata are shown on the map. The most reliable indication of a buried object is where the GPR detects an anomaly in the same location on perpendicular traverses.

A magnetic survey was completed using a GEM GSM-19FG Overhauser gradiometer, a unit with two magnetometers. The lower sensor was carried at a height of 51 cm, and there was a 103 cm vertical space between the two sensors. One person operated the readout console while a second carried the sensors. Measurements were taken every 0.5 m along the grid lines. In total, 1,247 pairs of measurements were made. The results were plotted as a series

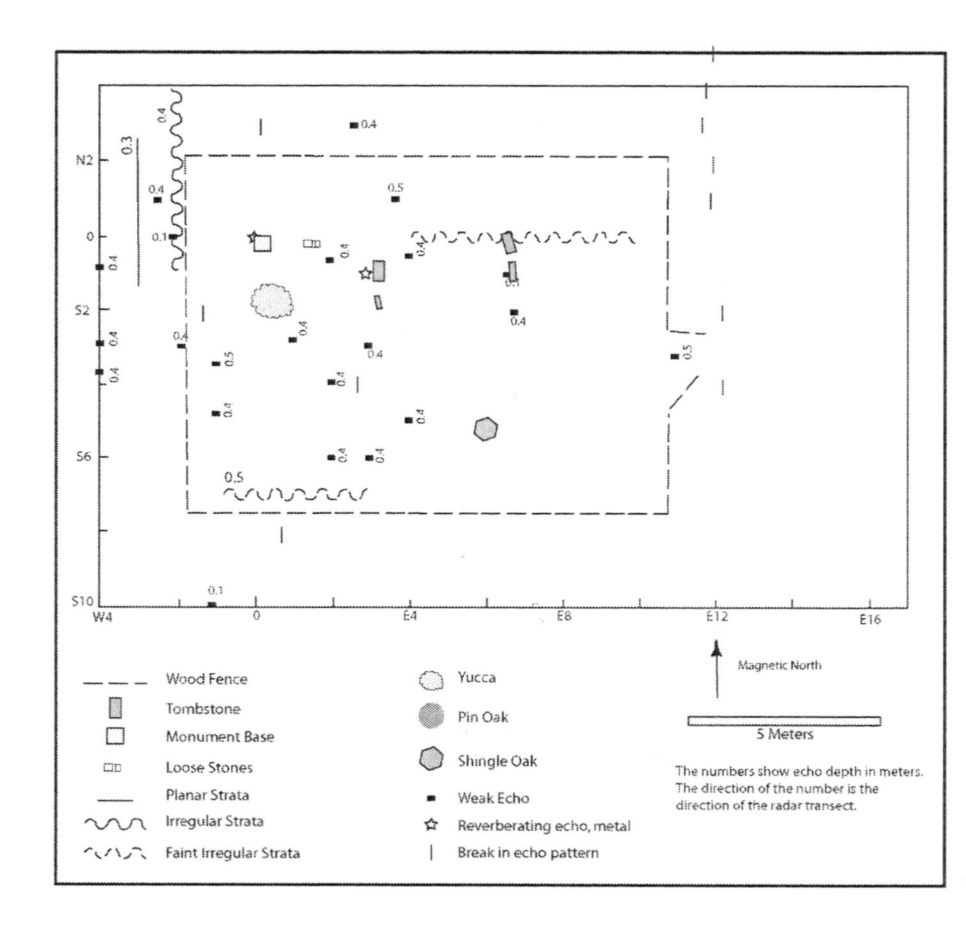

FIGURE 7-16
Interpretation of profiling completed by the GPR unit. Redrawn from DeVore and Bevan (1995, figures 33 and 35).

of maps, showing the readings as isobars (figure 7-17). Most of the high magnetic anomalies are the result of iron nails in the posts of the fence; the gate area shows up particularly well. However, several smaller anomalies show up inside the cemetery, away from the fence. DeVore and Bevan (1995:23) used a computerized model of dipolar magnetic anomalies to interpret these measurements and estimate their depth and an estimated iron weight. These are shown in the final site interpretation (figure 7-20).

A conductivity survey was also conducted in the cemetery, using the Geonics EM38 (figure 7-18). DeVore and Bevan (1995:21) used the machine to look for contrasting soil that could be filling the grave shafts. An electronic data logger was used with the instrument to record the measurements as they were taken. Measurements were made at 0.5 m intervals across the grid. The strong high readings in figure 7-18 match the high and low readings from the magnetic field data in figure 7-17 and probably reflect metal between the set of two low readings (they look like "dumbbells") and what is probably metal in the center of the isolated lows.

A profile across the cemetery was also performed using an electrical resistivity meter (figure 7-19) to look at the electrical stratification of the soil. A distinct change in the resistivity of the soil occurred at about 0.5 m, suggesting that the soil has a greater proportion of clay at that depth.

The final interpretation of the geophysical results relies on a combination of all the methods used (figure 7-20). Hopefully, looking at the results of any one of these methods will make it clear why it is always best to use a combination of methods to provide interpretations. The GPR readings are not clear and there is little clustering of echoes or confirmation of anomalies with perpendicular readings. There are no echoes below a depth of 0.5 m, and the resistivity reading suggests that the soil becomes quite clayey at this depth. Ground-penetrating radar does not work well in clay. The oak trees also have large roots and they caused false patterns on the radar profiles. The conductivity map shows low values at the two trees, as the machine had to be lifted slightly to move over the roots. The faint conductivity lows near two of the tombstones are too faint to interpret.

Both the conductivity and the magnetic surveys were strongly affected by metal from the fence, particularly the gate hinges. The triangles in figure 7-20 represent the strong magnetic anomalies not associated with the fence, and probably reflecting subsoil iron or brick. DeVore and Bevan (1995:26) feel that while coffin nails are too small to be seen through this survey, the anoma-

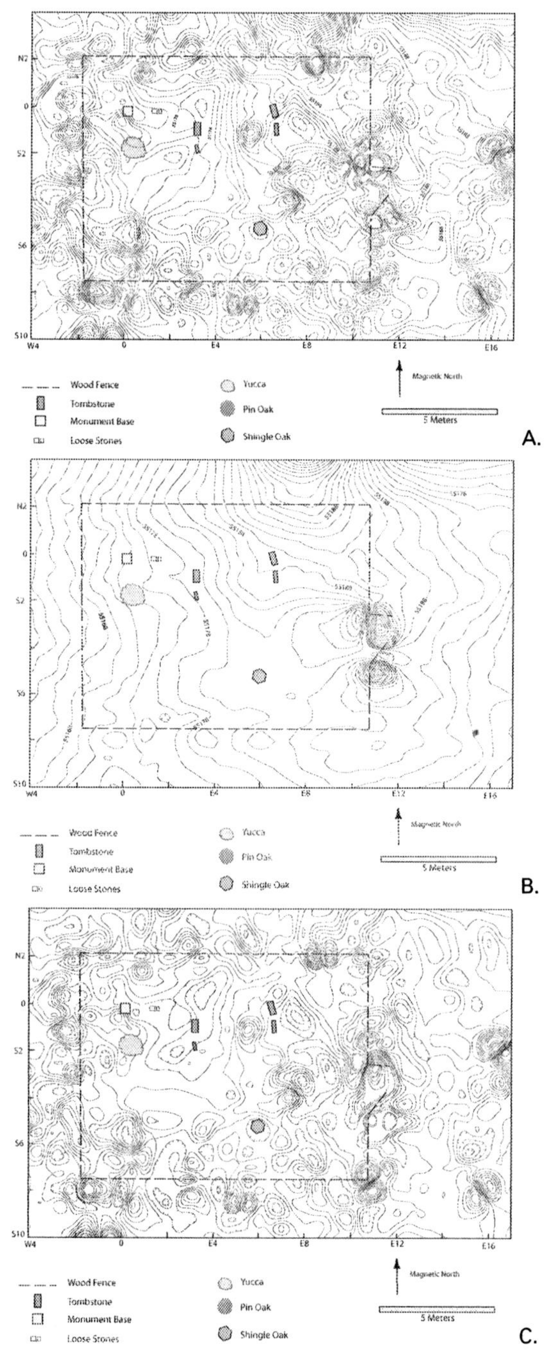

FIGURE 7-17

A. Magnetic field data from lower sensor. B. Magnetic field data from upper sensor. C. Magnetic gradient data.

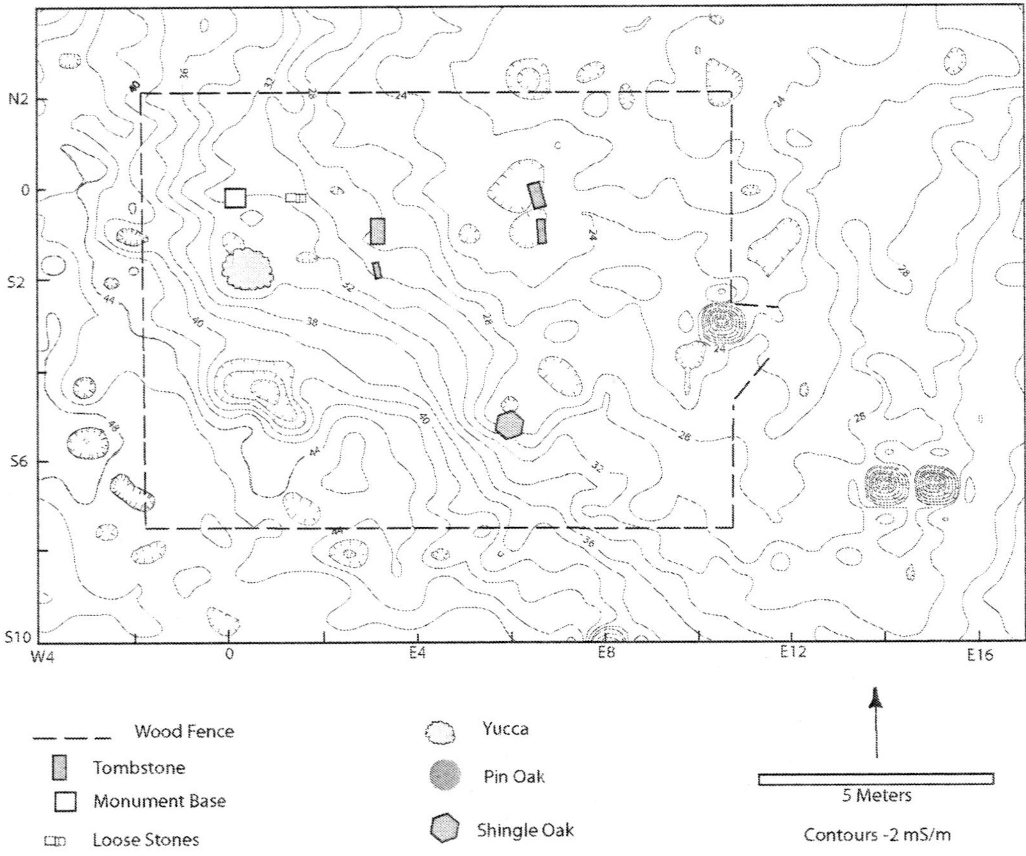

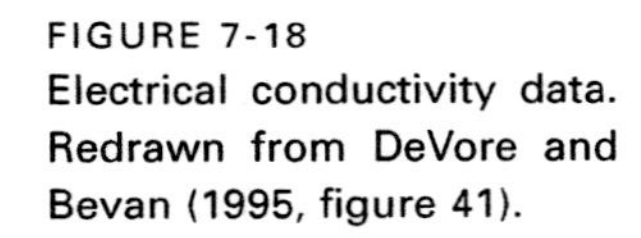

FIGURE 7-18
Electrical conductivity data. Redrawn from DeVore and Bevan (1995, figure 41).

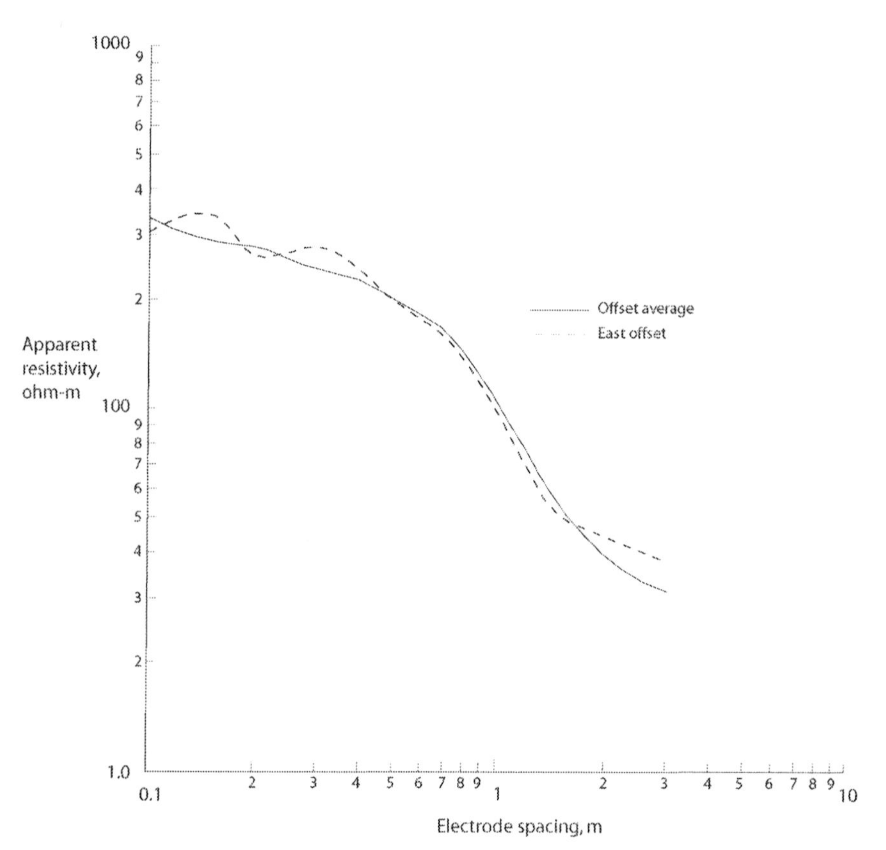

FIGURE 7-19

Resistivity sounding profile (DeVore and Bevan 1995, figure 32). Array along the line designated N1, center at the line designated E8.

lies could reflect other coffin hardware. Also, iron in the soil may accumulate in the subsidence depressions over graves. Note, however, that these anomalies are not patterned near the gravestones. To determine if these reflect graves, they would have to be excavated.

While this is not an example of how well these methods may work under the best of circumstances, it is a realistic overview of the frequently ambiguous results of a geophysical survey. Small amounts of surface metal, such as the nails in the fence, may obscure the relatively faint geophysical changes in the soil due to disturbance of the ground when digging a grave. Clay soils will hamper GPR readings and it is best to inspect the soil before going to the expense of bringing out the equipment and operator. Even had all the analyses

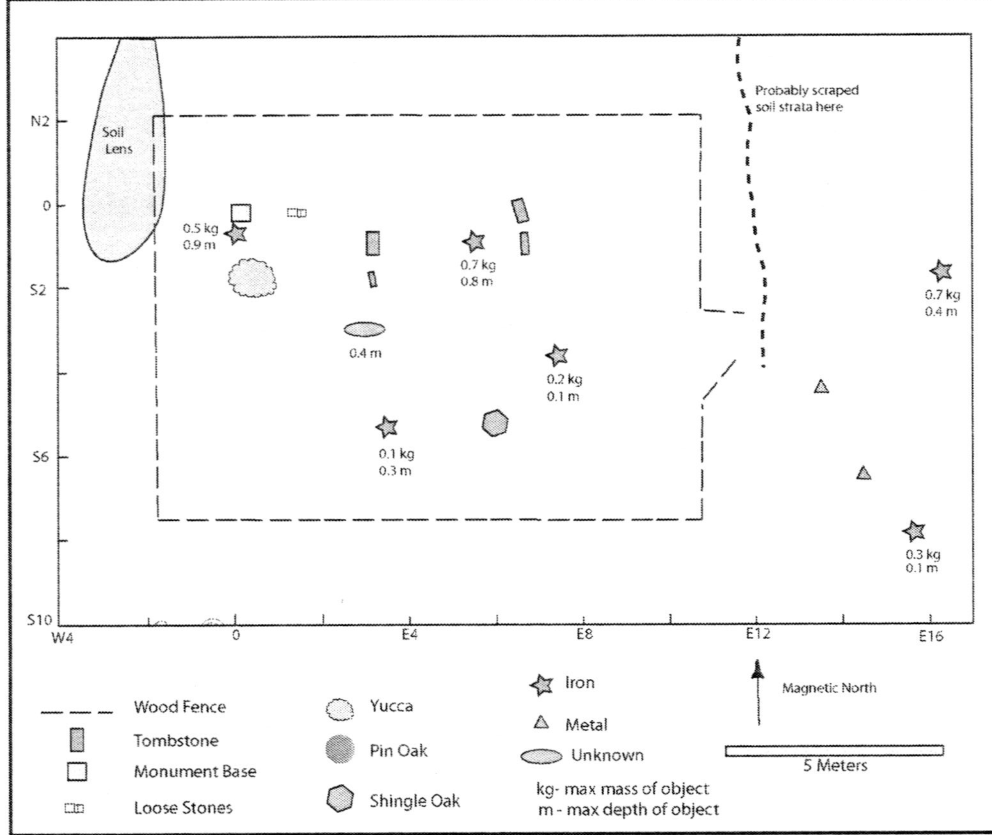

FIGURE 7-20
Interpretation of the combined geophysical analyses at the Perschbacher Cemetery (DeVore and Bevan 1995, figure 37).

pointed toward anomalies in the same location, these would need to be excavated, or "ground-truthed," to determine their origin.

Nickel (2000) conducted a similar example of the use of multiple remote sensing devices to locate graves in a historic cemetery. His results were more positive and found that a combination of the magnetometer, resistance meter, and GPR could detect subtle anomalies consistent with a grave. The radar alone detected an anomaly at 95 percent of the marked graves.

Each of the methods discussed above has its strengths and weaknesses. Table 7-2 outlines some of the basic strengths and weaknesses of each of the methods. The major points are that all methods have their weaknesses and that combining multiple methods is the best solution.

SUMMARY

The general procedure for the location of buried remains is as follows:

1. Obtain as much information from witnesses as possible. If there are investigators working on the case, they will also have relevant information.
2. Examine the topography of the general area and determine from the witness and investigator information what location methods will be relevant to the case.

   —Could there be any surface indications?
   —Are the remains recent enough to detect with a probe?
   —Is a cadaver dog available to assist?
   —Will excavation by a backhoe or shovels be needed to find the grave?

3. Conduct a pedestrian search over the area and look for surface remains, disturbed soil or vegetation, or areas where animals have been digging. If there are holes in the soil, look in them and examine the back dirt for remains.
4. If at all possible, have cadaver dogs search the area at the same time as the pedestrian inventory.
5. The use of a metal detector may, if there is not too much other debris, indicate the location of metal on clothing.
6. Use a probe on disturbed areas to determine if the odor of decomposing remains is present. If so, use the probe to determine the extent of the area where the smell originates and dig a test trench through that area.

Table 7-2. Advantages and limitations of grave location methods

Method	*Advantages*	*Limitations*	*Equipment Cost*
Aerial photography	Works on vast and inaccessible areas	Difficult to obtain good photos of usable scale; dependent on vegetation cover; doesn't detect subsurface objects	Can range from high to low, depending on whether the area has to be flown particularly for the project
Cadaver dogs	Quick, effective	Not all dog/trainer teams are equally reliable	Services frequently volunteered
Electrical resistivity	Less sensitive than electromagnetics to aboveground metal objects and power lines	Dependent on soil moisture	Middle
Electromagnetic (EM) survey	Susceptible to interference by objects with magnetic or electrical properties	Does detect subsoil objects; relatively small equipment	Middle
GPR	Equipment fairly universal; continuous measurements; deep soil penetration	Poor in stony or clay soils; poor in areas with moisture; may be difficult to get equipment in areas of rough topography	High
Magnetometers	Fairly universal; works deep in the subsoil; relatively simple to operate; most models fairly portable	Sensitive to noise from metal on the surface and small objects in topsoil; interpretation is not simple	High
Metal detectors	Quick, simple to operate	Shallow depth penetration; only finds metal	Metal detector frequently owned by police departments
Pedestrian survey	Quick, simple	Anomalies may not be related to case; untrained people may miss topographic and vegetation anomalies	Cost of people-power
Probes	Quick, simple, effective	Rocky soils make probes hard to use, may damage remains if pushed into them	Probe is about $75
Soil testing (phosphate or Zn/Cu)	May detect grave areas even when nothing other than body stains remain	Elements may not accumulate enough	Low
Topography and vegetation	Quick	Anomaly may not be related to case	Low
Trenching	Thorough method of a subsurface search	May damage remains if not careful	Backhoe rental, manpower for hand-dug trench
Witness	Fairly exact location, tied directly to the case	Reliability, memory	Low

7. If a backhoe cannot be used to search for the grave, then assess the potential for remote sensing methods.
8. When other methods are exhausted, use a backhoe with a finishing bucket to dig test trenches through the area until the archaeologist is sure that the area is either undisturbed or until the grave is found.
9. If the grave is not found, write a narrative of how the search was conducted and clearly document on a map what areas were searched. It is likely that further searches will be conducted later, and it is important to be clear on what areas were searched and how. This will ensure that work is not replicated and that later investigators will not assume the search was carried into areas that it was not.

GLOSSARY TERMS

electrical resistivity

electromagnetic induction meter

GPR

magnetometer

remote sensing

SUGGESTED READING

Bevan, Bruce W.

1991 The Search for Graves. *Geophysics* 56 (9): 1310–19.

Davenport, G. Clark

2001a Remote Sensing Applications in Forensic Investigations. In Archaeologists as Forensic Investigators: Defining the Role, M. Connor and D. D. Scott, editors, special issue, *Historic Archaeology* 35 (1).

2001b *Where Is It? Searching for Buried Bodies and Hidden Evidence.* Sportwork, Church Hill, Maryland.

France, Diane L., T. J. Griffin, Jack C. Swanburg, J. W. Lindemann, G. Clarke Davenport, V. Trammell, C. T. Armburst, B. Kondratieff, A. Nelson, K. Castellano, and D. Hopkins

1992 A Multidisciplinary Approach to the Detection of Clandestine Graves. *Journal of Forensic Sciences* 37 (6): 1445–58.

8

Excavating Human Remains

EXHUMATION GOALS

The classic questions of forensic anthropology determine whether the remains do, indeed, constitute a forensic case. As discussed in chapter 6, the first question is whether the remains are human or nonhuman. If the remains are not human, there is no reason to exhume them as a forensic case (actually, people who deal with violations in game regulations do investigate nonhuman remains, but that is a topic for another volume). The second classic question is whether the remains are recent or old. If the remains are those of a pre-Columbian Native American or historic settler, then the archaeologist has a different situation than if the remains are those of a modern individual. This is often more concretely shown by the context of the remains than by the remains themselves. If the remains are buried with stone tools and a clay pot, the answer will be different than if there is a 9mm bullet below the ribs. Examining a skeleton without seeing it in context can make determining whether it is modern or historic much more difficult than it need be.

Having established that the remains are, indeed, relatively modern, the archaeologist will want to determine whether the grave is primary or secondary. A primary grave is where the remains initially rested; a secondary grave is where the remains were reburied after having been disinterred. In a primary grave, the remains will be in anatomical position. If the remains are not in anatomical position, the changes should be interpretable as disturbance by rodents or other scavengers, or by natural processes (e.g., water erosion). If the bones are in anatomical position it does not mean that the remains were not moved. The remains may have been moved before the flesh decayed. Such a move may only be detectable if soil from the first location adheres to the body and is significantly different from soil from the second location. If the body is even partially skeletonized at the time it is moved, it is much easier to tell that the grave is a secondary location. It is unlikely that all the bones will be present and in anatomical position in the secondary grave. Remains moved after the remains are skeletal are frequently buried in bundles, and the excavator may even find remains of the container used to carry them.

Another goal is to determine, if possible, whether the scene is an execution site as well as a burial site. Clearly, if the grave is secondary, it is unlikely that the scene is an execution site. However, if cartridge cases as well as bullets are found in the grave, this is probable. Many times, the result of this portion of the investigation will be inconclusive from the physical evidence. The actual evidence to answer the question may come from witness testimony and the archaeologist will need to be prepared to discuss whether the physical evidence is consistent with witness testimony.

The final goal of the excavation is to re-create the activities at the scene. This will start with the last question: Was the deceased alive when he or she arrived at the scene? How was the site accessed? Did the people involved have to walk to it or could they have driven? What were the likely routes? If the deceased was already dead, what was the condition of the remains? What was it wrapped in or wearing?

THE GRAVE AS A TAPHONOMIC UNIT

Most taphonomic processes operate at the ground surface. Abrasion, weathering, scavenging, and trampling all occur when the bone is on the surface. Generally, the sooner the bone is buried beneath the surface for good, the better preserved it will often be (Lyman 1994:405). Post-burial effects on the remains include both mechanical and chemical effects. Mechanical effects may include deformation of the remains due to the weight of the soil above them. The chemical effects include the decomposition of the organic material by bacterial action, and the effects of soil pH, aeration, and water regime (Chaplin 1971:16–18). Highly basic sediments tend to inhibit bacterial activity and the organic fraction of skeletal tissue decays more rapidly in an aerobic than anaerobic environment (Rolfe and Brett 1969:226–29).

Hochrein (2002a) outlines six geotaphonomic aspects of the burial environment: stratification, tool marks, bioturbation, sedimentation, compression-depression, and internal compaction. All are relevant to examining in detail the history of the grave and reconstructing past events. *Bioturbation* describes how soils—and other objects—are mixed in the grave through animal and plant action. Tool marks on the side of the grave itself can help determine how the grave was excavated. The impressions of shovels, picks, and axes can sometimes be found on the undisturbed soil on the edge of the grave, as well as the foot and knee prints of the original excavator (Hochrein 1997). When large machinery is used, such as a backhoe, sometimes the tire tread of the machine can be found at the bottom of the grave. Other times, the impression of the teeth on a backhoe can be found in the undisturbed soil at the edge of a grave. Based on what is known about the case, the archaeologist may be able to develop hypotheses about what should be found, and test those hypotheses during the excavation.

As the fat in bodies break down, the natural hydrolysis process can produce a substance called *adipocere* (Janaway 1987:131) (figure 8-1). Adipocere is often described as looking like suet or cheese. The formation of adipocere is dependent on a series of factors that include soil chemistry, moisture, temperature, and available lipids (Gill-King 1997:103). Adipocere formation is thought to result from the chemical saponification of organic fatty acids in the presence of alkali (e.g., lime or calcium carbonate) (Mant and Furbank 1957). It is more frequent in the remains of females and infants, as the body composition of females and infants has a higher fat content. The high water content of fat cells may in fact offset an environmental lack of water (Gill-King 1997:102).

Relating the amount of adipocere formation to postmortem interval is difficult. Adipocere may appear as early as a few days following death (Gill-King 1997:101) and has been observed in burials as old as 122 years (Manhein 1997:470). Sledzik and Micozzi (1997:485) state that "presence of adipocere is an artifact of decomposition suggesting that a minimum length of time has passed since death, but it may not always be useful in determining the postmortem interval." In most graves, adipocere formation tells us little about the length of the postmortem interval.

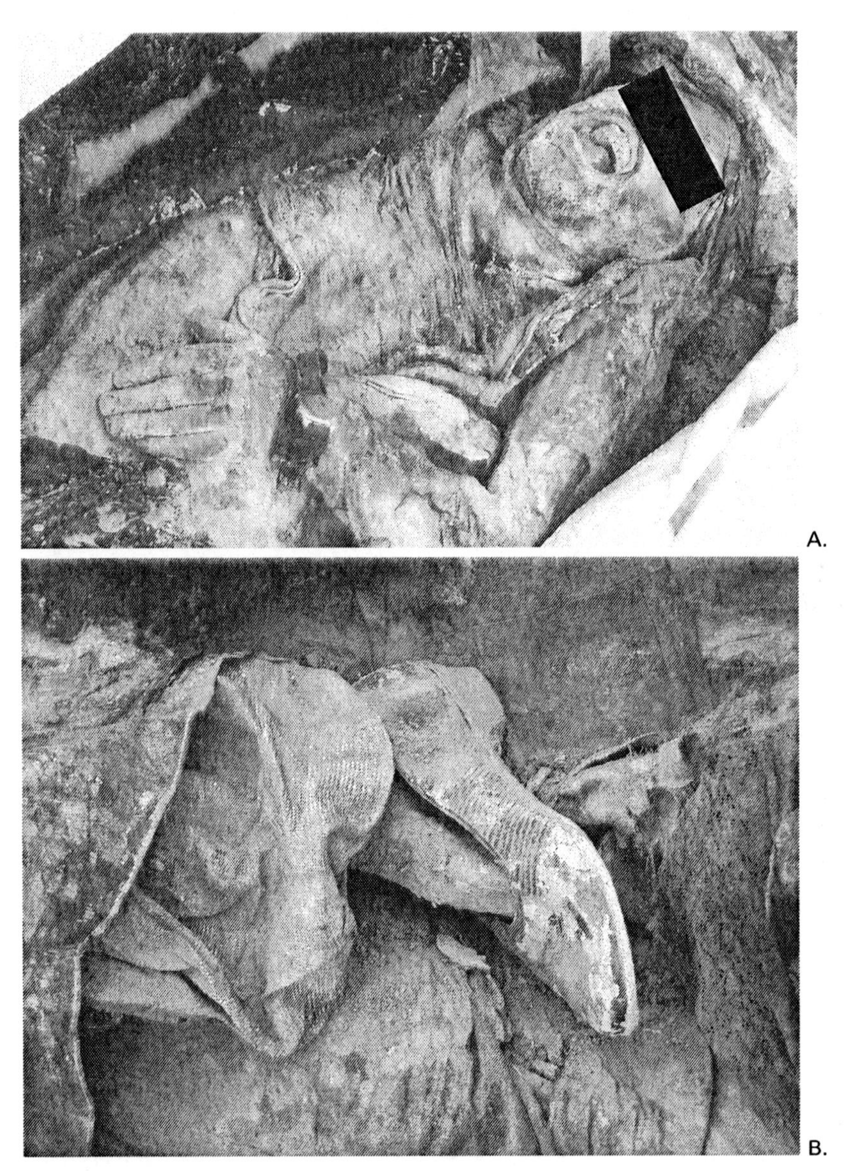

FIGURE 8-1
A. A 1993 execution excavated in 1998. Adipocere can keep facial hair in place, assisting in the identification of the individual. Excavation by the Bosnia and Herzegovina Federation Commission on Missing Persons. B. A 1986 killing uncovered in 2004. Adipocere can be seen on the foot in the shoe. From the Al Hatra, Iraq, excavation by the U.S. Army Corps of Engineers, St. Louis District for the Regime Crimes Liaison Office, U.S. Dept. of State.

Single and mass death sites have taphonomic differences that have been noted in archaeological bone beds. Discussing surface remains in a buffalo kill site, Todd (1987:149) points out the decomposing body fluids in a mass death site keep the animal hides moist and enhance their potential for rapid decay and consumption by invertebrate scavengers. The bones on the exterior of the body mass may be subject to weathering, but the bones on the interior of the body mass may be better preserved (Frison and Todd 1986:34). In buried sites the decomposition fluids also concentrate within the grave pit. The fluids may take years to disperse through the soil. If the grave was dug into soft rock or hard subsoil, the fluids will be concentrated around the bodies. This keeps the bodies in a moist environment, and they tend to saponify, as do remains under water. Thus, bodies in the center of a large body mass may be well preserved after years of burial.

Graves with poor drainage and multiple layers of bodies tend to trap moisture, even if only the moisture from the decomposing remains themselves. This moisture enables the formation of adipocere. Adipocere seems to last much longer in mass graves than in single graves, probably due to the differences in drainage. While it might seem contradictory to have mummified tissue, skeletonized remains, and adipocere tissue in the same grave, it is possible and is dependent on the moisture available to the remains. Moisture is essential for both decomposition and adipocere formation.

> Adipocere formation depends on the hydrolysis of fat to fatty acids, and cannot take place without an adequate supply of water. This water is derived not only from the exterior of the body but also from the interior, dehydrating the underlying tissues and organs including the muscles themselves. Thus adipocere formation retards the action of putrefactive organisms.
>
> It was found at exhumation, as would be anticipated from the above, that there was an outer layer of adipocere surrounding a layer of mummified muscle tissue. Some mummified muscle tissue was usually found incorporated in the deepest layers of adipocere. (Mant 1950:45)

Mass graves tend to create their own microenvironments toward preservation (Haglund, Connor, and Scott 2001; Mant 1950). Mant (1950:33) notes that in a mass grave the bodies in the center of the grave are much better preserved than those in the periphery of the grave. Mant did his research after World War II, exhuming graves for the Nuremberg tribunal. Also related to

World War II were the 1943 German excavations in Poland, investigating mass graves in the Katyn Forest. A professor of forensic medicine and criminology at Breslay University summarized the condition of these bodies: "The stages of decay were found to vary in accordance with the position of the bodies in the pits. Whilst mummification had taken place on the top and at the sides of the mass of bodies, a humid process could be observed caused by the damp nearer the center" (Buhtz 1943 in FitzGibbon 1977:142).

The German investigators attributed the preservation of the remains to the microenvironment created by the mass grave:

> In the mass graves at Katyn the murdered captives were packed so tightly together (either dead or dying) and sealed over with copious quantities of solid soil, that the putrification process was slowed considerably. For example, in the "L" shaped grave. . . the initial interment was estimated to be almost 3000 bodies. These bodies were packed together so tightly that decaying and decomposing fluids of each body penetrated, imbibed, and infiltrated other dead bodies within the grave. (official statement concerning the mass murder at Katyn 1943, as quoted in Lauck 1988:53)

That desiccated tissue, skeletal remains, and adipocere formation were encountered in the same grave is consistent with a combination of factors, including the alkaline soils, the clay content of the soil at the bottom of the grave, and that bodies were buried pressed together and in multiple layers.

WORKING THE BURIAL SCENE

Establishing the Scene Perimeter

When first setting up an area to search intensively or in which to begin exhumations, a scene perimeter needs to be established. Usually placing crime scene tape around the area is an effective method. Only people with a reason to be near the exhumation should be allowed within this perimeter. A record should be kept of all the people who enter and exit and the times at which they do so. Given the large number of people who frequently feel they are necessary at an exhumation, it is sometimes useful to set up a double perimeter. The first perimeter excludes the public, the curious, and the media. The second perimeter excludes anyone not actually working at that moment on the exhumation. This includes VIPs, workers on a break, photographers not taking photographs, or anyone else not needed at that moment on the exhumation. The second perimeter can be close enough that people can view the exhumation, but are not in the way of the workers. If there are a large number of people who need to see the exhumations, then setting up a video camera and having the picture run to a remote location can ease congestion at the scene.

If the perimeter is too small then the workers are crowded. The perimeter needs to be large enough that the excavations cannot be photographed with a zoom lens from outside the perimeter. Tarps, or other material, need to be set up to shield the excavation. Media may also use helicopters to look at the excavation, so be aware of security issues from above, as well as from ground level.

Safety

In the United States, the Occupational Safety and Health Administration (OSHA) office of the Department of Labor has guidelines for safe excavations. Many other countries have similar government offices and regulations. If the guidelines of these offices are not followed, the exhumations should be shut down.

Site conditions that should be considered in planning the excavation include traffic, nearness of structures and their conditions, soil type, surface and ground water, overhead and underground utilities, and the weather (OSHA 1995:3). The standards established by OSHA require excavators to determine the estimated locations of utility installations—sewer, telephone, fuel, electric, water lines—that may be encountered during excavation. Utility companies should be asked for the exact locations of their lines. If the excavations are near a public traffic area, then all workers should have and use warning vests with reflecting material.

The chief danger in excavations over 1.5 m deep is cave-ins. Soil may weigh over 45 kg for only a third of a cubic meter. A full cubic meter of soil may weigh more than 1225 kg. This weight is almost equivalent to that of a car in a space less than that of an office desk (Brown et al. 1998:1). Someone trapped by a cave-in will probably be seriously injured. If a wall does fail, several additional failures near the original location will probably quickly follow. First, the bottom of the wall will fall into the trench. The erosion at the base of the trench leaves the upper soil unsupported, and this may then fall into the excavation. Rescuers coming to the aid of those trapped by the first failure may themselves be trapped by later failures (Brown et al. 1998:2).

If the excavation is deep, then a competent person should inspect the excavations and surrounding areas for potential cave-ins on a regular basis. These areas should be inspected after a heavy rainfall or other conditions occur (e.g., blasting) that could destabilize the soil. The sides of the excavation should be sloped or benched to prevent cave-ins. For excavations not more than 6 m deep, a slope of 1.5 m horizontal to 1 m vertical is safe in most soils. If that is not possible, the side of the excavation should be supported with wood or jacks.

During any excavation, but particularly during deep excavations, materials or equipment that could fall or roll into the excavation should be kept away from the edge. Water in the excavation can be another hazard. If water accumulates in the hole, it has the potential to destabilize the sides and cause a cave-in. Water should be removed by using either buckets or a pump, and the soil should be allowed to dry before the excavators continue.

Another hazard in large, deep excavations can be the entrance and exit to the hole. If the sides of the excavation are well sloped, then workers may be able to walk up and down the slope. However, many soils are slippery when wet and there is a potential for workers to slip coming in or out of the grave. Ladders, steps, ramps, or some other safe means of entering and exiting the area should be supplied.

Graves

Single Graves

Once it has been determined that it is likely there is a grave, the area to be excavated needs to be determined. The common methods of doing this include

1. looking for surface changes in soil, vegetation, or micro-topography;
2. using a probe or pin flag to feel the differences in compactness between the disturbed and undisturbed soil, or
3. using a small trench to determine the perimeter of the soil changes.

Changes in soil, vegetation, or micro-topography will result from the fact that the soil in the grave is disturbed and less compact than the soil outside the grave. The area over the body may sink as the body decomposes, leaving a shallow indentation in the ground. In some soil types (particularly clay soils) a crack may form between the compact undisturbed soil and the loose disturbed soil, as the loose soil falls into the indentation and away from the undisturbed soil. In a disturbed area, there may also be some subsoil showing on the surface, mixed with the upper soil horizons.

The soil in the grave will be less compact than the undisturbed soil outside the grave. A practiced individual can feel this change in the soil using a tile probe and can outline the disturbance. Even the pin on a pin flag can sometimes be used to feel the change in soil compactness and outline a disturbed area.

It can be difficult to determine the outline of the grave based on the surface characteristics. Digging a narrow (20–40 cm) trench across the area where the grave is presumed to be will often show the soil changes characteristic of a disturbance. For a single grave, a trench the width of a shovel may reveal two edges of the grave. Once that is found, a second trench, perpendicular to the first, can be used to locate the opposite two edges of the grave. (See chapter 7, "Test Trenches.")

Once the area to be excavated is located, a grid extending past the edges of the grave can be established. For a single grave, a rectangle 3 m wide and 5 m long may be sufficient. A few quick measurements can give the excavator an idea of a good size for the excavation. The first corner is fairly arbitrary. It can be marked with a 6-inch nail, tied with flagging tape so it can be clearly seen. If possible, push the nail slowly into the ground, trying to feel if the nail hits anything. If it does, move it slightly and see if the object can be avoided. Take a tape measure and place a second nail the distance from the first the width of the area to be excavated in the direction that you wish the width of the grid to be.

The position of the next two nails can be triangulated (see chapter 4 and figure 4-8). Place a string, close to the ground, tied to the nails. Nylon string is preferable to cotton, as it does not stretch. Using brightly colored surveyor's string helps to keep workers from tripping over the string. Take a magic marker and mark the meter intervals on the strings. Name the squares they form, mark these on the map—and the grid is laid out. If appropriate, nails can be placed at the meter intervals and string laid out between them. However, this can be difficult to work around, and, in a small excavation, with a little care the excavators can tell which items came from which squares without the string.

Screening stations should be set up at enough of a distance from the hole that the dirt will not fall back into the hole. Soil from the excavation can also be bagged and screened at a later date. If this method, or any method other than screening all the soil, is used, then all the soil excavated should be placed in a pile on a tarp. This way, if at some point a reason for screening the soil is seen, then it is still possible to do so. If untrained individuals are used as screeners, then a small display of smaller bones and fingernails might be useful, so that the inexperienced screeners can see examples of what they should be collecting.

Before excavation, and before removing any vegetation, use a metal detector in the unit to ensure that any cartridge cases or other small items that may be on the edges of the grave are found. Carefully remove dead vegetation or leaves that lay on top of the unit. This can be done by square meter, and the leaf litter taken to the screening area for the screeners to go through more carefully. Use root clippers or a saw to remove any small trees or plants. The ground surface should be clearly visible. The excavators may see a clear depression or even cracks in the soil at the edge of the grave where the fill has pulled away from the undisturbed soil. Any anomaly like this should be recorded.

A flat shovel can be used to remove the next layer, whether it is grass or something else. This will be done using a technique called *skim shoveling*, where the shovel is used to remove only 2–3 cm of soil across the surface. The entire surface of the unit will be taken down these 2–3 cm, square meter by square meter. The people working the screens should know which square meter the soil in their screen came from. Using different colored plastic buckets for each square is an easy way to do this. The workers can continue downward in small increments, across the entire grid, square by square, until the grave pit is clearly delineated.

At this point, there are two goals. One is to dig around the body (or bodies), leaving it (or them) on a pedestal (figure 8-2). But the excavator also needs to remove the fill from the inside of the grave before destroying the grave pit, so that any tool marks on the edge of the grave can be seen and documented. Working from one side of the grave to the other side, the excavator can remove the fill inside the grave. Often, the unconsolidated soil from inside the feature will fall away from the edge of the consolidated soil outside the feature, delineating the edge of the grave. Again, the excavators should go down 2–3 cm using trowels, then across, so that one area is never greatly deeper than the others. They should also work square meter by square meter, sending the soil to the screens separately. If the excavators find material in the grave fill, above

FIGURE 8-2
Leaving the bodies on a pedestal and excavating the surrounding soil to a level below the remains allows the workers plenty of room. Excavation by the Bosnia and Herzegovina Federation Commission for Missing Persons.

the body, it should be documented, mapped, placed in a clearly labeled bag, and logged into the evidence log.

Using a wet-dry vacuum around the edge of the grave pit can remove loose dirt from the edge, and expose potential tool marks without the marks being contacted by the tools used in the excavation (Hochrein 1997:180). If any tool marks are seen, they should be photographed and a narrative description written; they should also be cast with dental gypsum, much the way shoe or tire print evidence is cast. Carefully digging the feature fill (the inside of the grave) ensures that any additional material that might have been buried is located and that the excavators are dealing with a single burial.

Trowels used should be flat mason's trowels (see chapter 3, on equipment). Rounded garden trowels do not allow as much control. The edge of the trowel should be held at about a 45 degree angle from the ground, angled away from the excavator. The trowel should then be used to scrape away a small amount of soil. The point of the trowel should never be stuck into the ground, as the excavator cannot see the damage the end of the trowel may be doing.

When the highest part of the body is reached, the excavators need to determine the position of the body in order to bring the entire excavation inside the grave to that level. As bone and artifacts are found in the ground, they should be left in place. This leaves them in context with the remainder of the material in the grave for the photographs and maps. It is also important that the investigators see all the material in context at one time. This helps immensely in the interpretation of the material in the grave. As the excavation proceeds below the material, each piece will be left on a soil pedestal exactly the size of the bone or artifact, which may expand slightly outward.

Making these pedestals requires some thought and skill. Their walls either need to be straight under the piece or expand slightly out. If the wall cuts under the object, then the weight of the piece will cause the pedestal to collapse. Loose, sandy soils will not hold much weight and the pedestal in such soil may need to be larger than in other soils. Clay soils can hold a lot of water and will shrink as they dry out, so the pedestal may need to be made slightly bigger than the artifact so that as the soil dries, it shrinks to the size of the piece. In clay, if a pedestal is cut to exactly the size of the object, then the pedestal will shrink smaller than the piece as the soil dries out and collapse under the weight of the artifact.

Two excavators can work on either side of the body, starting from the highest part of the body and working toward the lowest. If the body is basically level, they should work from the crania to the feet. This procedure helps to ensure that dirt does not fall on areas that have already been cleaned. If the soil allows or the bone is soft, use brushes or bamboo sticks when working near the bone. Sharp-edged trowels can leave cut marks on the bone. Leave all the bones and evidence in the ground until everything is exposed and can be photographed and drawn together. Never pull a partly exposed bone out of the ground. First, this can easily break off the end of the bone in the ground. Second, if the bone is in anatomical position, it is easy to find the next bone in sequence at the end of the element exposed. Third, if the bone is adjacent to a piece of evidence, then you lose context for the evidence.

If the remains are skeletal and not clothed, then working from the crania to the abdominal cavity is also frequently the fastest method. The ribs and vertebra are among the most complicated areas to expose and may be more difficult to access after the limbs are fully exposed. The soil surrounding the ribs should be removed, but enough soil left directly underneath to support the ribs so that they do not fall sideways. After this, the limbs can be exposed from the proximal to the distal. As the hands and feet contain lots of easily disturbed small bones, they should be the last things to be exposed (Hester, Shafer, and Feder 1997:266).

If the soil is hard, it will tend to break apart in peds (see chapter 5). It may be easiest to use a chopstick or other implement to pry up the soil by the peds. Lifting a ped will usually leave the bone in the ground. Clothing can be a big help in excavation. It can be *gently* tugged on to dislodge loose soil. Use discretion, however, for if the clothes are rotten, it may not be possible to tug on them at all, and they may be very difficult to excavate around.

If there is a chance the skeleton is female, the excavator needs to be aware of the possibility of a fetus in the abdominal area. The skeletal elements of a fetus make a quarter look large. If there is any indication of small bones in the lower abdomen, then all of the soil from the abdomen should be collected and searched in the laboratory. Even better, if the remains are clothed, leave the soil in the abdomen, lift the adult remains with the clothing into a bag, and collect the soil in the lab.

Juvenile and infant skeletons require much care. The younger the individual, the more care is needed. Skeletal elements of infants are extremely small. With younger individuals, excavating around the remains and pedestaling them as described above is still the best method. However, it may be best at this point to document the remains, and carefully cut through the pedestal, placing the small bones and the soil in a bag. The skeletal elements can then be separated out in the laboratory with good lighting and magnification. The small bones in an infant, such as the bones inside the ear, will almost certainly have to be magnified for identification.

If soil from around an infant or fetal burial is collected, it should not be screened. The screen will crush the bone and the smallest skeletal elements may be smaller than the soil particles. The soil can be searched on a clean, well-lighted surface. A magnifier with a ring-light is useful. The soil should be picked through using a small, artist's touch-up brush. Bones should be picked up with the brush and placed in a vial. Handling these very tiny skeletal elements with either the fingers or a tweezers is likely to crush them.

Hair should be looked for on the head and the crotch, and should be collected and bagged. There can be a great deal of hair in the head area, and excavators may decide to sample the hair, obtaining enough to look at the color, the cut, and any potential chemical treatments (dying, streaking, permanent, straightening, etc.). Excavators should be aware of the position of and look for the hyoid bone, and possible thyroid tissue.

Specialized samples are discussed in more detail below. These include bugs, pollen, soil, or other specialized material. If the specialist (entomologist, botanist, or palynologist) can be part of the team at the site and collect his or her own samples, the results tend to turn out best. This allows the expert to see the context of the sample with the remains and keeps the investigator from having to testify in a field in which he or she may not be qualified.

This portion of the excavation is complete when enough soil is removed, both from the top and the sides of the remains, to allow the body to be freely lifted. If the remains are on their side, the excavations need to be deep enough that they are totally below the side of the body. The soil on either the back or front, whichever is closer to being the bottom, needs to be left to support the remains, but the other side needs to be completely cleared off.

Small Multiple Graves (Two to Six Individuals)

If multiple individuals are buried in a single grave, this should become clear during the removal of the grave fill. If a second individual is found below or adjacent to the first, the direction and extent of the remains needs to be determined. When the grave fill is removed, the edges searched for tool marks, and the body mass is defined, then the body mass needs to be pedestaled. A trench around the body mass should be dug; it should be large enough for the workers (figures 8-2, 8-3, 8-4). If working with a backhoe, then the workers can throw any soil not to be screened into this trench, and it can be taken in a wheelbarrow to where it can be removed with the backhoe. Any soil from near the remains should be placed in buckets or wheelbarrows and transported to the screen.

The cleaning of the remains should start from the highest portion of the body mass. If the grave is relatively level, then the cleaning of the remains should start from the center of the body mass and move outward. In working this way, the areas once cleaned do not have to be walked over or worked over, and recleaned. The rule of thumb for body removal in graves with multiple individuals is that the last person in is the first person out.

Evidence clearly associated with a set of remains is usually logged with the case number of that body. Evidence not clearly associated with a single set of

FIGURE 8-3
Leaving the remains on a pedestal while excavating allows the excavator to ensure that all material adjacent to and below the body is easily seen. Excavation conducted by Sri Lankan forensic experts.

remains is logged independently, although the map, notes, and photographs should show to which case numbers the material was closest.

Mass Graves (More than Six Individuals)

Larger graves (and the seven used here as a cutoff is totally arbitrary) present a number of challenges not seen in the smaller graves (Haglund, Connor, and Scott 2001; Haglund 2002). Maintaining access to the central remains for body removal, while cleaning the surrounding remains, can be a challenge, as can the disposal of the soil from the excavation (also called the back dirt). A large mass of bodies (figure 8-4) creates differences in decomposition that become more noticeable the larger the mass of remains. Other large graves (figure 8-5) do not have large body masses that create the differences in decomposition, but share the logistical challenges of a large excavation.

As discussed above, the larger the grave, the greater the range of preservation likely to be present. In a large grave of several hundred, the outer bodies may become skeletal relatively quickly, but the interior of the body core may be well preserved. Haglund (2002) calls this a "feather edge effect." At a grave

FIGURE 8-4
Mass grave where the partially decomposed remains were thrown into a pit dug with heavy machinery. Excavations by the Bosnia and Herzegovina Federation Commission on Missing Persons.

of over five hundred individuals in Kigali, Rwanda, the grave itself was shaped rather like a flower, with the bodies in the upper layers spread further out than the lower bodies. The upper bodies were skeletons. The lower portion of the grave had been dug into soft shale, which held both the groundwater and the moisture from the decomposition fluids. Thus, the lower bodies were saponified, and relatively well preserved (Haglund, Connor, and Scott 2001).

As with any feature, the size should be defined before it is excavated. As the overburden is removed from a large grave, the excavator should look for the edges. This may be most easily done by placing two trenches, perpendicular to each other, over the grave (called *cross-trenching*). This should give the excavator an idea of the location of the sides of the grave. If the grave fill can be differentiated from the undisturbed soil, then the outline of the grave should be traced all around the edge.

If the grave was dug using heavy machinery, it is probably going to take heavy machinery to remove the overburden to the depth of the remains. This

FIGURE 8-5
Mass grave where the bodies were deposited neatly in rows, in body bags. Excavation at Glumina by the Bosnia and Herzegovina Federation Commission on Missing Persons.

will make it harder to look for tool marks or other indications of how the grave was dug. The excavators should look for teeth marks on the side of the grave showing the teeth of the original front-end loader or backhoe bucket. There may also be traces of a ramp used to access the bottom of the grave with the machine. On the ramp, or at the bottom, may be imprints of the tires, or treads, of the machine.

It may also not be possible to follow the "last person in, first person out" rule of thumb in a very large grave. For one thing, groups of individuals may have been dumped in the grave on different sides in different loads of bodies to the grave, or a group of people may have walked in under their own power at the same time, then been shot. In some mass graves, the bodies are laid neatly side by side in rows in a long trench (figure 8-5). In a case such as this, where the bodies were buried in an organized manner, the bodies can be numbered at one time, documented in sequence, and lifted in sequence.

In other mass graves, where bodies are not buried in an organized fashion (figure 8-4), Haglund, Connor, and Scott (2001) describe an excavation method that has worked satisfactorily. The excavators work in two teams: a documentation team and a body removal team. Working in groups of about ten bodies at a time, the documentation team completes the mapping, notes, and photographs of the next ten bodies to be removed on one side of the grave. If the bodies are not laid neatly in the grave, deciding on the next bodies to be removed takes some investigation to reveal which remains are least encumbered by other remains. Bodies are not numbered until they are ready to be removed, to cut down on errors. It is also easy to label two portions of the same body with different case numbers when the intervening portions of the remains are covered with other bodies.

The body removal team then comes in and lifts the remains. On fleshed remains, this may entail lifting limbs of some bodies in order to free the target remains. Skeletal remains present more of a challenge and portions of remains may need to be documented and partially removed to get to the remains below. If this is done, then both the portion removed and the articulating portion left in the ground need to be carefully labeled. No more than two skeletons on each area should be partially removed, or confusion will inevitably result. At no point should personnel in the team change, if skeletons have been partially removed. The same people that partially removed one skeleton should remove the remainder of that same skeleton.

In graves where heavy machinery was used to bury the remains, it is not uncommon to find disassociated body parts. This also happens at sites where the remains were buried after they were partially decomposed. Should isolated body parts be found, they should be catalogued separately from the complete sets of remains. A "partial remains" log can be started that numbers the assemblage, and gives the location, photograph numbers, and a brief description of the remains. Including the partial remains in the same numbering system as the complete remains ensures confusion during the examination, when the partial remains are reunited with the remaining body parts.

Documentation

Before removal, the body should be photographed, mapped or sketched, and notes taken. Standard terminology for describing body position is found in Sprague (2005:37–55). If the bones are fragile and possibly will not come out of the ground in one piece, then measurements of the long bones may be noted at this time as well. Detailed photographs should be taken of any apparent injuries, particularly those that have broken, or cracked, the bone. Gunshot wounds often badly fracture the bone. Once the bone is moved, it may fall apart. It can be painstakingly reconstructed in the laboratory, but the field documentation shows that the material was fractured when it was uncovered, and not during transport or storage.

Field notes should be relatively skimpy next to most archaeological field notes. There should be nothing in them that could be contradicted by later analysis, and absolutely no theorizing. *At no point* should the archaeologist write a potential cause of death in the notes. If there is a 9mm hole in the skull, there is simply a 9mm hole, or circular defect, in the skull, not a gunshot wound. The pathologist has the responsibility of determining cause of death, and he may determine that the hole was caused by a 9mm ice pick. Inconsistencies among experts cause defense attorneys great joy, and may make a strong case weak.

Notes that are not on forms should be kept in a single notebook for each case. Notes for multiple cases absolutely should not be kept in the same notebook. The court can subpoena these notes and the archaeologist may have to turn over the entire notebook. There is no reason to turn over to the attorney material on other cases. The notes in the book can be in the form of a log, starting with the request for assistance (when it came in, who called, and with whom the archaeologist talked).

Removing the Burial

If the remains are fleshed, the head and the hands and feet should be placed in bags to preserve any trace evidence. A paper bag placed over the hands can be taped over the forearm. This will also help keep decomposing fingers from falling off during lifting or transport. If the arms are spread they should be moved to lie on the chest before the body is moved. The legs also, can be brought together, if they are not already. The opened, labeled body bag can be placed along the side of the grave. One person should be by the bag, on the side opposite the grave, to help keep the body bag open. At least two people, and possibly three, should be used to lift the remains. The remains should be kept level and placed in the bag.

When the body is in a container, such as a box, tarp, or carpet, the container is never opened at the scene. The container, with the body inside, is removed and placed in the position in which it was recovered on a sterile sheet or in a body bag.

If the body is partially decomposed, the crania and some cervical vertebrae may separate from the body. The excavator will probably be able to tell if this is the case while placing a bag over the head. If that is the case, they should be lifted first and placed into the body bag. Enough vertebrae should be lifted with the head so that the remaining vertebrae will be easily packed inside the shirt collar.

If the remains are skeletal and clothed, the clothing should not be removed. The clothing may have holes from gunshots or stab wounds. The pathologist needs to see the clothing in situ on the body. A body bag can be used with skeletal remains as well. Lifting should start with the head and a skeletal inventory be conducted as the elements are removed from the ground into the body bag. Skulls and mandibles may need to be wrapped with packing, both for transport and to minimize tooth loss. If the clothing is relatively intact, the body should be lifted in a manner similar to that used with fleshed remains. The arms, in the sleeves, can be brought onto the chest and the entire thoracic area lifted in the shirt to the body bag. Each hand should be bagged separately in a clearly labeled bag. The lower extremities can be lifted in the pants, skirt, and/or pantyhose. It may be easiest to bend the knees, flexing the lower part of the body, bring the bundle into the body bag, and then straighten the legs out. If there are shoes and socks, these will hold the feet bones together.

Body bags should be supported in the middle when moved. Preferably they should be moved on a stretcher, but if one is not available, either three people should carry the bag or one person needs to hold both one end and the middle.

Fragile materials can be lifted in a block with the soil that surrounds them (figure 8-6). The material should be excavated as cleanly as possible, then isolated on a pedestal until the excavator is sure nothing is below the object (figure 8-6A). At this point, a consolidant or adhesive can be applied to help hold the material together during the lifting process. The consolidant can be put into a spray container and sprayed over the material until it is saturated. However, there may be problems in using these consolidants in samples that will be analyzed for DNA or other biochemical portions of bone. If the material is bone that may be analyzed for DNA, then it would be best to leave some of the bone untreated. If any chemicals are used, this should be noted on the field records, and the name of the chemical used recorded.

FIGURE 8-6
Using plaster bandages to help lift fragile bone. A. The bone (here a bison metatarsal) is first pedestaled and cleaned as much as is possible without breaking it. B. A damp paper towel is placed over the bone to separate it from the plaster. The plaster bandages are laid over the paper towel. After the plaster has dried, the pedestal will be carefully undercut and a rigid piece of metal or wood slid underneath.

Materials used to help to lift friable materials include plaster of paris, plaster bandages, and gauze bandages. All these are readily available in pharmacies in most countries. Plaster of paris is a white powder consisting of calcined gypsum. The plaster should not come into direct contact with an object so it is separated from the object by a layer of cloth or aluminum foil. But when applied over an object, the plaster forms a rigid support. Plaster bandages are gauze bandages with dry plaster of paris throughout. They are much easier to use than plaster of paris without the gauze, and are quick and easy to apply over objects. The plaster should be thoroughly dry before the bone is lifted.

Once the friable material is surrounded by a stable casing, the pedestal can be undercut, frequently simply by sliding a shovel through it, and the material removed. The adhering soil is usually best removed in the laboratory. The material, its casing, and the adhering soil should immediately be packaged for transport. Wrapping it in bubble wrap and placing it in an appropriately sized box is frequently a good way to package the material with its casing.

The excavation is not complete when the body is removed. Frequently, there will be a gray soil beneath the body, soil saturated with decomposing body fluids. The body fluids may stain the soil so that it is impossible to determine the bottom of the grave pit. This material needs to be dug until the excavator is sure that they are outside the grave pit. At that point, a metal detector should be used in the excavation. If the person was shot near the grave, cartridge cases may be buried well below the bottom of the pit. Bullets may fall from decomposing remains and into the ground below the body. Rodents, or the weight of the remains, may have moved objects below the bottom of the pit. When the archaeologist is sure nothing remains in the excavation, the empty grave should be photographed and described.

Before the scene is released, soil saturated with decomposition fluids should be removed or buried. Both family and media are likely to visit the grave site, and there is no need to have the decomposition smell in the area. Before release, the scene should be policed so that it looks—and smells—clean.

Evidence Management

Throughout the excavation, pieces of evidence will be unearthed. Each should be numbered in some sequential system agreed upon by the archaeologist and the law enforcement evidence custodian. No numbers should be skipped in forensic cases, or the lawyers may imply that evidence was lost. The location of each piece of evidence should be recorded on the site map, and the piece photographed in the ground before removal. The evidence should be placed in a bag properly labeled with the evidence number, case number, date, time, the initials or name of the person who collected the piece, and map number or location.

An evidence log should be kept and a description of each piece of evidence and its number written in the log. The log should also include the date the item was collected, roll and frame numbers of relevant photographs, the tape numbers of relevant videotapes, and the map number or location of the object in the grid. The object should be labeled only insofar as the collector is absolutely sure of what the object is.

Inconsistencies between field labeling and later identification by an expert in the lab can lead to difficulties in court. If a bullet is collected, then the log should read "suspected bullet." Unless the person who enters the log is the person who will testify in court that this is a 9mm bullet, then the initial log should not read "9mm bullet." For instance, if the initial field log reads "9mm bullet" and the firearms expert later identifies it as a bullet from a .22, there will be no 9mm bullet in the final inventory of evidence from the scene. The lawyers may ask, "Who lost the 9mm bullet? Who planted the .22 caliber bullet?" The answers will be—and are meant to be—embarrassing. The "experts" look less than expert.

Packaging

The material in the ground is supported by soil. As it is taken out of the ground and denied this support, good-quality packing supplies, the proper packing of materials, and attention to packing the vehicle for transport can determine whether the materials are still intact on arrival at the laboratory. If the material is excavated and transported to a laboratory the same day, much less care is needed in packaging. However, if it will be several days or a month until the material is unwrapped and properly treated, packaging becomes very important.

In general, wet materials should be kept wet and dry materials dry until all can be stabilized in a controlled environment. However, wet materials will begin to grow mold once exposed to the air, so it is important to either refrigerate them or move them to a supervised environment quickly. Cleaning soil that was wet and dried on bone can damage the bone. So either the bone should be cleaned, then dried, or the bone should be kept damp until it can be cleaned.

Material can be kept damp by including sheets of wet polyethylene foam inside the packaging and sealing the artifact and wet foam in polyethylene sheeting. Wet objects can also be placed into sealed plastic containers to retain their moisture. Notes should be written directly on the container that this object needs to be refrigerated or stabilized immediately on reaching the lab.

Silica gel is also useful in packing objects. Silica gel is chemically inert and is used as a drying agent in packing moisture-sensitive materials. It can be bought as self-indicating crystals that change from blue to pink as the silica gel absorbs moisture. The silica gel needs to be included with the material in a sealed, airtight container (e.g., a mason jar or ziplock bag) to be effective.

Ancillary Studies

Ancillary studies are secondary studies that may not be useful in all, or even many, buried-body cases. But when the evidence is there to be used, these studies can be critical. For this reason, all excavators should be aware of these types of studies, of what they can tell the investigator, and of what type of data is needed for the analysis. If a decision is made that a type of evidence is not important, the archaeologist may end up revisiting that decision on a witness stand. So it may be better in some cases to take the samples and do the analysis, even if it results in no useful information.

Botany

The plants in or near remains can help to determine the time since death and sequence of events, and place people or objects at the scene (Hall 1997; Coyle 2004; Dupras et al. 2006:69–73). When a grave is dug, the plants in the area are disturbed and the roots are cut. Cut roots may show the grave edges. Roots grown through the grave, or the remains, may yield an estimate of length of time since the disturbance, as some species of plants show annular rings, both in the plant and the root. Some plants are quite short-lived and their presence in a grave may indicate the season in which the grave was dug. Plant remains on clothing, blankets, or tarps may indicate that those items were at a grave scene, if they match the plants at the scene. Plant fragments on the body or at scenes that do not match the plants growing at the scene may indicate that the body was moved, and may help to determine from where the remains were moved.

If the investigator suspects that the plant remains will be useful in establishing time since death or placing people or objects at the scene, then they should contact a local botanist and take samples of plants from around the scene. Most plant samples can be dried without harming their value for identifying the species (Hall 1997:358). However, a botanist on-scene may identify seeds, algae, or other plant-related material that others would not.

Collected plant remains should, if possible, be pressed for preservation. A phone book or a catalogue is good to use to collect samples and newspaper works as well (Dupras et al. 2006:71).

Palynology

Pollen is everywhere and on everything. Forensic pollen analysis has been used mainly to place people or objects at crime scenes. Studies on soil surface pollen content suggest that there is sufficient variation between areas to distinguish between areas, even when they may be relatively close (Horrocks, Coulson, and Walsh, 1998). In one case, pollen analysis was used to differentiate a crime scene and alibi scene that were seven meters apart (Horrocks and Walsh 1999).

Pollen samples can be collected from shoes, soil, clothing, or almost any object. A comparative pollen sample from the location will need to be taken, and this should be done by the palynologist completing the analysis. The object from which the pollen will be taken should be put in a plastic or paper bag immediately to protect it from collecting more of the ambient pollen that surrounds us at all times. The palynologist will wash the pollen from the object and compare the assemblages of pollen, looking for similar percents of plants and for the occurrence of unusual or unique plants.

Entomology

Much of the decomposition of soft tissue is driven by insects. Information on the type of insects present and their distribution on the body can be used to estimate the time since death, drug use before death, the position and presence of wounds, and whether the body was moved since death (Anderson and Cervenka 2002:174). Most forensic entomologists would prefer to collect the data themselves at the scene, rather than to work with material collected by other people. The American Board of Forensic Entomology certifies trained specialists and can be contacted for the names of certified forensic entomologists around the country. The second alternative to having a specialist on-site is to contact one over the telephone, describe the scene, and talk to the specialist about collecting the specimens.

Insect evidence that needs to be collected can include eggs, larvae (maggots), pupae, pupal cases, and the insects themselves. Each stage of insect life requires a different collection technique (Anderson and Cervenka 2002) and may be collected in different areas in and around the remains. Eggs may be around wounds and body openings. Maggots may be found near wounds and body openings, but will be found throughout the remains as decomposition progresses. Pupae may be in and around the body, up to a meter away. The empty pupal cases will more often be hidden, perhaps a few centimeters under the soil or in the folds of the clothing. Insects may be crawling on the remains or flying above them, or found in the soil and vegetation.

For each stage, a sample of material should be collected and preserved alive and another sample collected that is immediately killed and preserved. The live samples will be hatched, as it can be difficult to determine insect species based solely on the egg or larvae. The length of time that it takes the material to hatch may also be useful in determining how long since it was deposited on the remains.

Firearms Identification

Bullets, cartridge cases, and cartridges are found during many forensic excavations. They are important as they can determine whether the scene is an execution scene as well as a burial scene. Marks or striae made on the bullets and cases when the gun is fired also show differences among weapon types, as well as among individual weapons. All should be excavated and handled carefully to avoid damaging the marks made by the weapon. Cartridge case and/or bullet depositional patterning may be very important as an aid in reconstructing the shooting scene. Cartridge, cartridge case, and bullet find locations should be routinely mapped and appropriate data collected for further investigation by a qualified firearms examiner.

Bullets found in the bottom of a grave have frequently fallen through the decomposing remains and so are not an indication that the weapon was fired in that location. Bullets found in trees do suggest that a weapon was fired at that location. Also, importantly, the bullet track into the tree may yield information about where the shooter was standing and in what direction he or she was firing, aiding in shooting scene reconstruction. If the investigator is not familiar with reconstructing bullet tracks, he or she should call a specialist before recovering the bullet. Simply digging the bullet out with a penknife, or other such object, will destroy the bullet track and may mark the bullet.

When most modern weapons are shot into the soil, the bullet may travel up to several meters below the ground surface. Depending on the soil type and the velocity of the projectile when fired, there may be a bullet track in the soil that can be seen through careful excavation. Most bullet tracks are too small for rodent holes and too large for insect burrows. If excavated for several centimeters, they will go straight and not turn to the side, as will tracks left by rodents or insects. Documenting the angle of the track may help to reconstruct where the shooter was standing. If the investigator wishes to recover the bullet, this should wait until all else at the scene is excavated, as the bullet track will probably be much deeper than anything else.

GRAVES WHERE THE BODIES HAVE BEEN REMOVED

Sometimes the investigator finds the grave, but not the body. When this happens, it is important to document that the body or bodies were there and were moved. Skinner, York, and Connor (2002) discuss the indications in many graves that remains were removed. One of the common, and important, indications is a pit that includes soil saturated in decomposition fluids. Other indications include disassociated body parts, clothing, or, in older graves, body silhouettes (see chapter 5). Intersecting pits, where one pit was dug to bury the remains and a second dug to remove the remains, is also an indication that a grave was disturbed. Equipment associated with body moving that may be in the area includes rubber gloves, parts of tarps or body bags, or shovels, stretchers, or other such equipment.

Where removal of remains from a grave is suspected, documentation of the original location of a burial is important in reconstructing the events that tie a murderer to a body (Skinner, York, and Connor 2002) or in verifying a witness statement. If there are scattered human bones, especially the small bones, if the ground surface is clearly disturbed, and if there are artifacts scattered on the surface, there may be reason to believe that a body has been removed from the area. The proposed grave area will need to be carefully exhumed and documented to strengthen that argument.

Documentation will include not only a map of the location of the artifacts, but also of the site topography, which will assist in detailing where the soil from the grave was put the first time, and the soil from the exhumation the second. During excavation, careful attention needs to be paid to the soil stratigraphy, especially to the grave cuts. Unless exactly the same soil was dug during the exhumation as was dug during the original inhumation, there will be evidence of two cuts in the soil. Screening or other examination of the grave fill is also necessary, as it is likely that small bones and pieces of evidence were left behind and are mixed in the fill.

An example comes from the small village of Zaklopača, which was a Muslim village before the Balkan War that spanned much of the 1990s. According to information from the judge in charge of the case, residents of the village were killed in their homes in 1992. A witness was watching from the hills surrounding the village as the bodies were buried. The bodies were brought to the grave area on tractors. The witness said the grave was dug with a mechanical excavator and was deep enough that only the scoop of the backhoe, rising out of the ground, was seen from the witness' position. The witness said the bodies of children were placed in the grave first, those of women and young boys next, and the adult males last. There were fifty-eight people missing from the village and presumed to be in the grave (Connor 1998c).

The Bosnia and Herzegovina Federation Commission for Missing Persons conducted the exhumations for humanitarian purposes. Attempts to locate the grave began around a pile of earth about fifty meters long, two meters wide, and less than one meter high. The adjacent area was used as a lumberyard and wood planks and a saw were placed throughout the area. Northeast of this area was a slight depression, the outlines of which continued into the adjacent fields not included in the scene perimeter. Throughout the area, the vegetation was uniform, suggesting that the area had not been disturbed during the recent growing season.

The exhumations continued for three days. The first day, the exhumation team began work by documenting the area defined by the witness with film and digital still photography, as well as video photography. The team made a sketch map of the area, moved the lumber, and cut the vegetation in the de-mined area (approx. 150 sq. m). When the initial documentation was complete, the team began to trench the area with shovels. The initial trench cut across the long axis of the de-mined area, between a stone barn and the saw, to the south of the mounded soil. In this trench, they hit groundwater, but no human remains.

The second day, a pump was used to remove the groundwater that had filled the trench overnight. A small tractor with a backhoe was used to cut a series of trenches perpendicular to the initial trench. The backhoe on this tractor was capable of digging a trench only slightly deeper than one meter. Near the initial trench, a sock containing foot bones, ankle bones, and some cloth was found. Digging with the backhoe was stopped when this was located and the area was investigated using hand tools. A soil change was seen in the profile of the side of the backhoe trench, and the exhumation team concluded that this change indicated the disturbance created by a grave. By the end of the second day, it was clear that the small backhoe was not capable of digging deep enough to uncover the grave.

The third day, a much larger backhoe was brought into the site. This was used to excavate a wall in the soil near where the sock containing foot bones was found. The digging unearthed a tire rim. A portion of a child's cranium was found in the rim. Hair and clothing, unassociated with any other remains, were also collected from the back dirt. Digging with the backhoe was stopped when a shoe, an adult cranial fragment, and several hand bones were seen in the profile of the trench. These were excavated with hand tools and photographed. The bones were collected and placed in plastic bags. The deepest material was about two meters below the original ground surface. The shoe was bent back on itself and the exhumation team concluded that it was likely that the shoe had been at the margin of the disturbance and was bent when the hole was filled. The skeletal elements and evidence seen in the trench were excavated with hand tools. The adjacent area was also excavated with hand tools to determine whether additional remains were nearby. The partial remains found were isolated and no additional materials were found adjacent to them.

At this point, the exhumation team determined that it was probable that the bodies had been moved from the grave. The backhoe was used to cut trenches around the margin of the disturbance, using the soil change as an indicator of the margin. When the team felt that the margin had been reached, a wooden stake was placed in the soil. This allowed the team to measure the size of the soil disturbance. The disturbed area was roughly twenty meters in diameter.

Note that there would have been two episodes of soil disturbance in addition to the Bosnian team exhumations: (1) the actual digging of the grave, and (2) the soil disturbance reflecting the digging to remove the bodies. The second episode of soil disturbance would overlap the first, and may have obliterated the evidence of the first event. It is likely that the area measured reflects the maximum of the two events, and is larger than the limits of either event by itself.

LATRINES, CISTERNS, AND WELLS

A body to dispose of . . . an existing hole in the ground. Almost anyone can put those two together. Latrines, cisterns, and wells can easily be used for body disposal, particularly in areas where they may not be used for a while. The main logistical concerns in exhuming bodies from these locations is to (1) ensure that they are structurally safe; (2) pump out or otherwise remove any standing water and, if necessary, create a sump to remove groundwater; and (3) construct a safe method of lowering and raising workers, soil, the equipment, and the remains. If there is not enough room inside the structure to work, heavy machinery can be used to dig a trench parallel to the structure so that it can be approached from the side (see below).

The Bosnia and Herzegovina Federation Commission on Missing Persons removed numbers of bodies from wells, cisterns, latrines, and caves for humanitarian reasons. Much of this country is a karst topography, with a limestone base. Poisonous gasses are always a concern here, and people above the ground are sure to keep in verbal touch with the excavators below ground to ensure that they are coherent. The author was present during the removal of a body from a stone-lined underground cistern in the small village of Kramer Selo (Connor 1988b). The interior of the cistern was accessed by a 40 cm-square manhole, covered by a metal plate. The cistern was about three meters deep and filled with over two meters of water. The body was floating, front down, in the water. The upper portion of the torso and arms could be seen floating in the water through the manhole. The skull and hands were no longer attached.

The team brought a pump and pumped the water out of the well. They used an extension ladder to get to the bottom of the cistern. The team head and the pathologist's assistant climbed into the cistern. The team head wore a climber's light attached to his head. They took with them a heavy-duty body bag with plastic handles on the side; they collected the remains and placed it into this bag. They tied rope around the handles and with the two men on the bottom pushing the bag up, the remains were pulled to the surface. The team then opened the bag and photographed the remains.

A challenge in these sites is working in a confined area and not stepping on, or otherwise placing the excavator's weight on, the remains. If the remains are skeletal, then dirt can be left over enough of the remains for the excavator to stand or kneel on until the remainder of the skeleton is exposed. The exposed skeleton can then be documented and removed and the excavator can shift to that portion of the area (where the skeleton has been removed) while the remainder is exposed and documented.

If there is not enough room to work within the confined area, then it may be possible to use heavy equipment to excavate the area adjacent to the well and come into the burial from the side.

LANDFILLS AND DUMPS

Dumping unwanted remains in the garbage or a dumpster is another way to dispose of an unwanted body. Remains placed in the garbage often end up in either a dump or a landfill. A dump is simply a pile of garbage; frequently it is an open hole in the ground where trash is buried. Dumping is illegal on public lands in the United States now, but can still be carried out on private lands and is common in many other countries. Contents of dumpsters in the United States end up in landfills. A landfill is a structure built into or on top of the ground that is designed to isolate trash from the surrounding environment. This is accomplished with a bottom liner and a daily covering of soil. A landfill is actually designed so that the trash will decompose little. Both dumps and landfills can be very difficult scenes in which to search for a body.

The author worked on one dump in Bosnia and Herzegovina that was the main dump for the city of Prozor (Connor 1998b). The dump was on the side of a steep hill and the slope ended in a creek at the bottom (figure 8-7). The engineers that looked at the dump estimated that there was approximately twenty-two tons of material on the hill slope. This included cars, car parts, animal carcasses, bags of household trash, and some munitions. During the war, twenty-two Bosniak men had allegedly been brought to the top of the dump, shot, and pushed over the edge. The witness was a man who had escaped by jumping forward when the shooting began. He then rolled down the slope to the bottom and ran partway up the other side until he was hidden in the vegetation. People in the surrounding area said that they saw smoke coming up from the area of the dump the next day and the presumption was that an effort may have been made to burn the remains.

FIGURE 8-7

Prozor dump, Bosnia and Herzegovina. Excavations by the Bosnia and Herzegovina Federation Commission for Missing Persons. A. An overview of the Prozor dump where families were looking for the remains of twenty-two men. B. The backhoe created a level surface on which to spread the garbage out. The garbage was then searched.

The Bosnia and Herzegovina Federation Commission for Missing Persons made several visits to the site before beginning exhumations, which were to be carried out for humanitarian, and not judicial, purposes. The garbage in the dump continually smoldered and when garbage was moved, it would occasionally burst into flames. The initial investigators walked the sides of the dump area looking for human skeletal elements and walked the bottom of the dump along the creek, including the area downstream of the dump itself.

Before the excavations began, the commission had several truckloads of water poured onto the dump in an attempt to put out the fires. This had limited success and throughout the excavations there were pockets of material that were hot to the touch, although the water had reduced the smoldering enough so that there were few areas that burst into flame when the garbage was moved.

The team completed as much of an inventory of the surface of the dump as was practical. Some of the area was extremely steep, and it was difficult to walk through. A small backhoe was brought to the bottom of the dump. The operator cleared a path at the bottom to the level of soil beneath the garbage. The path that the operator cleared was level and served as an area in which the garbage could be spread out and examined. The team worked through the garbage as it was moved. An anthropologist worked with the team at all times to help the team differentiate human from nonhuman bone. Many of the skeletal elements were fragmented and burned to the point that this could not be done visually. Due to the large amount of nonhuman bone in the dump, it was assumed that fragments were nonhuman unless they had marking that showed otherwise. No definitely human skeletal elements were located, and the team left the site without finding the remains of the men.

The Plattsmouth County Police Department, led by Police Chief Brian Paulsen, used a similar method, on a much larger scale, to look through the Plattsmouth County landfill for the remains of a missing three-year-old child, Brendan Gonzalez. Gonzalez's father confessed to killing the child and said he had put the body, rolled in a blanket, in a specific dumpster. On the inside of the dumpster, police did find traces of the child's blood (Paulsen and Dunning 2005).

A landfill is much more organized than a dump, and the police worked with the landfill operators to determine the potential location of the material deposited on the target day from the address of the dumpster. The landfill was prepared by removing the overburden from the designated area. The operation included three stages: (1) a farmhouse used to brief searchers each morning; (2) the "pit" where the backhoe dug waste from the landfill; and (3) the search pad where the waste was spread and examined (Paulsen and Dunning 2005).

The searchers strongly suspected that the body would be mummified or fleshed despite the fact that the remains would have been deposited in January and the search took place in July and August. This inference was based on the slow decomposition of material in landfills. Indeed, during the search, meats, such as turkey carcasses, were found that had little or no decomposition and were interspersed with material dated from November and December (Paulsen and Dunning 2005).

A backhoe removed the trash from the dump into a dump truck. An officer monitored the backhoe at all times from a position in which he could see the garbage being removed from the pile. The boy's father had told police that he wrapped the body in a blanket to absorb the blood, and most large pieces of cloth were removed and examined by this officer before they reached the search pad (Paulsen and Dunning 2005). Access to the pit was limited due to the possibility of a trash avalanche, and the wish to minimize the number of people who could be hurt.

The dump trucks moved the garbage to the search pad where waiting backhoes spread it out (figure 8-8). The search pad was approximately 100 feet by 60 feet approximately (30 m by 18 m) and was considered large enough to spread the waste for examination (Paulsen and Dunning 2005). Volunteers, including police from a number of jurisdictions, first responders from throughout the region, and eventually local volunteers, raked through the garbage. These people were supplied with the address of the housing complex the dumpster was in and a range of nearby addresses, as well as the date the body was deposited. They were also shown items of clothing similar to those the boy was wearing when he was killed, as well as a knife similar to the one used. When they found envelopes, bills, or other materials that might include a date or date and address that corresponded to the target date and address, then the entire team was notified and the garbage searched even more closely.

A cadaver dog was also used, both where the garbage was being removed and where it was being searched. The dog was able to identify blood on clothing and in hospital waste. Unfortunately, the body of the boy was never found

FIGURE 8-8
A. Garbage from the landfill being loaded into the dump truck. B. The truck being dumped on a prepared surface. C. Searchers looking through the material for specific clothing items or items with the target date and addresses.

despite the fact that over 82 metric tons of trash were moved and searched (Paulsen and Dunning 2005). Brendan Gonzalez weighed approximately 16 kilograms.

In general, the only way to search a landfill or dump is to identify the area most likely to contain the remains and use heavy machinery to spread out the garbage so it can be searched. The process is extremely time-consuming. In working on a dump, where the remains will decompose quickly, training personnel to identify human bone is essential. In landfills, material will not decompose as quickly, but depending on the time lag between the death and the deposition of the remains in the landfill, it may be necessary to have anthropologically trained individuals on-site.

SUMMARY

A general procedure for the recovery of buried remains is as follows:

1. Delineate the outline of the ground disturbance believed to be a grave through differences between disturbed and undisturbed soil.
2. Photograph and map this disturbance.
3. Determine the depth and extent of the body mass.
   A. If this is a large grave, then there is a need for a test trench about one meter wide across the grave to determine the extent and depth of the remains. This test trench will extend to the top of the remains. A second trench, perpendicular to the first, will provide additional information on the extent and depth of remains in the opposite direction.
   B. In smaller graves, this information may be gained through slit trenches, probes, or shovel tests.
4. If this is a deep grave, excavate a trench around the outside of the disturbance with sufficient room to stand and work on the remains inside the disturbance.
   —If this is a large grave, before excavation the team will need to plan:
      (1) where to put the soil removed from the grave where it won't be in the way, but can be used to fill in the hole left by the excavation;
      (2) how to drain the grave should it rain during the excavation or the excavation hit groundwater; and
      (3) how to ensure access to the remains without anyone having to step on other remains.

—If it is a large grave that was mechanically dug, then the soil at the top of the grave may need to be removed before it is outside the reach of the backhoe. The testing done during step 3 should allow this to be done safely, but there is always the risk of hitting a body with the backhoe. Therefore, the backhoe should be carefully monitored at all times.

5. Excavate the disturbed soil using hand tools as much as possible. The disturbed soil may contain debris from the grave digging and deposition episode. Also there may be tool marks on the interface of the disturbed soil and undisturbed soil that will be important evidence.
   —If tool marks are found, then uncover the mark, document it, and dig through it. If a body overlays part of the mark, then leave the portion of the graveside with the mark intact until the body is removed so that the tool mark can be documented in its entirety.
6. As the remains are reached, clear all soil from around the remains.
   —Collect and bag hand and foot bones as they are found. Clearly label the bags and keep them in a place where they will be reassociated with the correct body when the bodies are removed.
   —Leave a pedestal of soil supporting body parts. Do not remove soil beneath the body so that limbs are left hanging unsupported in the air.
   —When finished, the remains should be clearly visible and supported on a body pedestal. If there is only one layer of remains, then the areas without remains should be excavated below the disturbed soil.
7. If possible, expose all the remains in the grave and document them before removing any remains. When all the remains are exposed:
   —Obtain good overall photographs.
   —Make a map showing the interrelationship of the remains. Even if taking survey information to make a map later, make a sketch map keyed to the survey data as a reminder when drawing the final map.
   —Ensure that overall measurements of the length, width, and depth of the grave are taken.
8. Document each body individually.
   —Obtain individual photographs of each body. Obtain close-up shots of trauma, particularly where the bones are shattered and will fall apart when the remains are lifted. This can be particularly important with skull shots. The entrance wound may be clearly visible when the skull is in

the ground, but the skull may be fragmented and fall apart when lifted. Reconstructing the skull in the lab to get the same information there as when it is lying in the ground is a tedious process.

—If any element is shattered, but lying in its entirety in the ground, then if possible, take the relevant anthropological measurements before the element is removed from the soil.

—Ensure that the body is correctly placed on the site map.

—Fill out a case form describing the remains and associated evidence and documenting the photograph numbers and numbers on the map associated with that case.

9. Begin removing the remains.

—Determine which body was placed in the grave last and remove it first.

—If partially decomposed, place bags around the hands and feet (if without shoes and socks) and tie to the long bones. Partially decomposed feet and hands tend to lose digits when moved, and this will keep the fingers and toes from falling off.

—Wrap crania and mandibles to ensure that teeth do not fall out.

—If there are shattered skeletal elements, bag or wrap the element so that all the pieces stay together.

—Finish the notes on each case with describing how many packages should arrive in the morgue associated with this case, for example, one body bag (fleshed remains) or fourteen brown paper bags (skeletal remains placed in bags).

—Search the area under the body for anything associated with that individual that was left behind.

10. When all the bodies are removed from the grave:

—Excavate the grave to undisturbed soil.

—Use a metal detector at the bottom of the excavation to ensure no bullets, cartridges, or other objects were pushed into the soil at the bottom of the grave.

—Create a profile of the bottom of the grave.

—Photograph the empty grave.

—Write a narrative justifying why the excavators feel that there are no further remains (can clearly see soil profiles; may have dug test trenches into bottom of grave and sides; probing and metal detectors show no further anomalies).

A general procedure for working with a body in a well, latrine, or cistern:

1. Drain any liquids and have a qualified person determine whether the structure is sound.
2. If there is room in the structure to work with the remains, then find a method of lowering personnel into the structure and soil and other materials out of it.
3. If there is not enough room, or the structure is not sound, then examine the possibility of using a backhoe to trench into the structure from the side.
4. Once safely in the structure, map, photograph, and document the scene.
5. Collect evidence and remove the body.
6. Clear the scene.

A general procedure for searching for a body in a landfill:

1. Determine a target area by establishing where garbage was dumped on a particular day.
2. Remove any overburden from the area and have the heavy machinery create a search pad.
3. As always when working with a backhoe, have a monitor work with the machine at all times.
4. Move the waste to the search pad, spread it out, and have people search through the material.

GLOSSARY TERMS

geotaphonomy

pedestal

SUGGESTED READING

Hester, Thomas R., Harry J. Shafer, and Kenneth L. Feder

1997 *Field Methods in Archaeology*. Seventh ed. Mayfield Publishing, Mountain View, California.

A thorough review of archaeological field methods.

Simmons, Tal

2002 Taphonomy of a Karstic Cave Execution Site at Hrgar, Bosnia-Herzegovina. In *Advances in Forensic Taphonomy: Method, Theory, and Archaeological*

Perspectives. William D. Haglund and Marcella H. Sorg, editors, pp. 263–75. CRC Press, Boca Raton, Florida.
Account of exhumations in a cave site—an area of extreme logistical challenges.

Stewert, R. Michael
2002 *Archaeology: Basic Field Methods*. Kendall/Hunt Publishing, Dubuque, Iowa.
A review of field methods written for people who know absolutely nothing about field work.

9

Evidence

The range of material culture found in a grave is greater than the range of the products found at a Wal-Mart. For the most part, neither investigators nor archaeologists will have difficulty identifying recent and common material. The difficulty comes with recognizing buried material after it has begun to decompose. Natural fibers, such as cotton, decompose relatively quickly, while synthetic materials may outlast the reader of this volume. The natural fiber in a natural-fiber shirt sewn with synthetic-fiber threads can decompose, leaving only the synthetic threads which may appear on photographs to be small roots. If there are only a small amount of these threads, an inexperienced excavator may miss them and reach a conclusion that the victim was buried without a shirt or without clothes—which information may then be incorrectly used to reconstruct the scene.

The decomposition of the body has an effect on the material buried with it. The proteins on the remains are broken down in decomposition and attract a range of bacteria. In addition, if the death was accompanied by a bacterial infection, bacteria may be widespread throughout the cadaver and hasten decay (Janaway 1987:132). As the proteins are broken down, the tissues can become increasingly liquid and an assortment of microorganisms can subsist in this strata. This stage of decomposition probably has the greatest implication for the preservation of any material with the body, particularly textiles (Janaway 1987:132).

Investigators then have a challenge identifying material affected by the decomposition of the remains. In addition, there may be a range of medical and dental appliances found in the grave. Relatively few people are familiar with the range of heart valves, pacemakers, and orthopedic devices that are implanted in people during modern surgical procedures. Yet these are important pieces of evidence as any modern implant device will have a serial number, which can be traced to the manufacturer. This can then be used as an aid to determine the identity of the person in whom it was implanted. In other words, the finding of any of these devices can lead directly to the identity of the deceased. Also, in the absence of any trauma, the presence of devices, such as a pacemaker, may provide insight to the possible reasons for the victim's death.

Ordnance may also occur in and around gravesites, particularly in post-conflict areas. Soldiers may actually be buried with live grenades and ammunition that they were carrying when they fell. The ordnance may become less stable over time, and it is worth being aware of what explosives a soldier may have been carrying on patrol or during a battle.

This chapter cannot be a comprehensive discussion of all types of material culture that could be found in a grave—that would be an exhaustive list of all the materials on this earth past and present. But the goal is to discuss some of the material culture types likely to be encountered. The types of evidence discussed here include clothing, dental and medical appliances, and ammunition components.

CLOTHING

Clothing is evidence that everyone will recognize and collect. However, not everyone can describe clothes well. Most people should use fairly generic descriptions for clothing (ladies' upper garment, for instance, rather than blouse or shirt). The exception is people who know the correct technical names for clothing and parts (e.g., the difference between a blouse and a shirt, or between a brassiere, a teddy, and a camisole). Many of these will be people who sew and make clothes. If you don't know the difference between a dart and gusset, then describe clothes generically.

Clothing color should, in most cases, not be described at the grave. Rather the color should be described after the clothes have been cleaned and dried. Soil, decomposition fluids, and moisture all change the color of the clothes, frequently making them appear darker or grayer than their original color.

Not all clothing materials decompose at the same rate. Textile fibers can be grouped into five main categories: (1) animal wool and hair, (2) silk, (3) plant stem fibers, (4) plant hair fibers (cotton), and (5) man-made fibers. As a rule, natural fibers decompose faster than man-made fibers. Even heavy cotton, such as that used in blue jeans, will decompose faster than rayon threads. Women's nylons may preserve for a relatively long time. Decomposed cotton underwear may be represented only by the man-made elastic around the waist and legs. Other cotton clothing may be represented by the synthetic thread used to sew the seams in the clothes. If the excavator is familiar with clothing construction (preferably someone who sews clothes), he or she may be able to suggest the type of garment from how the threads are arranged—which show where the seams were. On the other hand, where the material in the clothes is synthetic, and the thread is cotton, the thread may decompose first, leaving the clothing in the pieces from which it was constructed.

Textiles may preserve when next to metal that is oxidizing. When next to copper, the copper ions act as localized biocidic agents (Janaway 1987:135). Iron corrosion may form a cast around textile fibers, which later decay. The cast, however, accurately reflects the dimension and surface morphology of the original fiber (Janaway 1987:135). Even small pieces of these casts may allow the identification of the textile weave. Janaway (1987:141) feels that the early stages of the decay/preservation process are critical to determining whether an identifiable textile or cast will be formed. There must be sufficient solid corrosion to deposit a layer of corrosion over the textile before the textile decays. This may depend on microenvironmental conditions such that it will vary both within a single grave and between graves. Occasionally, textile impressions will survive on bone. At the Little Bighorn Battlefield, the impression of a burlap bag was found on bone (figure 9-1).

Shoes generally preserve well. Most are combinations of leather and plastic, both of which preserve for a long time. While leather is a natural material, it has been tanned, which is a method of preserving hide. Given a moderately dry environment, leather will last for decades in the ground. Many sneakers are a combination of cotton and leather or plastic, so that while the cotton may decay, other parts of the shoe will still be found. Some cheaper shoes are partially made of cardboard and these will decay quickly.

Many times clothing tags will survive, although they may no longer be attached to the clothes themselves. Excavators should take care behind the neck

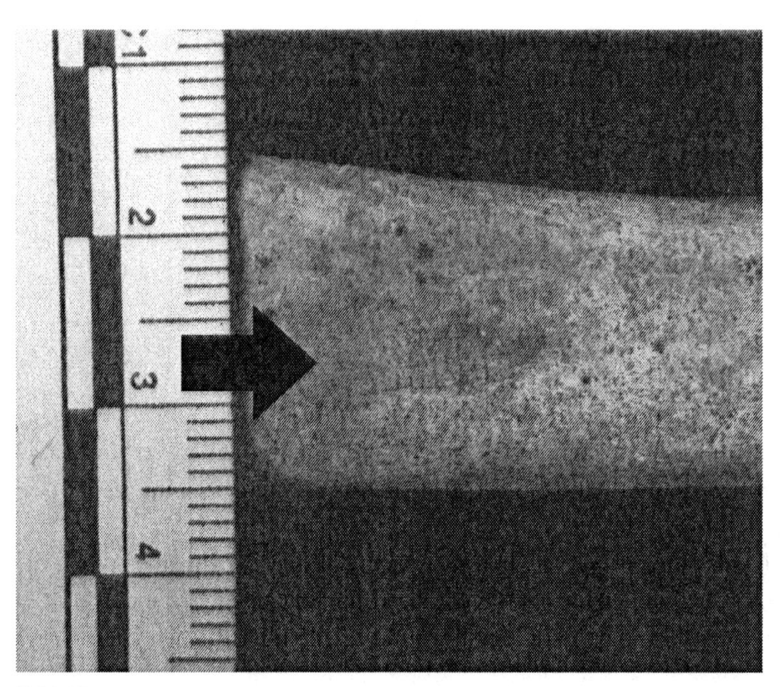

FIGURE 9-1
Cloth impressions on bone. The bone is from Little Bighorn Battlefield. It had been collected from the battlefield and interred in the Custer National Cemetery in a burlap bag at an unknown date (Scott, Willey, and Connor 1998:177). When the remains were exhumed for analysis in 1992, the burlap bag no longer existed, but the impression of the bag on the bone was clear.

of a victim, around the waistband, and around the lower torso, so that small, partially decomposed labels can be found. Many times these will contain the name of the store where the clothes were bought and the size of the piece, both potentially useful bits of information.

MEDICAL APPLIANCES

There is an enormous range of medical appliances that might be found, including both those used in the past and those used today. Some are obvious, some might easily be overlooked. All are important, as they provide information for identifying remains. Under the United States Safe Medical Devices Act, the Food and Drug Administration of the Department of Health and Human Services requires that implants be traceable. This act went into effect March 1, 1993 (Ubelaker and Jacobs 1995:168). Even prior to 1993, many manufacturers marked implants with a manufacturer's stamp and a unique serial or production number. Ubelaker and Jacobs (1995) provide information on the identifiers used by nine companies.

This section, again, is not meant as an exhaustive overview of such appliances. Hopefully, however, this brief introduction will raise the excavator's awareness of this category of evidence. Like clothing, unless the excavator is well versed in medical appliances and terminology, generic descriptive terms should be used when an item is found and recorded. This will avoid a misidentification on an evidence log as the pathologist's report will be more precise and accurate in terminology.

Dental Appliances

Most dental appliances are relatively easily recognizable. Since they're frequently attached to either the mandible or maxilla, there's relatively little danger of their not being collected with the skeleton. Fillings and restorations are not classified as dental appliances. These are where cavities in the teeth have been removed and the hole filled with an amalgam, gold, or other substance. Dental appliances should be noted in the field notes, especially if they are detachable or have the potential to become separated from the body at any point.

Dental work can, of course, be used to identify individuals. Such identification is often based on the characteristics of the teeth and dental work. Individuals who are edentulous (have no teeth) may have a full set of dentures that may be difficult to identify. A variety of labeling techniques are available (Richmond and Pretty 2006) and if marked, the denture may provide a simple method of identification.

The quality and amount of dental work can also give an indication of social-economic status or the life history of an individual. People with older, high-quality dental work, but who needed additional work when they died, may have fallen on economic hard times in recent years. Dental work done in detention facilities may also be distinctive.

Crowns

The crown of a tooth is the part of the tooth external to the gum. When the natural crown is broken or damaged, then frequently an artificial crown will be placed on the tooth. These can be obvious, such as those made with gold or gold veneer. Others can be made of porcelain that matches the teeth so well that they are difficult to detect.

Dentures

A denture is an artificial replacement for one tooth or several teeth. Thus, bridges, partial plates, and dental plates are all different types of dentures. A common classification for partial dentures is the Kennedy classification (Krol, Jacobson, and Finzen 1990:25). The main classifications are based on where the missing teeth are (the edentulous areas):

Class I—There are missing teeth on both sides of the mouth and they are located behind (posterior to) the remaining natural teeth.

Class II—The main group of missing teeth is on one side of the mouth and is behind the remaining natural teeth.

Class III—The main group of missing teeth has natural teeth both behind and in front of it.

Class IV—There is a single area of missing teeth in front of (anterior to) the remaining natural teeth.

Dentures are made of a vast range of material, including wood (usually older dentures), aluminum, other metals, or a variety of plastics (figure 9-2).

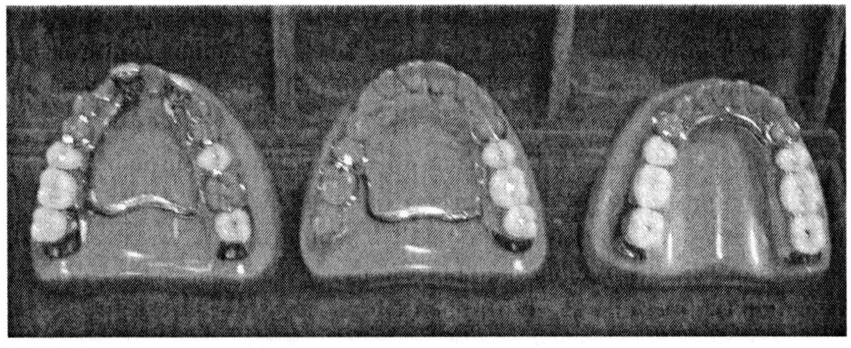

FIGURE 9-2
Dentures. The denture on the far left is Class III, where the main group of missing teeth has natural teeth both in front of and behind the remaining natural teeth. The middle denture is a Class II where the main group of missing teeth is on one side of the mouth. On the far right is a Class I denture, where there were missing teeth on both sides of the mouth behind the remaining teeth.

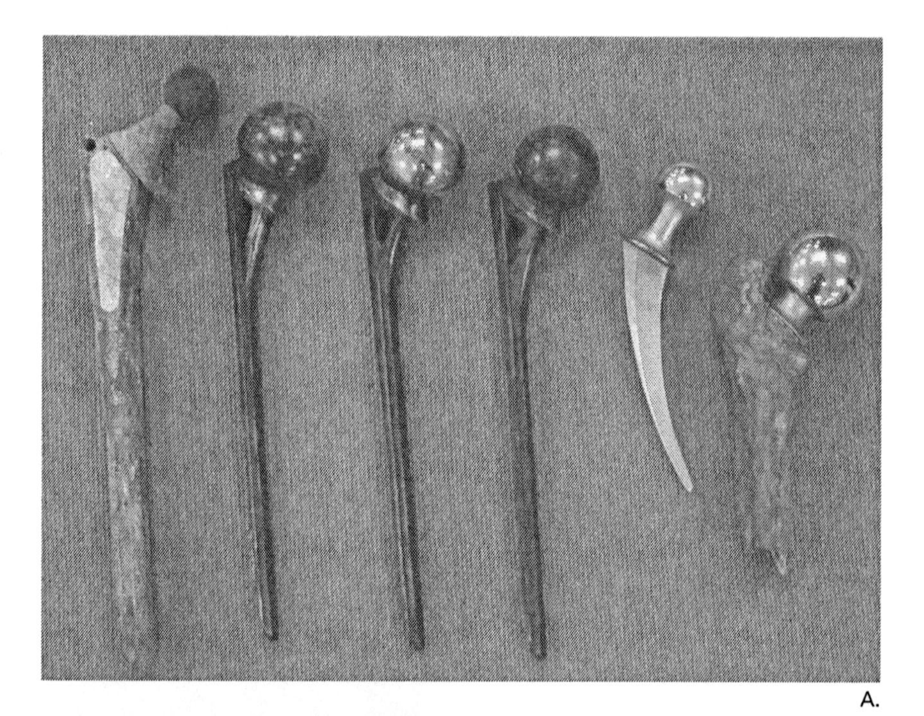

A.

B.

FIGURE 9-3
A. Ball joints used to replace the proximal portion of the femur. B. Modern hip replacements tend to have substantial plastic components. The ball would replace the proximal end of the femur and the plastic portion would replace the acetabulum.

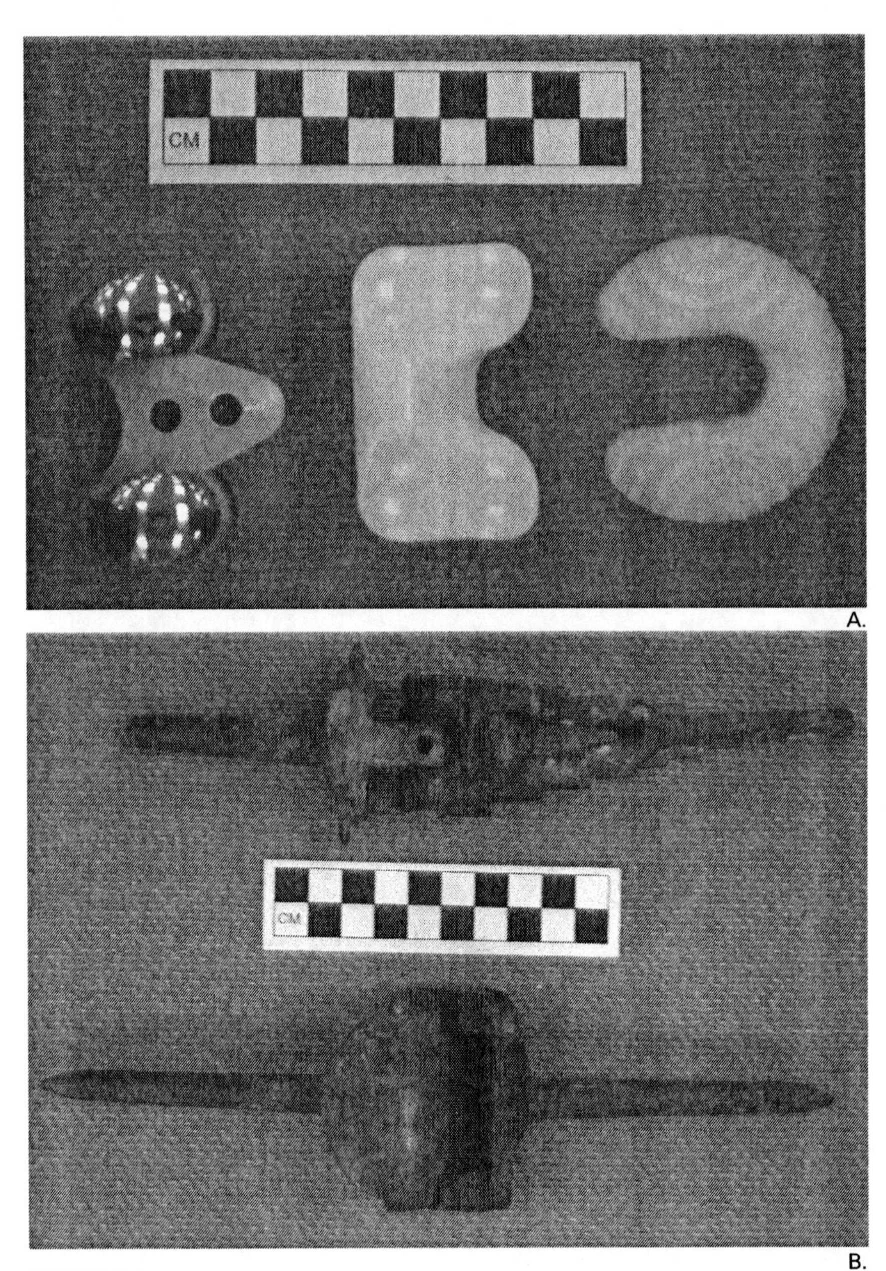

FIGURE 9-4
Components used in knee replacements. A. Modern knee replacement components. B. Older components, where one side replaces the distal end of the femur and one side replaces the proximal end of the tibia.

Orthopedic Appliances

Orthopedics is the branch of medicine that relates to skeletal deformities or problems. Most people are aware of many orthopedic devices, but since these devices are usually implanted where they don't show, relatively few people have actually seen them (see figures 9-3 and 9-4). Many actually look similar to hardware that can be bought commercially. Particularly in a surface scatter of material, screws and pins could easily be mistaken for hardware. The primary difference is that most medical pins and screws are made of special noncorrosive materials, such as titanium or plastics.

Surgical Devices

Modern surgery is frequently closed with a biodegradable surgical thread. But occasionally the use of staples or buttons is warranted (figure 9-5). Aside from staples and buttons, some nonbiodegradable sutures may be found on occasion. One form of nonbiodegradable suture is silver wire, sometimes used prior to the 1980s in combination with rubber or plastic tubing to promote drainage

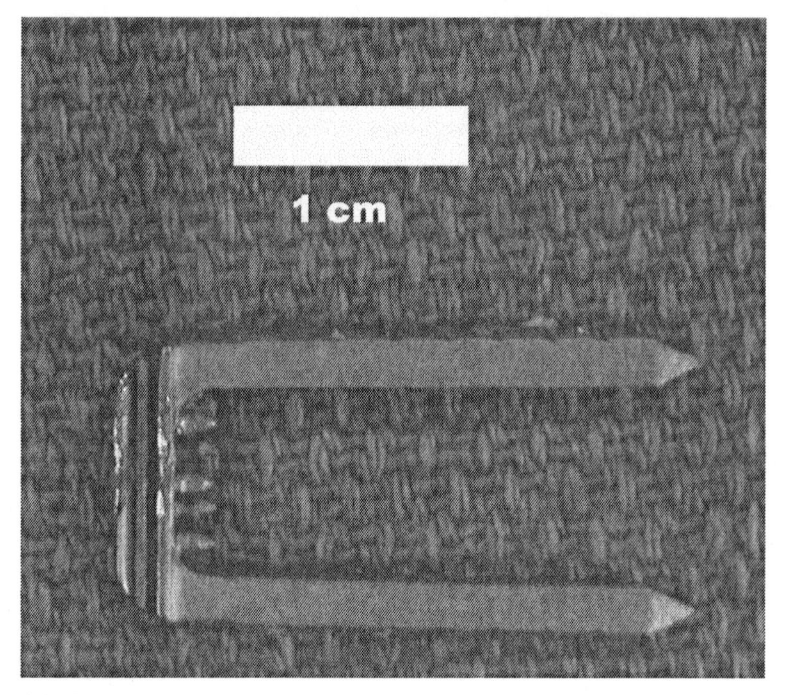

FIGURE 9-5
A surgical staple.

in wounds. Various forms of drainage tubes, catheters, and shunts, along with medical needles or syringes, can occasionally be found with remains; these are often associated with the burial of those dying of wounds in hospitals or aid stations. Most often these appliances and medical items are associated with remains that had to be buried in haste, such as after mass disasters or conflict situations.

Other medical materials associated with bodies can include nonbiodegradable bandages or surgical tape. Yet another occasionally recovered medical item is a cast. Casts are made from plaster of paris and this can survive in the ground for long periods of time. Plaster of paris has given way in the last decade or two to a variety of other materials including plastics and moldable polymers. These man-made materials will preserve in buried situations for years.

Other Appliances and Implants

A variety of appliances and implants are put into the human body today. There are too many to list them all here, but this section may help to give the reader some sensitivity to these devices.

Heart operations are becoming increasingly common, as are the implants. Heart valves (figure 9-6) appear less common than pacemakers, but can be present in a body's thorax, as are pacemakers. Pacemakers come in two major types. A single-chamber pacemaker regulates only a single heart chamber. The dual-chamber pacemaker has two leads and regulates two chambers.

Stents are small wire devices used to open blood vessels and increase the blood flow (figure 9-7). They come in a variety of shapes, sizes, and diameters, and can be cut to the necessary length.

Even contraceptive devices can be found with human remains (figure 9-8). Intrauterine devices (IUDs) are made of copper wire and plastic and seem to have a long life span.

FIREARMS AMMUNITION COMPONENTS AND EXPLOSIVE ORDNANCE

The term *ammunition components* refers to the components of firearms ammunition. This can include cartridges, bullets, and cartridge cases (figure 9-9). Once again, unless the excavator is familiar with proper terminology of ammunition and ordnance, it is best to make generic descriptions in notes and on evidence logs and allow trained firearms identification experts to make the final identification. A *cartridge* is the ammunition for the modern firearm. It consists of a bullet, primer, cartridge case, and propellant (e.g., gunpowder).

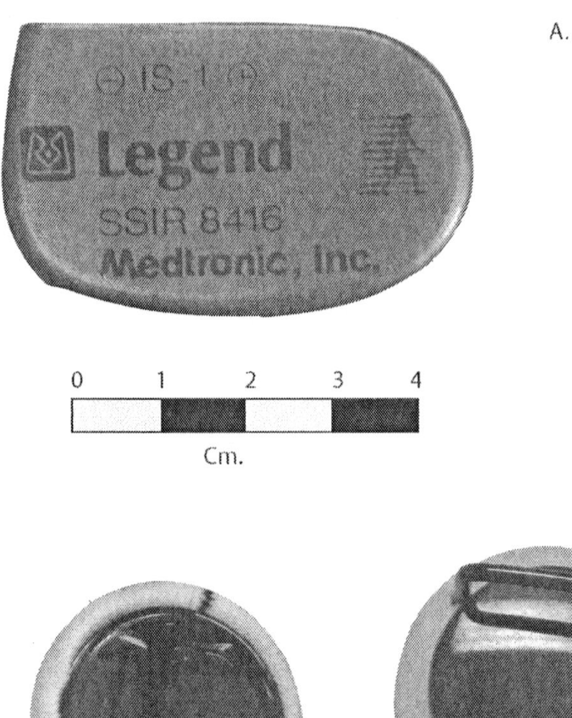

FIGURE 9-6
A. Pacemaker, Medtronic Legend. Note the serial number on the implant. B. St. Jude mechanical heart valve.

When struck, the primer produces a spark that ignites the powder. The ignition of the powder produces gas, which propels the bullet from its position seated in the cartridge case. Bullets are nonspherical projectiles in weapons. Other projectiles may be round balls (usually associated with older, black-powder weapons) or shot.

Most modern weapons are *rifled*. Rifling produces helical grooves in the bore of a firearm barrel. The rifling is what causes the bullet to spin when fired, which

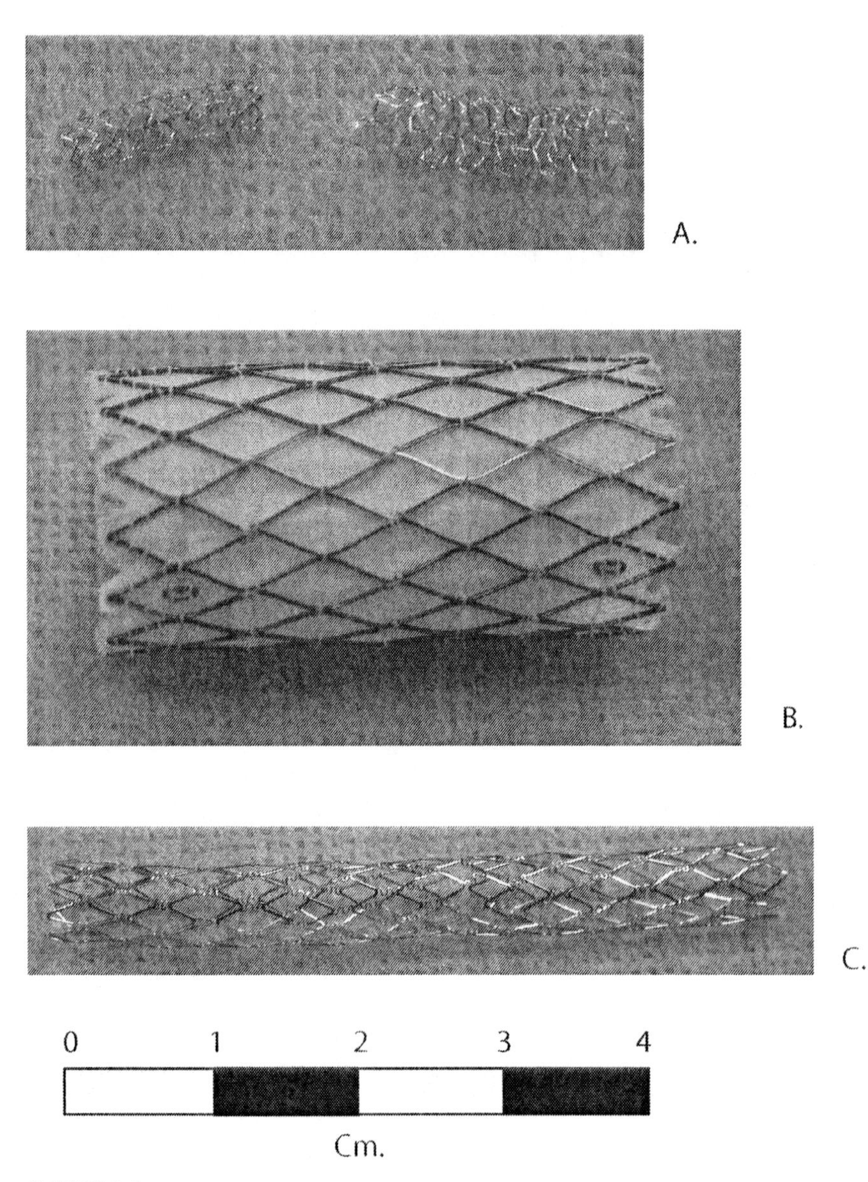

FIGURE 9-7
Stents. A. ACS stent. B. Aorta stent. C. Corinthian stent.

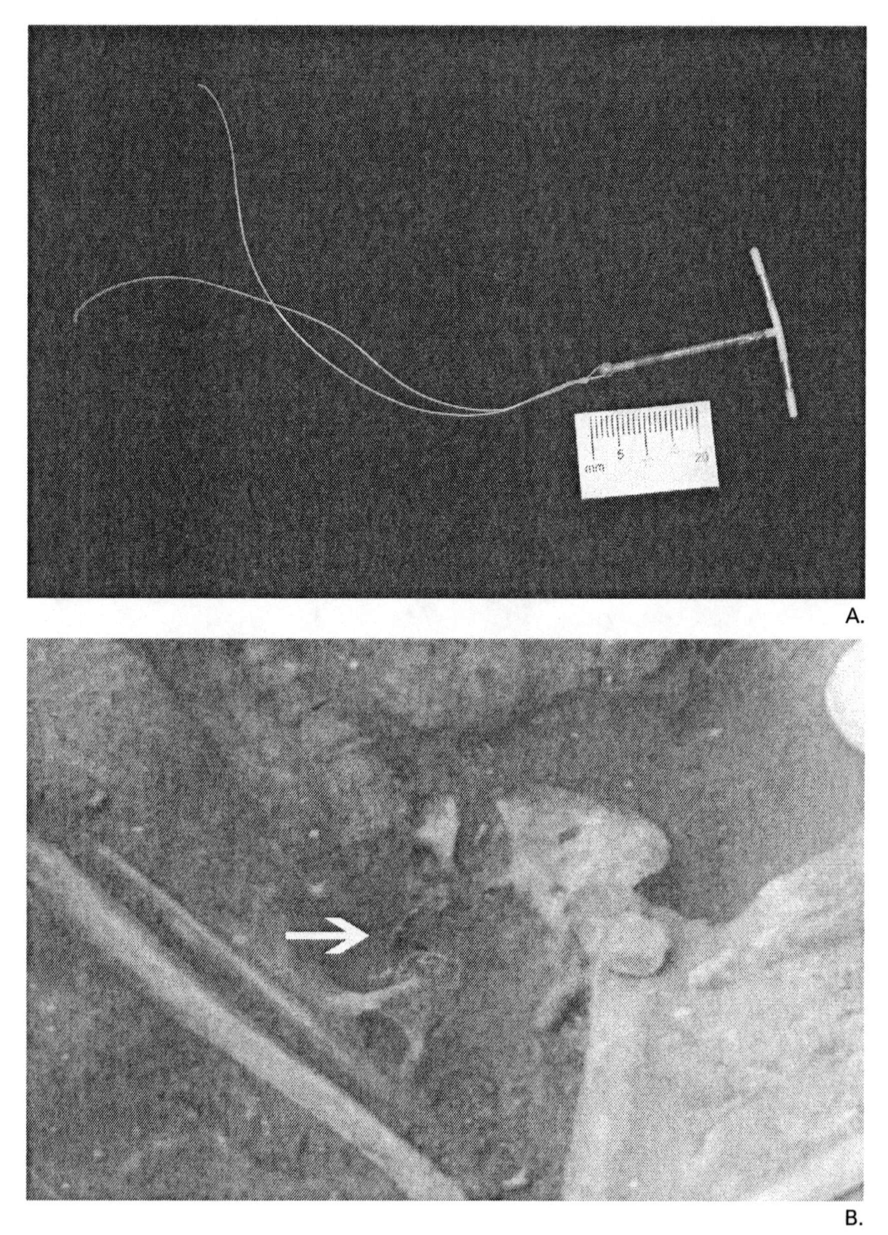

FIGURE 9-8

A. Intrauterine contraceptive device (IUD). Courtesy Planned Parenthood of Nebraska and Council Bluffs. B. Arrow points to IUD found with skeleton. Excavation conducted by Sri Lankan forensic experts.

helps to keep the bullet to a straight path. The marks of the rifling are impressed on the bullet as the bullet is propelled down the barrel of the gun (figure 9-9). The grooves in the rifle barrel leave raised areas on the bullet (called *grooves*) and the raised areas in the barrel leave grooves in the bullet called the *land*. The raised and depressed impressions on the bullet are the negative impressions of the original land and groove marks in the rifle barrel. The combination is called the land and groove imprint on the bullet. The land and groove imprints on the bullet reflect the type and manufacture of the firearm from which the bullet was

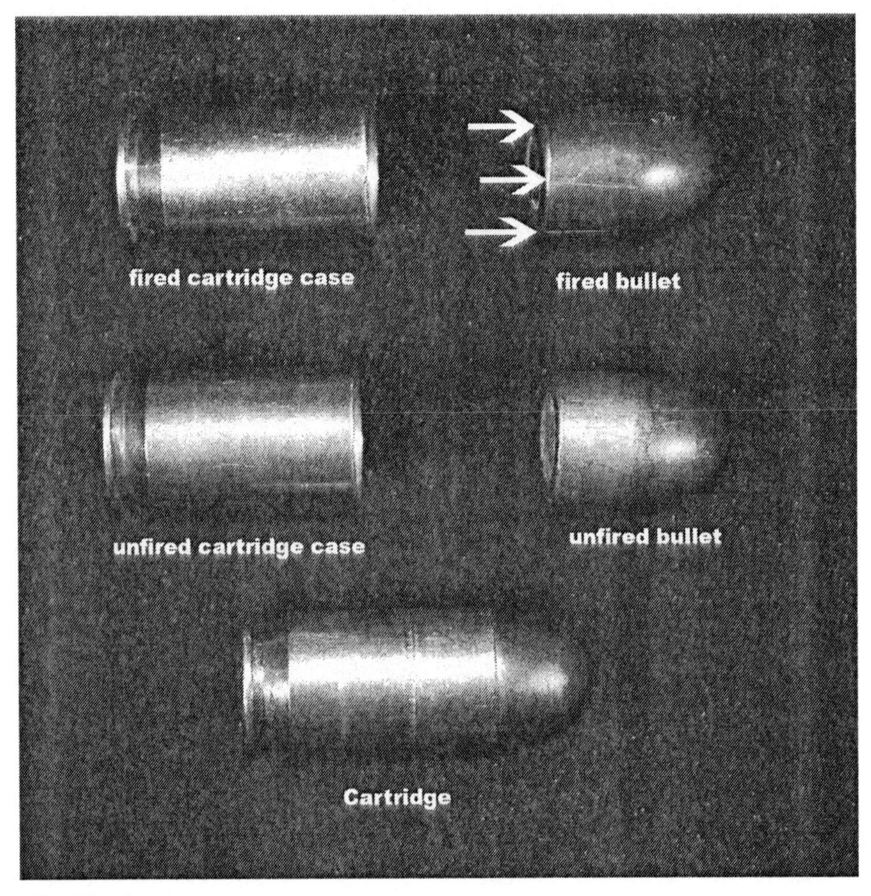

FIGURE 9-9
Basic ballistic terminology. The cartridge includes both the bullet and the cartridge case. At this angle, there is no difference between a fired and unfired cartridge case. However, on the fired bullet, the arrows point to the striations created by the land and grooves on the inside of the barrel of a rifled weapon.

fired. The land and grooves on each weapon are unique, so that bullets can be matched to the exact weapon from which they were fired.

There are two main types of modern cartridge: the rim fire and the center fire. The center-fire cartridge has a primer within the center of the base, or head, of the cartridge. A rim-fire cartridge contains a priming mixture inside the outer rim cavity of the head of the cartridge; it is struck on the rim to set off the cartridge, rather than in the center.

To ignite the propellant, modern firearms use a small metal pin, called the *firing pin,* released by the trigger. Each firing pin leaves a mark unique to that weapon on the cartridge (figure 9-10), allowing the cartridge to be matched to the weapon from which it was fired.

As the bullet leaves the firearm, the cartridge case is slammed back onto the breech face of the weapon. This contact creates an impression of the breech face on the head of the cartridge case. The extractor then pulls the case from the weapon chamber and the ejector pushes it out of the firearm. Both the ejector and the extractor may leave marks on the cartridge case, which may be identifiable to a weapon.

FIGURE 9-10
The head of a cartridge case. This type of cartridge is called a center-fire cartridge because the primer that contains the charge is located in the center. When the firing pin on the weapon strikes the primer it leaves a firing pin mark. The arrow on the cartridge case on the left points to a firing pin mark, which shows that the cartridge has been discharged. The cartridge case on the right has not been fired.

A *headstamp* on a cartridge is either a raised image or an impression on the head of the cartridge case. These stamps generally indicate the manufacturer of the cartridge, the caliber of the cartridge, the year of production, and which plant it was manufactured in. There are many headstamp guides that can help in interpretation of the stamps (Barnes 2003; White and Munhall 1963).

When a firearm is discharged, smoke or residue from the ignition of the propellant comes out of the muzzle. This firearms discharge residue can adhere to both clothing and skin in the vicinity of a weapon being fired (Heard 1997). There is not much data on how long this residue might last in the grave with decomposition fluids, but it is well worth being careful of the clothing of individuals with suspected gunshot wounds until the clothing can be tested for gunshot residue.

Small arms cartridges, even when found intact in a grave or on the surface nearby, are not dangerous. Unfired small arms cartridges, less than .50 caliber or 17.5 mm, can only be exploded when placed in a firearm or subjected to high heat, such as a fire. If a cartridge is subjected to fire and explodes, there is little or no danger to anyone more than three feet or one meter away from the object, and then the danger is limited to bits of the cartridge case being blown outward. These are likely to cause only small cuts or bruises. The projectile will only travel a few inches or centimeters and at such low velocity it is not even likely to bruise a person. Regardless, live or unfired ammunition should be handled with care and properly stored when gathered as evidence in a case.

Larger or heavier calibers of ammunition, such as heavy machine gun rounds, grenades, rocket propelled grenades (RPG), artillery shells or projectiles, mortar bombs, land mines, aerial bombs, missiles, and other such heavy ordnance may be encountered in a grave or in association with conflict burials. If heavy ordnance is known or expected to be encountered in a recovery situation, it is important to have properly trained personnel available to identify, excavate, and remove these potentially dangerous and deadly pieces of ordnance. In some cases, land mines, aerial bombs, and other antipersonnel devices may have time-delayed fuses, or they may have deteriorated to the point that they are unstable. In these cases only properly trained ordnance disposal personnel should deal with the explosive device. They may be able to defuse the item, but more than likely they will destroy it by blowing it up in place. Obviously this could be disruptive to a scene or site, but a well-trained explosive ordnance specialist can minimize the damage to the site or feature—although in some cases discretion is the better part of valor in conflict situations.

In recent conflict situations, buried bodies may be booby-trapped as an unwelcome gift to those charged with recovery. Proper safety training and careful excavation are required in these situations, along with calling in trained explosive ordnance specialists when high explosive munitions are encountered. Under no circumstances should an excavator attempt to move or remove a potential high explosive device without proper training or authorization from trained explosive professionals. To date, killers in most homicide situations outside of conflict areas have not gotten sophisticated enough to booby-trap graves, but one must always be aware of the possibility.

SUMMARY

Clothing, dental restorations, dentures, medical materials, and medical appliances, as well as cartridge cases, bullets, cartridges, and explosive ordnance devices are just a few of the many pieces of evidence that can be found in association with or during the excavation of a grave. All evidence can be important and needs to be collected and properly preserved to be of value. This chapter focuses on some of the less well-known or harder to recognize pieces of evidence that can be found with a body. In addition, the chapter describes firearms-related evidence that is often encountered at scenes and in graves. Small arms cartridges, cartridge cases, and projectiles are easily identified and can be handled quite safely. On the other hand, handling and disposing of heavy caliber machine gun rounds or components, artillery shells, aerial bombs, land mines, and other forms of high explosives should be left to trained professional explosive ordnance experts. These items can be entirely benign or extremely dangerous, and only those properly trained can tell the difference.

GLOSSARY TERMS

bullet
cartridge
cartridge case
firearms discharge residue
groove
land

SUGGESTED READING

U.S. Department of Justice

2003 *Quick Reference Guide for IBIS Users.* Bureau of Alcohol, Tobacco, Firearms, and Explosives, U.S. Department of Justice, Ammendale, Maryland.
A short, well-written reference on ammunition components.

10

Documentation

FIELD RECORDS

Written and photographic documentation is necessary for all professional exhumations. While many people prefer to document exhumations through notes, standardized forms ensure that the necessary information will be gathered from each case and each feature investigated. In a large project, standardized forms ensure that everyone is collecting the same information in a consistent manner. The forms can also be used to provide a checklist of necessary data so that those who do not deal with buried-bodies scenarios on a regular basis record a useful data set.

All records of the excavation need to be maintained in a secure location in their original condition. The original field notes, once finalized, should be provided to the primary investigating agency, which should provide a receipt for the notes. They can then be entered into evidence in a timely manner and stored in approved law enforcement evidence storage facilities. In this way there can be no argument that the notes were later altered.

While it is not possible to identify all types of field and project records that may be needed, the following are primary documentation for most projects. For large projects or offices, standardized forms can be part of the customary protocol and used as a matter of course. All participants need to be reminded that all documents are subject to subpoena and should be written as if they had to be submitted to court.

Grave Assessment Form

The grave assessment form is completed in the field in the course of an initial examination of a potential grave (figure 10-1). This should include the information necessary for someone else to locate the grave area, an assessment of whether it actually is a grave site, and information on the steps and equipment necessary for excavation (shovels, backhoe, permission from the utility companies, etc.). The location should be exact, having been determined using

Nebraska Wesleyan University
Forensic Science Program
Grave Assessment Form

Area: *Happy Acres Subdivision*

Feature No.: *1-4*

Date: *July 19, 1999*

Recorded By: *Kimberly Bayer*

Location (UTM or Latitude/ Longitude): *34T 07300411E 4791515N*

Description of area: *The area where the team concentrated the examination is in the north portion of the Happy Acres subdivision. The Buna River bounds the area to the south and east, Route E73 to the west, and Highway 72 to the north. The locale contains a dirt road and a house. The witness indicated an area to the east of the house (see accompanying sketch map).*

Witnesses: *Karin Black Juntask*

Who is allegedly in the grave: *Herman Juntask*

Witness information: *Mrs. Juntask says that during the night of July 17 1999, she woke to find her husband and her adult son in a fight on the porch outside the house. Afraid for her son's safety, she grabbed the frying pan on stove (inside the house by the sliding door) and slammed her husband's head with it. Repeatedly. She and her son placed a garbage bag over the dead man's head, placed their soiled clothes in another garbage bag, and her son buried the body somewhere near the river behind the house.*

Remarks and Evaluation: *There are several disturbed areas (see sketch map) that have no obvious function. Recommend returning with probe and, if possible, cadaver dog.*

FIGURE 10-1
Sample grave assessment form.

UTMs, latitude/longitude, or township/range and taken from either a topographic map or a GPS unit.

The assessment also includes a narrative description of what the area looks like, and, if necessary, a description of how to access the area. The form includes information on why the investigator thinks a grave is in the area. Often, this is information from a witness. Finally, the investigator needs to evaluate the grave and suggest the next step in the investigation. This may include information on whether a backhoe would be useful or logistically feasible.

Supervisor's Journal

This document is kept in many forms, usually in a notebook. Many types of surveyor's books have waterproof pages and graph paper on one side for sketches. Handheld microcassettes can also be useful. In whatever form, the supervisor's journal represents a daily log and record of field and administrative activities related to the project. If a notebook is used, then a separate notebook should be used for each project. Notes are subject to discovery, and should the notebook be subpoenaed then only the notes for that project, and not others, would be included in the notebook. In archaeological projects, archaeologists are encouraged to record their impressions and thought processes. This is not true for forensic work. Any impressions, thoughts, or comments that should not be read in court should not be included in the notes. Likewise, any impressions that may be contradicted by lab technicians after they have cleaned material or by physical anthropologists or pathologists in the laboratory should not be included. Thus, an archaeologist sees a "circular defect" in a skull; the pathologist interprets this as a gunshot wound. At no point does the archaeologist see a gunshot wound, in case the pathologist later ascribes the defect to another cause.

The journal may include observations on daily tasks undertaken and who was assigned them and what was completed. On a large project, it may also include the case numbers and evidence numbers of the material excavated that day (figure 10-2).

Survey and Mapping

In electronic mapping, the records are frequently kept in an electronic data collector that should be downloaded in a computer daily (see chapter 4). The raw data should be printed out and kept as a paper record of the day's activities. The top of the printout should include the site and the day's date. There should

Nebraska Wesleyan University
Forensic Science Program
Supervisor's Journal

Project: *Obara* Page: *4 of 7*
Date: *July 22, 1996* Name: *I. M. Kologist*

General:

Crew left HQ at 7:30 a.m. and traveled via convoy to Obara Site. Today the crew consists of SD, DDS, RH, and JC. RH will continue to act as photographer, SD, and DDS continued to clean and excavate bodies from the graves exposed so far. JC used the probe in surrounding areas to look for additional remains. I continued working on the site sketch map and kept up the evidence log as SD and DDS uncovered material.

Rain today in p.m. No tarp up over graves, so worked until it became heavy and stopped so that we wouldn't damage small bones that were difficult to see in the overcast skies.

Feature 4:
Included three cases, Case 6, Case 7, and Case 8. All skeletal. SD and DDS excavated these and did the case forms and the feature form. All three were lifted today and will be sent to the morgue tonight with their documentation. SD and DDs used metal detector at the bottom of the grave after the cases were lifted (no hits), then shoveled until sterile soil was reached.

Feature 5:
SD and DDS began skim shoveling at the top of this feature when they finished Feature 4. By end of day, they have reached about two feet below surface, and no remains.

Feature 6:
Located today with probe by JC. Clear decomp smell coming from probe

FIGURE 10-2
Example of a supervisor's journal.

be enough annotation on the notes that someone aside from the surveyor can easily understand what the notes mean. Computerized data are subject to discovery and should be preserved as evidence. Raw data files should be downloaded and the first copy to disk maintained as original evidence.

Survey data collected by hand should be recorded in either a series of data sheets or a survey notebook. The survey notes should include columns for point number, point description, distance, vertical angle, and horizontal angle. In addition, at the beginning of each set-up there should be a description of the mapping station, the distance of the instrument above the ground, and then back shots to two known points.

Sketch maps of the area surveyed are good ancillary documents for either type of notes. A series of sketch maps will allow someone other than the surveyor to understand the notes far more quickly than working through the survey data.

If using colored pens or pencils to draw diagrams, remember that the notes will be duplicated for other agencies, prosecutors, defense attorneys, and other experts. In all likelihood, those copies will be generated on a black-and-white copy machine, and the meaning of the colors lost. Better to use crosshatching or dashed and dotted lines to portray differences.

Photographic Records

Crime scene photography is a specialty in itself and this short paragraph on documentation in no way replaces more substantial discussions of this specialized field (see Osterburg and Ward 2004, appendix 2). However, the photographic record is part of the necessary suite of documentation at the buried-body scene. The rule of thumb is to be generous in making a photographic record as the chance for the same photographs will never happen twice. A photograph log is designed to document field photography (figure 10-3). Photographers should record the date, direction, location, site, as well as a general description of each exposure. If using film, each roll of film should have written on it the roll number in permanent marker, and this should correspond to the roll number in the logbook.

If using a digital camera, then the roll number should correspond to the number on the memory card. The numbering for the camera should be set back to one for each site. If possible, the memory cards should be downloaded after every field session and a CD burned as a backup, before the files on the memory cards are erased. If a CD writer is not available in the field, then the cards should still be downloaded, but not erased, so that the files on the computer function as a backup.

Feature Form

All graves are features, though not all features are graves (see chapter 2). Thus, when investigating a feature that is an alleged grave, it is safer to consider it a feature until proven a grave.

Nebraska Wesleyan University
Forensic Science Program
Photographic Record

Location: Happy Acres   Page 1 of 1

Roll Number: 2   Film Type: Fujichrome 200

Neg. No.	Date Taken	Photographer	Description (include direction photo taken from)
1-3	7/19/99	Bayer	Overview of alleged grave area take from east to west
3-6	7/19/99	Bayer	Overview of alleged grave area take from north to south
7-9	7/19/99	Bayer	Overview of alleged grave area take from west to east
10-12	7/19/99	Bayer	Overview of alleged grave area take from south to north
13-15	7/19/99	Bayer	Feature 1. From w to e. Disturbed area that could be potential grave.
16-18	7/19/99	Bayer	Feature 1. From n to so. Disturbed area that could be potential grave.
19-21	7/19/99	Bayer	Feature 2. From w to e. Disturbed area that could be potential grave.
22-24	7/19/99	Bayer	Feature 2. From n to so. Disturbed area that could be potential grave.
25-27	7/19/99	Bayer	Feature 3. From w to e. Disturbed area that could be potential grave.
28-30	7/19/99	Bayer	Feature 3. From n to so. Disturbed area that could be potential grave.
31-33	7/19/99	Bayer	Feature 4. From w to e. Disturbed area that could be potential grave.
34-36	7/19/99		Feature 4. From n to so. Disturbed area that could be potential grave.

FIGURE 10-3
Sample photographic record log sheet.

The feature form is a summary record of the detailed observations of the features recorded or tested in the field. If the feature is not a grave, the form can be used to document the testing that determined that there were no human remains present. If the feature is a grave, the form can be used to

Nebraska Wesleyan University
Forensic Science Program
Excavation –Feature Summary Sheet

Feature No.: 4 Location: *Happy Acres*

Date Summarized 8/16/01 Recorder: *I.M. Kologist*

Dates Feature was Excavated: 8/15 -16/01

Size of Excavation: *2 m north to south and 1.5 m east to west*

Size of Feature: *1.8 m north to south and 0.82 m east to west*

Feature Background/ Witness Information: *Witness was victims' wife, participated in the killing, but son buried father somewhere outside. This was the fourth feature in this area we investigated to see if it was a grave.*

Location Method (Check all that apply) ☐ Witness Testimony ☐ Probe ☐ Backhoe

Notes: *Probe had definite decomp smell when used.*

Recovery Method: ☐ Backhoe ☐ Shovel ☐ Trowel or hand tools

Screening: ☐ None ☐ Small Screen used for hands and feet ☐ All soil around remains

Other notes on recovery methods: __________

Evidence Numbers Associated with Feature: *None*

Case Numbers Associated with Feature: *None*

Roll Numbers of Photographs: E6

How was the feature originally excavated and what is the evidence for that:

The feature was excavated by shovel as the grave for a medium-sized dog. The dog skeleton and LOTS of hair were found in the feature.

FIGURE 10-4
Feature form.

document which case and evidence numbers were associated with the grave (figure 10-4).

Case Excavation Sheet

Each case that is excavated should also have a synopsis written on a case excavation sheet. This should summarize the basic data relevant to that case, including photograph numbers, the survey shots, and any evidence associated with the human remains. Descriptions of clothing should be extremely basic, as colors and even descriptions can change in the morgue when such material is cleaned and examined under morgue conditions (figure 10-5).

Nebraska Wesleyan University - Forensic Science Program
Excavation -- Case Record

Case No.: ____1____________ Location: __Happy Acres Feature 3__

Date: ___8/16/01___________ Recorder: __I.M. Kologist___________

Size of Excavation: ___2m north to south and 1.5 m east to west___

Other Cases in Same Excavation Unit: _None____________________

Other Cases in Same Grave: __None___________________________

Recovery Method: ☐Shovel ☒ Trowel or hand tools ☐ Remains were pedestaled
Screening: ☐ None ☐Small Screen used for hands and feet ☐ All soil around remains
Other notes on recovery methods: ____________________________

Objects recovered with Case in Excavation (not given separate evidence numbers):
☐ None ☐ Bullets ______ ☐ Cartridge Case _______

☐ Clothing __Not only was there clothing on the victim, but there was a garbage bag full of clothing that witnesses said belong to the killer and the person who buried him.

☐ Jewelry ____________________________________

☐ Personal Items __Cigarette lighter____________________

☐ Other____________________________________

Field Photos:
Date_8/15___ Roll _4___ Neg. _3-20__ Date_8/16____ Roll __6__ Neg. 15-22

Date_8/15___ Roll 5__ Neg. __1-15__Date________ Roll _____ Neg. _______

Method of packaging:
☒ All remains and objects placed in single body bag
☐ Remains placed in ______ (number) paper bags and objects in _____ additional bags
☐ Other. Describe:____________________________

Site Map:
☐ Case placed on site map by surveyor. Date _8/16_ Shot numbers _42-65_______
Include sketch map of individual case with form.

FIGURE 10-5
Sample case excavation form.

Chain of Custody Form

The moment any material is excavated it becomes evidence and it is important to maintain the chain of custody. In other words, the investigators must know where the material was at any time so that if there is any question about the material being altered, that question can be addressed. In many courts, any disruption in the chain of custody can cause the evidence to be inadmissible. Any material that leaves the custody of the excavation team for any reason, for example, so an investigator can have a relative examine the material, should be noted on a chain of custody form. If DNA samples are sent to a lab, then the lab needs to sign for their receipt on a chain of custody form, and when they are given back to the morgue, the morgue needs to sign to show the material is back in its custody (figure 10-6).

All law enforcement agencies use customized chain of custody forms, of which the original is maintained in the case file and copies provided to any other individuals involved.

THE FINAL REPORT

The grave exhumation reports will be part of a larger investigation report (Groome 2001). Coordinating with the other authors of the investigation report is necessary so that information is not repetitive or contradictory. Even if the exhumation report is meant to stand alone, it is essential to coordinate with others working on the case so that no conflicting statements are made.

Clear, precise language is key in the report (Groome 2001:269). This is also a formal report and it should be written as such. Sentences should be simple whenever possible, consisting of subject, verb, and predicate, and written in active tense. This is particularly important when working on international projects where English will not be the first language of all participants.

The report should contain the following sections:

1. Abstract or executive summary—A summary, no longer than a page, of what was investigated and the results.
2. Project background—Explaining the political or investigative context, and how the exhumations fit into that.
3. Participants—A list of excavators, anthropologists, pathologists, and observers who participated and their institutional affiliations. If some were

Nebraska Wesleyan University
Forensic Science Program
Evidence Transfer Sheet
Chain of Custody Record

Object: ____

____

____

Transferred From:	**Transfer To:**
Signature: ____________	Signature: ____________
Name ____________	Name ____________
Title: ____________	Title: ____________
Institution: ____________	Institution: ____________
Date: ____________	Date: ____________
Transferred From:	**Transfer To:**
Signature: ____________	Signature: ____________
Name ____________	Name ____________
Title: ____________	Title: ____________
Institution: ____________	Institution: ____________
Date: ____________	Date: ____________

FIGURE 10-6
Sample chain of custody form.

responsible for writing sections of the report, then the authorship of each section should be clear (as it should be on the title page).

4. Methods—An outline of how the exhumations were completed, what protocols were followed, and explanation for any deviations from the protocols.
5. Physical evidence—This section should describe each grave located and the evidence associated with each grave. It should describe each case located

within each grave, and every piece of physical evidence found for each case. In a full investigative report there should also be sections on documentary evidence and testimonial evidence. However, if the report describes grave exhumations, it is likely that it will focus on the physical evidence recovered.

6. Conclusions—This section should contain a reconstruction of the events at the grave site based on the physical evidence obtained. The reconstruction of events should be based solely on the physical evidence and should not exceed the expertise of respective contributors. In a historical archaeological site, the final reconstruction usually incorporates any oral history or documentary accounts that exist. This is not true in a forensic case. The physical evidence needs to stand alone to verify or discredit witness or documentary evidence. Incorporating witness testimony or information from documents into the reconstruction means that the physical evidence cannot be used as independent verification of the veracity of other types of evidence.

SUMMARY

1. Written and photographic documentation is necessary for all professional exhumations. Standardized forms ensure that the necessary information will be gathered from each case and each feature investigated.
2. All documents are subject to subpoena and should be written as if they had to be submitted to court.
3. A project is not complete until the final report is submitted and accepted.

11

The Professional Forensic Archaeologist

THE ROLE OF THE FORENSIC ARCHAEOLOGIST

Defining the Forensic Archaeologist

Training for many forensic archaeologists has been of the on-the-job variety. In the United States, most anthropology departments that teach forensics do so as part of physical anthropology. In the United Kingdom, there are now several programs that give degrees in forensic archaeology. However, since forensic casework is sporadic, most archaeologists who practice forensic work also work on historic or prehistoric sites and have jobs that involve education or cultural resource management. Investigators with an archaeological background spend most of their careers doing other work and being periodically called to buried-body sites.

There are few professionals who make a living doing forensic archaeology. The Register of Professional Archaeologists (RPA) considers a professional archaeologist an individual with an advanced degree (MA, MS, PhD, or DSc) in archaeology, anthropology, or other appropriate discipline, with a specialization in archaeology, from an accredited institution. The individual must have designed and executed an archaeological study, and reported on an archaeological study in a scope equivalent to a master's thesis or PhD dissertation. The individual must have a minimum of one year (fifty-two weeks) of field and laboratory experience, gained in blocks of at least four-weeks duration. This includes a minimum of eight weeks each of excavation, survey, laboratory, and research experience supervised by an RPA or RPA-equivalent archaeologist. Only with this level of experience can an individual begin to approach the depth and breadth of experience necessary for forensic work.

In addition to the RPA credentials, to engage in forensic work the archaeologist should have a demonstrated knowledge of human osteology and osteological techniques, as well as a knowledge of the type of material culture likely to be encountered. At some point, the archaeologist should have learned the protocols of criminalistics, either through courses in forensic archaeology or anthropology or by working with a law enforcement agency. Archaeologists who work in forensics without appropriate training open themselves to personal liability and charges of professional negligence (Crist 2001:47). Trial experience, or at least deposition experience, is critical. Mistakes made by untrained archaeologists make it harder for the law enforcement community to continue to include archaeologists in their investigations.

The British Council for the Registration of Forensic Practitioners has implemented criteria for the registration of forensic archaeologists. Two referees comment on the nominee's professional qualifications and the background information provided by the nominee, including his or her training, membership in relevant professional bodies, teaching/lecturing, relevant research publications, professional archaeological experience, and "fitness to practice." The "fitness to practice" section consists of the applicant's certification that he or she has read the Code of Conduct for Forensic Practitioners, is physically and mentally healthy, has never been disqualified as a forensic practitioner, has never been convicted of a serious crime, nor has legal actions pending against him or her.

As a minimum, the applicant needs to list three cases on which he or she has worked. From this case log, the assessors choose cases on which they would like to see more information and the applicant is asked to summarize his or her involvement in the case. The applicant is also asked to show:

1. Ability to understand archaeological problems; ability to excavate, record, plan, and draw sections rapidly
2. Familiarity with electronic and conventional methods of survey and aerial photography, and an understanding of advantages and limitations of relevant geophysical techniques

3. Basic knowledge of human skeletal components and their anthropological significance and familiarity with skeletal terminology
4. Broad knowledge of police structure, criminal investigation, and scene of crime infrastructure
5. Broad knowledge of appropriate legal frameworks, including court systems, disclosure, and chain of evidence or chain of custody
6. Ability to give advice confidently, to acknowledge the boundaries of one's expertise, to recommend others as appropriate, and to work independently but within a team
7. Ability to provide reports orally and in writing to colleagues, to communicate succinctly without excessive terminology, and to give evidence lucidly in court
8. Understanding of the evidential requirements of other scene-of-crime personnel, such as a forensic scientist or entomologist
9. Ability to keep up to date with developments in the field and to take active steps to maintain competence

As of this writing, the RPA is the closest American certification equivalent. Many law enforcement personnel looking for someone with archaeological expertise go to their local universities, as the institutions will often provide the archaeologist free of charge as part of their community service programs. This, unfortunately, results in many archaeologists who have no forensic background and no understanding of crime scene protocol being involved in cases.

What the British qualifications make clear is that forensic archaeology is a graduate or postgraduate specialty. Also, a forensic archaeologist must be part of the greater archaeological community in order to keep in touch with methodological and technical innovations in the field. Historic archaeologists are much more likely to have the necessary background in modern material culture than prehistoric archaeologists.

Forensic work requires a moral and ethical commitment. "One cannot 'dabble' in forensic science or treat it as a hobby" (Crist 2001:45). A forensic archaeologist may not be able to talk about his or her cases, much less publish on them. The forensic archaeologist must be willing to work to understand the needs of law enforcement, must take seriously the need to stay current in the discipline, and must take the reporting of responsibilities seriously. There can be no forensic cases that are not written up for years after the field work, as happens with traditional archaeological excavations. The archaeologist must take seriously that this work is, literally, a matter of life and death.

The Archaeologist in Death Scene Investigations

There are five phases in death scene investigation: discovery, recovery, laboratory analysis, law enforcement processing, and sometimes adjudication (Crist 2001:45). The archaeologist plays the biggest role in discovery and recovery. In this, the archaeologist must work under the chief investigator and within the protocols of the jurisdiction with which he or she is working.

Particularly important to follow are the rules of evidence and the protocols involving the chain of evidence or chain of custody. Archaeologists are not used to having to account for artifacts in as detailed a manner as law enforcement accounts for evidence. Not doing so, however, can cause the evidence to be tossed out of court. Material cannot be taken to an unsecured laboratory for analysis. If the archaeologist is to look at remains or associated material, it is best to leave the material in the police laboratory and conduct the analysis there, rather than take it to the archaeological lab. Few archaeological labs have the security required to secure the chain of custody and assure the court that the evidence has not been tampered with.

Differences in documentation between archaeological and forensic notes need to be taken seriously as well. Field notes, and certainly the reports, will be given to the opposing side during discovery. Any speculation in the documents beyond the expertise of the archaeologist will be used to discredit the archaeologist and the side for which he or she is testifying. This can include graveside notes referring to the gender and age of the skeleton. The archaeologist needs to be careful to be generic enough that he or she will not contradict the results of the osteological analysis. If the archaeologists and the police technicians are both producing maps of the area, they need to coordinate to ensure the maps are consistent, as any inconsistencies are likely to be exploited by the opposing attorney.

This conservatism needs to be extended to conversations on the scene (Crist 2001:46). If the archaeologist does not have the training in osteology to be completing the analysis that will be submitted to court, he or she should not be making statements about the skeleton. The archaeologist will probably be asked to make estimates of the skeleton's age, sex, and identifying characteristics, so that the law enforcement personnel can use the information for identification. However, these statements may well be recorded into the notes of the scene made by the investigators and be available to the attorneys. Discrepancies between these graveside autopsies and the official analyses may need to be explained in court, which will leave the archaeologist looking less than expert.

The court experience itself is something that many archaeologists have not experienced. It is the job of the opposing prosecutor to find the flaws in the expert's testimony. If the opposing attorney can also unnerve the expert, the expert may appear as if he or she is not sure of the findings. This is the attorney's job and most attorneys are very good at it. Many forensic institutions hold seminars in expert witness testimony and expose the student to testifying in a mock court. This type of seminar is an excellent experience for anyone who may need to testify, but has not yet done so.

THE FUTURE OF FORENSIC ARCHAEOLOGY

The history of forensic archaeology, as outlined in the first chapter, has been tied to forensic anthropology. But forensic anthropology is changing in some dramatic ways. The use of DNA testing for the identification of skeletal remains means that the osteological study, while still necessary, often takes a secondary role. Meanwhile, species identification using DNA and protein immunoassay techniques on small bone samples is also making the osteological knowledge of whether a bone is human or nonhuman less critical. These have been two major roles of physical anthropological knowledge in forensics. The role of physical anthropology in the examination of skeletal remains and determination of cause of death will continue, but the actual cause of death is always the legal purview of the pathologist.

Physical anthropologists, though, brought with them to forensics the archaeological techniques of body recovery and the location of sites. The skills archaeologists bring to a buried-body case continually seem to be useful. In their role in a buried-body case, archaeologists are paralleling, to some degree, the role of the investigator. In the law enforcement field, there is a push for law enforcement personnel to become increasing professional and for that to be reflected in college degrees and certification programs. As these trends continue, it is likely there will be some blending of forensic archaeology and investigation. There are already forensic archaeology courses where investigators can learn archaeological techniques for use in their cases. There are master's degree programs in forensic archaeology, where either archaeologists or investigators can pursue this unique blend of knowledge.

The examination of the qualifications of forensic archaeologists earlier in this chapter makes it clear that forensic archaeologists should be full-time archaeologists with their fingers on the pulse of the innovations within the discipline. The necessary experience in searching for features, excavating, and soils can most easily be gained through traditional archaeological work. This experience can then be applied to forensic work. For most archaeologists, forensic work will probably continue to be a part-time specialty, as it has been with physical anthropologists.

However, simply because most archaeologists do not practice forensic work full-time does not mean that training, qualifications, or certification should be ignored. Hopefully, this chapter has made it clear that working in forensics requires a commitment to the vocation. In the near future, we need to see the major professional organizations take this commitment seriously and establish certifications for professional forensic archaeologists.

Appendix

Supplies and Services

This list is supplied for information only. No endorsements or other representations are implied by inclusion in this list.

Armor Forensics
13386 International Parkway
Jacksonville, FL 32218
800-852-0300
www. redwop.com
A forensic supply company for everything from barrier tape to fingerprint kits.

Cabela's
One Cabela Drive
Sidney, NE 69160
800-237-4444
www.cabelas.com
An outdoor outfitter for everything from generators to tarps.

Forestry Suppliers, Inc.
P.O. Box 8397
Jackson, MS 39284
800-647-5368

www.forestry-suppliers.com
Basic archaeological and mapping supplies, including mapping templates and Munsell color charts.

Lynn Peavey Company
P.O. Box 14100
Lenexa, KS 66285
800-255-6499
www.lynnpeavey.com
Supplies for crime scene investigations, including biohazard suits and photography supplies.

U.S. Geological Survey
www.usgs.gov
Several locations, including:
Box 25286
Federal Center
Denver, CO 80225
503 National Center, Room 1-C-402
12201 Sunrise Valley Drive
Reston, VA 20192
USGS sells topographic maps for everywhere in the United States.

Glossary

absolute date—The determination of age with reference to a specific time scale, such as the calendar. For example, an event occurred at 5 p.m., 24 April 1989. Compare with *relative date.*
activity area—An area within a larger site where a specific activity occurred.
artifact—Any portable object made, used, or modified by humans.
assemblage—A group of artifacts which cluster together at the same time and place.
association—The co-occurrence of an artifact with other material.
attribute—A minimal characteristic of an artifact that cannot be further divided. An important attribute of a cartridge case is the caliber.
azimuth—A horizontal angle measured clockwise from a north baseline.
bullet—A nonspherical projectile used in a firearm with a rifled barrel.
cartography—The science or art of making maps.
cartridge—Ammunition used in modern firearms consisting of the cartridge case, primer, propellant, and projectile(s).
cartridge case—The container for all the components in a cartridge.
clay—A mineral, or soil, particle less than 0.002 mm in diameter. Clay has a sticky feel when wet and may be shaped into a ribbon when pressed between the fingers.
cognitive map—An interpretive framework of the world that exists in the mind(s) of the person/people who created the site and affects actions and decisions.

context—The interrelated conditions in which an artifact occurs, for example, its association with its matrix, other artifacts, features, and the environment.
cremains—The ash, bone fragments, and teeth that remain when a person is cremated.
Daubert v. Merrell Dow Pharmaceuticals, Inc.—A 1993 Supreme Court ruling that outlines the criteria on which expert testimony will be allowed.
deduction—The process of developing testable statements from the theories; these statements must be verified against observations.
diachronic—Relating to phenomena as they change over time.
discovery—The process before a trial where each side turns over its information on the case to the other side.
ecofacts—Non-artifactual organic and environmental remains that have cultural relevance.
electrical resistivity—A remote sensing technique that uses probes inserted into the ground to measure variations in the underground resistance to electrical current. Changes in variations may indicate a subsurface feature, such as a grave.
electromagnetic induction meter—A machine that provides a measurement of the electrical conductivity of the soil. Variations in the conductivity may indicate a subsurface feature, such as a grave.
feature—A non-portable artifact; something made or used by people that cannot be moved. A grave is a feature.
firearms discharge residue—Also known as gunshot residue (GSR). The residue consists of the components of the smoke that comes out of the muzzle when a firearm is discharged.
formation process—A process that affected the way in which archaeological material came to be buried or distributed. This might include the activities of humans or animals, as well as natural or environmental phenomena or events.
Frye v. United States —A 1923 Supreme Court decision that outlines criteria for expert testimony based on what was generally accepted by the relevant scientific community. This has been replaced in many jurisdictions by Daubert.
geotaphonomy—The study of the geophysical characteristics of, and changes in, subterranean features associated with the interment of buried evidence (Hochrein 1997).

GPR—Ground penetrating radar. A system that transmits radar waves through the ground, giving a picture of the soils beneath the surface. Can be used to find underground features, such as a grave.
GPS—Global positioning system. A net of satellites over the earth that send signals with their positions to the earth. A GPS receiver picks up these signals and uses them to triangulate the position of the receiver on the earth.
groove—A helical indentation in the bore of a forearm barrel which gives the projectile a rotary motion. On the bullet, the impressions of the grooves are raised above the land impressions.
hypothesis—A tentative assumption made in order to test an empirical conclusion.
indictment—A written list of the charges brought against a defendant.
induction—The process by which a theory, or hypothesis, is formed from observed facts.
land—Lands are the areas between the helical grooves in the bore of a rifled firearm. On bullets the impressions of the lands are below the impressions of the grooves.
latitude—Angular distance north or south from the earth's equator measured through 90 degrees.
law of superposition—Under most conditions, the oldest soil layers are on the top and the youngest on the bottom.
longitude—Angular distance east or west from a standard circle (meridian) drawn from pole to pole.
magnetometer—A machine that measures variations in the magnetic properties of soil. The three most common types of magnetometers are the fluxgate, the cesium, and the proton. Variations in the magnetic properties of the soil can be used to find underground features, such as a grave.
matrix—The physical material in which artifacts are embedded or supported.
motion—Request filed by either side in a trial that may affect the judge's decisions. Motions may request that certain evidence be allowed or that it not be allowed, or request a change in venue if there has been too much publicity in the trial.
Munsell chart—A commercial color chart used to standardize the description of soil color.
paradigm—A set of assumptions, concepts, values, and practices that consti-

tutes a way of viewing reality for the community that shares that set, especially in an intellectual discipline.
ped—A natural soil aggregate.
pedestal—Noun. In archaeological excavation, a support of soil left below an object as the unit is excavated.
pedestal—Verb. To create a support of soil below an object as the excavations continue, leaving the object in its original position.
pedology—The study of the morphology, genesis, and classification of soils.
pH—A measure indicating the degree of acidity or alkalinity in soil.
relative date—A chronological framework without reference to a fixed time scale. In other words, Action A happened before Action C, but after Action D. Compare with *absolute date.*
remote sensing techniques—Techniques that investigate and define an object without direct contact with the object.
sand—Mineral particles 0.06 to 2.00 mm in diameter. Sand particles are visible to the naked eye and feel gritty when the soil is moistened and rubbed between the fingers.
scientific method—The method that distinguishes the sciences from other disciplines, based on the formation and testing of hypotheses.
silt—Mineral particles between 0.002 and 0.060 mm in diameter. Particles cannot be seen with the eye, but soils with a large silt fraction will have a "soapy" or "silky" feel and are only slightly sticky when moistened and rubbed between the fingers.
site—A distinct spatial clustering of a residue of human activity.
stratification—The physical placement of layers of material, such that the oldest is at the bottom and the youngest at the top.
stipulation—The facts in a case that everyone agrees to before a trial. Evidence supporting these facts then does not have to be discussed in the trial.
surveying—The branch of applied mathematics that is used to determine the area and contour of any portion of the earth's surface and accurately delineate that on paper.
synchronic—Phenomena occurring at a single point in time.
taphonomy—The study of processes that affect organic material, such as corpses or bones, after death.
theory—A plausible or scientifically accepted hypothesis, or set of hypotheses, offered to explain phenomena.

township—A division of territory in surveys of U.S. lands containing thirty-six sections, or thirty-six square miles.
triangulation—An operation for finding a location by means of bearings from two known points a fixed distance apart.
Universal Transverse Mercator (UTM)—A metric division of territory that covers the world.
verification—In the scientific method, the process of checking predictions against observations, and assigning greater or lesser credibility to the body of theories on the basis of the outcome.
weathering—The effects of saturation, desiccation, and temperature changes on bone.

References

Akridge, Glen

1994 The Sloan Site Revisited: Preliminary Report on the Soil Samples. Field notes, *Newsletter of the Arkansas Archaeological Society* 260:5–9.

Anderson, Gail S., and Valerie J. Cervenka

2002 Insects Associated with the Body: Their Use and Analyses. In *Advances in Forensic Taphonomy: Method, Theory, and Archaeological Perspectives*, William D. Haglund and Marcella H. Sorg, editors, pp. 173–200. CRC Press, Boca Raton, Florida.

Baby, R. S.

1954 Hopewell Cremation Practices. *Ohio Historical Society Papers in Archaeology* 1:1–7.

Barnes, Frank C.

2003 *Cartridges of the World*. Tenth ed., revised and expanded. Krause Publications, Iola, Wisconsin.

Bass, William M., and William H. Birkby

1978 Exhumation: The Method Could Make the Difference. *FBI Law Enforcement Bulletin* 47:6–11.

Beard, Lorna, Jerry Hilliard, and Glen Akridge

2000 Historical and Chemical Traces of an Ozark Cemetery for Enslaved African-Americans: A Study of Silhouette Burials in Benton County, Arkansas. *North American Archaeologist* 21 (4): 323–49.

Behrensmeyer, Anna K.

1975 The Taphonomy and Paleoecology of Plio-Pleistocene Vertebrate Assemblages East of Lake Rudolf, Kenya. *Bulletin of the Museum of Comparative Zoology* 146:473–578.

1976 Fossil Assemblages in Relation to Sedimentary Environments in the East Rudolf Succession. In *Earliest Man and Environments in the Lake Rudolf Basin,* Y. Coppens, F. Clark Howell, Glen Isaac, and R. Leakey, editors, pp. 383–401. University of Chicago Press, Chicago.

1978 Taphonomic and Ecologic Information from Bone Weathering. *Paleobiology* 4:150–62.

1982 Time Resolution in Fluvial Vertebrate Assemblages. *Paleobiology* 8:211–28.

1990 Transport-Hydrodynamics: Bones. In *Paleobiology: A Synthesis,* D. E. G. Briggs and P. R. Crowther, editors, pp. 232–35. Blackwell Scientific Publications, Oxford.

Bennett, Joanne L.

1999 Thermal Alteration of Buried Bone. *Journal of Archaeological Science* 26 (1): 1–8.

Berryman, Hugh E.

2002 Disarticulation Pattern and Tooth Mark Artifacts Associated with Pig Scavenging of Human Remains: A Case Study. In *Advances in Forensic Taphonomy: Method, Theory, and Archaeological Perspectives,* William D. Haglund and Marcella H. Sorg, editors, pp. 487–95. CRC Press, Boca Raton, Florida.

Bethell, Phillip

1989 Chemical Analysis of Shadow Burials. In *Burial Archaeology: Current Research, Methods, and Development,* C. A. Roberts, F. Lee, and J. Bintliff, editors, pp. 205–14. B.A.R. International Series, 211, B.A.R., Oxford.

Bevan, Bruce W.

1991 The Search for Graves. *Geophysics* 56 (9): 1310–19.

1996 Geophysical Exploration in the U.S. National Parks. *Northeast Historical Archaeology* 25:69–84.

1998 *Geophysical Exploration for Archaeology: An Introduction to Geophysical Exploration.* Midwest Archaeological Center Special Report No. 1. Midwest Archaeological Center, National Park Service, Lincoln, Nebraska.

Biek, L.

1970 Soil Silhouettes. In *Science in Archaeology: A Survey of Progress and Research*, D. Brothwell and E. Higgs, editors, pp. 118–23. Praeger, New York.

Binford, Lewis R.

1964 A Consideration of Archaeological Research Design. *American Antiquity* 29:203–310.

1981 *Bones: Ancient Man and Modern Myths*. Academic Press, New York.

Bleed, Peter

2000 Will the Marshalltown Be Forever Golden? *SAA Bulletin* 18 (4):21.

Blumenschine, Robert J.

1986 Carcass Consumption Sequences and the Archaeological Distinction of Scavenging and Hunting. *Journal of Human Evolution* 15 (8): 639–59.

Boas, Franz

1904 The History of Anthropology. In 1974, *The Shaping of American Anthropology 1883–1911: A Franz Boas Reader*, George W. Stocking, Jr., editor. Basic Books, New York.

Boaz, D.

1982 *Modern Riverine Taphonomy: Its Relevance to the Interpretation of Plio-Pleistocene Hominid Paleoecology in the Omo Basin, Ethiopia*. PhD dissertation, University of California, Berkeley. University Microfilms, Ann Arbor.

Brain, C. K.

1967 Bone Weathering and the Problem of Bone Pseudo-Tools. *South African Journal of Science* 63:97–99.

1981 *The Hunters or the Hunted? An Introduction to African Cave Taphonomy*. University of Chicago Press, Chicago.

Brinker, Russell

1969 *Elementary Surveying*. Fifth ed. International Textbook Company, Pennsylvania.

Brodsky, Stanley L.

1991 *Testifying in Court: Guidelines and Maxims for the Expert Witness*. American Psychological Association, Washington, D.C.

Brown, Larry C., Kent Kramer, Thomas L. Bean, and Timothy J. Lawrence

1998 *Trenching and Excavation: Safety Principles*. NASD Database, Ohio University Extension.

Carson, E. Ann, Vincent H. Stefan, and Joseph F. Powell
2000 Skeletal Manifestations of Bear Scavenging. *Journal of Forensic Sciences* 45 (3): 515–26.

Chandler, C., P. Cheney, P. Thomas, L. Trabaud, and D. Williams
1983 *Fire in Forestry,* vol. 1. *Forest Fire Behavior and Effects.* John Wiley and Sons, New York.

Chaplin, R. E.
1971 *The Study of Animal Bones from Archaeological Sites.* Seminar Press, London.

Clark, Anthony
1990 *Seeing Beneath the Soil: Prospecting Methods in Archaeology.* B. T. Batsford, London.

Connor, Melissa A.
1998a Prozor Exhumations. State Commission on Missing Persons (23 Sept.–27 Oct. 1998). Forensic Monitoring Project Report, Physicians for Human Rights, Tuzla, Bosnia and Herzegovina.
1998b Rogatica Exhumations Conducted by the State Commission on Missing Persons (1–4 Sept. 1998; 15 Sept. 1998). Forensic Monitoring Project, Physicians for Human Rights, Tuzla, Bosnia and Herzegovina.
1998c Zaklopača Exhumation Conducted by the State Commission on Missing Persons. 22–24 June 1998. Physicians for Human Rights, Tuzla, Bosnia and Herzegovina.

Connor, Melissa A., and Kenneth P. Cannon
1991 Forest Fires as a Site Formation Process in the Rocky Mountains of Northwestern Wyoming. *Archaeology in Montana* 32(2):1-14.

Connor, Melissa A., Kenneth P. Cannon, and Denise C. Carlevato
1989 The Mountains Burnt: Forest Fires and Site Formation Processes. *North American Archaeologist* 10 (4): 293–311.

Connor, Melissa A., and Douglas D. Scott, editors
2001a Archaeologists as Forensic Investigators: Defining the Role. Special issue, *Historical Archaeology* 35 (1).

Connor, Melissa A., and Douglas D. Scott
1998 Metal Detector Use in Archaeology: An Introduction. *Historical Archaeology* 32 (4): 76–85.
2001b Paradigms and Perpetrators. In Archaeologists as Forensic Investigators:

Defining the Role, M. Connor and D. D. Scott, editors, special issue, *Historical Archaeology* 35 (1): 1–6.

Cook, J.

1986 The Application of Scanning Electron Microscopy to Taphonomic and Archaeological Problems. In *Studies in the Upper Paleolithic of Britain and Northwest Europe*, D. A. Roe, editor, pp. 143–63. British Archaeological Reports International Series 296, Oxford, U.K.

Correia, Pamela Mayne, and Owen Beattie

2002 A Critical Look at Methods for Recovering, Evaluating, and Interpreting Cremated Human Remains. In *Advances in Forensic Taphonomy: Method, Theory, and Archaeological Perspectives*, William D. Haglund and Marcella H. Sorg, editors, pp. 435–50. CRC Press, Boca Raton, Florida.

Coyle, Heather M.

2004 *Forensic Botany: Principles and Applications to Criminal Casework*. CRC Press, Boca Raton, Florida.

Crist, Thomas A. J.

2001 Bad to the Bone?: Historical Archaeologists in the Practice of Forensic Science. In Archaeologists as Forensic Investigators: Defining the Role, M. Connor and D. D. Scott, editors, special issue, *Historical Archaeology* 35 (1): 39–56.

Davenport, G. Clark

2001a Remote Sensing Applications in Forensic Investigations. In Archaeologists as Forensic Investigators: Defining the Role, M. Connor and D. D. Scott, editors, special issue, *Historic Archaeology* 35 (1).

2001b *Where Is It? Searching for Buried Bodies and Hidden Evidence.* Sportwork, Church Hill, Maryland.

DeVore, Steven, and Bruce W. Bevan

1995 *Pioneer Family Cemeteries at Scott Air Force Base, St. Clair County, Illinois.* National Park Service, Rocky Mountain Regional Office, Interagency Archeological Services, Denver, Colorado. MIPR NSA 94-235.

Dirkmaat, Dennis

2002 Recovery and Interpretation of the Fatal Fire Victim: The Role of Forensic Anthropology. In *Advances in Forensic Taphonomy: Method, Theory, and Archaeological Perspectives*, William D. Haglund and Marcella H. Sorg, editors, pp. 451–72. CRC Press, Boca Raton, Florida.

Doolittle, Jim, and Michael Kaschko
1990 Geophysical Surveys on Guam and Saipan, December 10–18, 1990. Memorandum to Joan B. Perry, USDA-Soil Conservation Service, Agana, Guam. 18 January 1990.

Dupras, Tosha L., John J. Schultz, Sandra M. Wheeler, and Lana J. Williams
2006 *Forensic Recovery of Human Remains: Archaeological Approaches.* Taylor and Francis, New York.

Equipo Argentino de Antropologia Forense (EAAF)
2005 Annual Report 2005: Covering the Period January to December 2004. Argentine Forensic Anthropology Team. Equipo Argentino de Antropologia Forense, Buenos Aires.

FitzGibbon, L.
1977 *Katyn Massacre.* Corgi Books, London.

Foth, H. D., and L. M. Turk
1972 *Fundamentals of Soil Science.* Fifth ed. John Wiley and Sons, New York.

France, Diane L., T. J. Griffin, Jack C. Swanburg, J. W. Lindemann, G. Clarke Davenport, V. Trammell, C. T. Armburst, B. Kondratieff, A. Nelson, K. Castellano, and D. Hopkins
1992 A Multidisciplinary Approach to the Detection of Clandestine Graves. *Journal of Forensic Sciences* 37 (6): 1445–58.

Frison, George C., and Lawrence C. Todd
1986 *The Colby Mammoth Site: Taphonomy and Archaeology of a Clovis Kill in Northern Wyoming.* University of New Mexico Press, Albuquerque.

Galloway, Alison, and J. Josh Snodgrass
1998 Biological and Chemical Hazards of Forensic Skeletal Analysis. *Journal of Forensic Sciences* 43:940–48.

Gifford-Gonzalez, Diane P., David B. Damrosch, Debra R. Damrosch, John Pryor, and Robert L. Thunen
1985 The Third Dimension in Site Structure: An Experiment in Trampling and Vertical Dispersal. *American Antiquity* 50 (4): 803–18.

Gill-King, H.
1997 Chemical and Ultrastructural Aspects of Decomposition. In *Forensic Taphonomy: The Postmortem Fate of Human Remains*, William D. Haglund and Marcella H. Sorg, editors, pp. 93–108. CRC Press, Boca Raton, Florida.

Goff, M. Lee
2000 *A Fly for the Prosecution: How Insect Evidence Helps to Solve Crimes.* Harvard University Press, Cambridge, Massachusetts.

Groome, Dermot
2001 *The Handbook of Human Rights Investigation: A Comprehensive Guide to the Investigation and Documentation of Violent Human Rights Abuses.* Human Rights Press, Northborough, Massachusetts.

Haglund, William D.
1992 Contribution of Rodents to Postmortem Artifacts of Bone and Soft Tissue. *Journal of Forensic Sciences* 37 (6): 1459–65.
1997 Dogs and Coyotes: Postmortem Involvement with Human Remains. In *Forensic Taphonomy: The Postmortem Fate of Human Remains,* William D. Haglund and Marcella H. Sorg, editors, pp. 367–82. CRC Press, Boca Raton, Florida.
2002 Recent Mass Graves, An Introduction. In *Advances in Forensic Taphonomy: Method, Theory and Archaeological Perspectives,* William D. Haglund and Marcella H. Sorg, editors, pp. 243–62. CRC Press, Boca Raton, Florida

Haglund, William D., Melissa Connor, and Douglas D. Scott
2001 The Archaeology of Mass Graves. In Archaeologists as Forensic Investigators: Defining the Role, M. Connor and D. D. Scott, editors, special issue, *Historical Archaeology* 35 (1).
2002 The Effect of Cultivation on Buried Human Remains. In *Advances in Forensic Taphonomy: Method, Theory, and Archaeological Perspectives,* William D. Haglund and Marcella H. Sorg, editors, pp. 133–50. CRC Press, Boca Raton, Florida.

Haglund, William D., Donald Reay, and Daris Swindler
1989 Canid Scavenging/Disarticulation Sequence of Human Remains in the Pacific Northwest. *Journal of Forensic Sciences* 34:587–606.

Haglund, William D., and Marcella H. Sorg (editors)
1997 *Forensic Taphonomy: The Postmortem Fate of Human Remains.* CRC Press, Boca Raton, Florida.
2002 *Advances in Forensic Taphonomy: Method, Theory, and Archaeological Perspectives.* CRC Press, Boca Raton, Florida.

Hall, David W.
1997 Forensic Botany. In *Forensic Taphonomy: The Postmortem Fate of Human*

Remains, William D. Haglund and Marcella H. Sorg, editors, pp. 353–63. CRC Press, Boca Raton, Florida.

Haskell, Neal H., Robert D. Hall, Valerie J. Cervenka, and Michael A. Clark
1997 On the Body: Insects' Life Stage Presence and Their Postmortem Artifacts. In *Forensic Taphonomy: The Postmortem Fate of Human Remains,* William D. Haglund and Marcella H. Sorg, editors, pp. 415–48. CRC Press, Boca Raton, Florida.

Haughton, Christine, and Dominic Powlesland
1999 *West Heslerton The Anglian Cemetery,* vol. 1, *The Excavation and Discussion of the Evidence.* Landscape Research Center, Yedingham, North Yorkshire.

Haynes, G.
1981 *Bone Modifications and Skeletal Disturbances by Natural Agencies: Studies in North America.* PhD dissertation. University Microfilms, Ann Arbor.

Heard, Brian J.
1997 *Handbook of Firearms and Ballistics: Examining and Interpreting Forensic Evidence.* John Wiley and Sons, New York.

Heimmer, Don H.
1992 *Near Surface, High Resolution Geophysical Methods for Cultural Resource Management and Archaeological Investigations.* Geo-Recovery Systems, Golden, Colorado.

Hester, Thomas R., Harry J. Shafer, and Kenneth L. Feder
1997 *Field Methods in Archaeology.* Seventh ed. Mayfield Publishing, Mountain View, California.

Heye, G. C.
1919 *Certain Aboriginal Pottery from Southern California.* Museum of the American Indian, Heye Foundation Indian Notes and Monographs 7. Heye Foundation, New York.

Hochrein, Michael J.
1997 The Dirty Dozen: The Recognition and Collection of Toolmarks in the Forensic Geotaphonomic Record. *Journal of Forensic Identification* 47 (2): 171–98.
2002a An Autopsy of the Grave: Recognizing, Collecting, and Preserving Forensic Geotaphonomic Evidence. In *Advances in Forensic Taphonomy: Method,*

Theory, and Archaeological Perspectives, William D. Haglund and Marcella H. Sorg, editors, pp. 45–70. CRC Press, Boca Raton, Florida.

2002b Polar Coordinate Mapping and Forensic Archaeology within Confined Spaces. *Journal of Forensic Identification* 52 (6): 733–49.

Holland, Thomas D., Bruce E. Anderson, and Robert W. Mann

1997 Human Variables in the Postmortem Alteration of Human Bone: Examples from U.S. War Casualties. In *Forensic Taphonomy: The Postmortem Fate of Human Remains*, edited by William D. Haglund and Marcella H. Sorg, pp. 263–74. CRC Press, Boca Raton, Florida.

Horrocks, M., S. A. Coulson, and K. A. J. Walsh

1998 Forensic Palynology: Variation in the Pollen Content of Soil Surface Samples. *Journal of Forensic Sciences* 43 (2): 320–23.

Horrocks, M., and K. A. J. Walsh

1999 Fine Resolution of Pollen Patterns in Limited Space: Differentiating a Crime Scene and Alibi Scene Seven Meters Apart. *Journal of Forensic Sciences* 44 (2): 320–23.

Hoshower, Lisa M.

1998 Forensic Archeology and the Need for Flexible Excavation Strategies: A Case Study. *Journal of Forensic Sciences* 43 (1): 53–56.

Houck, Max, and Jay Siegel

2006 *Fundamentals of Forensic Science*. Elsevier, New York.

Hunter, John R.

1996 Locating Buried Remains. In *Studies in Crime: An Introduction to Forensic Archeology*, John Hunter, Charlotte Roberts, and Anthony Marsh, editors, pp. 86–100. B. T. Batsford, London.

Hunter, John, and Margaret Cox

2005 *Forensic Archaeology: Advances in Theory and Practice*. Routledge, London.

Hunter, John, Charlotte Roberts, and Anthony Marsh

1996 *Studies in Crime: An Introduction to Forensic Archeology*. B. T. Batsford, London.

Janaway, Robert C.

1987 The Preservation of Organic Materials in Association with Metal Artefacts Deposited in Inhumation Graves. In *Death, Decay and Reconstruction: Approaches to Archaeology and Forensic Science*, A. Boddinton, A. N. Garland, and R. C. Janaway, pp. 127–48. Manchester University Press, Manchester.

Jenny, Hans

1941 *Factors of Soil Formation*. McGraw-Hill, New York.

Joyce, Christopher, and Eric Stover

1991 *Witnesses from the Grave: The Stories Bones Tell*. Little, Brown and Company, Boston.

Kemeny, John G.

1959 *A Philosopher Looks at Science*. D. Van Nostrand, New York.

Kennedy, Kenneth A. R.

1999 The Wrong Urn: Commingling of Cremains in Mortuary Practices. In *Forensic Osteological Analysis: A Book of Case Studies*, Scott I. Fairgrieve, editor, pp. 141–50. Charles C. Thomas, Publisher, Illinois.

Komar, Debra

1999 The Use of Cadaver Dogs in Locating Scattered, Scavenged Human Remains: Preliminary Field Test Results. *Journal of Forensic Sciences* 44 (2): 405–8.

Krol, Arthur J., Theodore E. Jacobson, and Federick C. Finzen

1990 *Removal Partial Denture Design. Outline Syllabus*. Indent. San Rafael, California.

Kurland, Michael

1997 *How to Try a Murder: The Handbook for Armchair Lawyers*. MacMillan, New York.

Lauck, John H.

1988 *Katyn Killings: In the Record*. Kingston Press, Clifton, New Jersey.

Li Ling, Xiang Zhang, Niel T. Constantine, and John E. Smialek

1993 Seroprevalence of Parenterally Transmitted Viruses (HIV-1, HBV, HCV, and HTLV-I/II) in Forensic Autopsy Cases. *Journal of Forensic Sciences* 38:1075–83.

Lufkin

1998 Taping Techniques for Engineers and Surveyors. Cooper Tools, Apex, North Carolina.

Lyman, R. Lee

1994 *Vertebrate Taphonomy*. Cambridge Manuals in Archaeology, Cambridge University Press, Cambridge.

Lyman, R. Lee, and Gregory L. Fox
1997 A Critical Evaluation of Bone Weathering as an Indication of Bone Assemblage Formation. In *Forensic Taphonomy: The Postmortem Fate of Human Remains,* William D. Haglund and Marcella H. Sorg, editors, pp. 223–48. CRC Press, Boca Raton, Florida.

Manhein, Mary H.
1997 Decomposition Rates of Deliberate Burials: A Case Study of Preservation. In *Forensic Taphonomy: The Postmortem Fate of Human Remains,* W. D. Haglund and M. H. Sorg, editors, pp. 469–81. CRC Press, Boca Raton, Florida.

Mant, A. K.
1950 A Study of Exhumation Data. MD thesis, University of London.

Mant, A. K., and R. Furbank
1957 Adipocere: A Review. *Journal of Forensic Medicine* 4:27–31.

Micozzi, Marc S.
1997 *Postmortem Change in Human and Animal Remains: A Systemic Approach.* CRC Press, Boca Raton, Florida.

Miller, G. J.
1975 A Study of Cuts, Grooves and Other Marks on Recent and Fossil Bones: II, Weathering Cracks, Fractures, Splinters, and Other Similar Natural Phenomena. In *Lithic Technology,* E. Swanson, editor, pp. 212–26. Mouton, The Hague.

Mondero, Jessica
2005 Experimental Study of the Decomposition of Child-Sized Remains in the Midwest: A Study of Summer, Surface Deposited Pigs. Paper submitted for Forensic Science 599. On file, Forensic Science Program, Nebraska Wesleyan University, Lincoln, Nebraska.

Morse, Dan F.
1997 *Sloan: A Paleoindian Dalton Cemetery in Arkansas.* Smithsonian Institution Press, Washington, D.C.

Morse, Dan, R. C. Dailey, James Stoutamire, and Jack Duncan
1984 Forensic Archaeology. In *Human Identification: Case Studies in Forensic Anthropology,* Ted Rathbun and Jane Buikstra, editors, pp. 53–63. Charles C. Thomas, Publishers, Springfield, Illinois.

Morse, Dan, Jack Duncan, and James Stoutamire
1983 *Handbook of Forensic Archaeology and Anthropology*. Rose Printing, Tallahassee, Florida.

Morton, Robert J., and Wayne D. Lord
2002 Detection and Recovery of Abducted and Murdered Children: Behavioral and Taphonomic Influences. In *Advances in Forensic Taphonomy: Method, Theory, and Archaeological Perspectives,* William D. Haglund and Marcella H. Sorg, editors, pp. 151–72. CRC Press, Boca Raton, Florida.

Murray, Raymond C.
2004 *Evidence from the Earth: Forensic Geology and Criminal Investigation.* Mountain Press Publishing, Missoula, Montana.

Nickel, Robert K.
2000 *An Evaluation of Geophysical Survey Instruments for Detecting Unmarked Graves at the Mission Cemetery, Spalding, Idaho*. U.S. Department of the Interior, National Park Service, Midwest Archaeological Center, Lincoln, Nebraska.

Occupational Safety and Health Administration (OSHA)
1995 *Excavations*. OSHA 2226. U.S. Department of Labor, Occupational Safety and Health Administration, Washington, D.C.

Olsen, S. L., and P. Shipman
1988 Surface Modification on Bone: Trampling Versus Butchery. *Journal of Archaeological Science* 15:535–53

Osterburg, James W., and Richard H. Ward
2004 *Criminal Investigation: A Method for Reconstructing the Past.* Fourth ed. Anderson Publishing, Cincinnati, Ohio.

Owsley, Douglas H.
1993 Identification of the Fragmentary, Burned Remains of Two U.S. Journalists Seven Years After Their Disappearance in Guatemala. *Journal of Forensic Sciences* 38 (6): 1372–82.
1995 Techniques for Locating Burials, with Emphasis on the Probe. *Journal of Forensic Sciences* 40 (5): 735–40.

Paulsen, Brian, and Tim Dunning
2005 Final Disposition: A Landfill Search for Brendan Gonzalez. Unpublished paper in possession of author.

Rebmann, Andrew J., Marcia Koenig, Edward David, and Marcella H. Sorg
2000 *Cadaver Dog Handbook: Forensic Training and Tactics for the Recovery of Human Remains*. CRC Press, Boca Raton, Florida.

Reed, Stewart, Nathan Bailey, and Oghenekome Onokpise
2000 *Soil Science for Archaeologists*. Florida Agricultural and Mechanical University and Southeast Archaeological Center, National Park Service.

Richmond, Raymond, and Iain Pretty
2006 Contemporary Methods of Labeling Dental Prostheses—A Review of the Literature. *Journal of Forensic Sciences* 51 (5): 1120–26.

Robbins, Elaine
2006 Archaeological Crime Fighters. *American Archaeology* 10 (2): 25–30.

Rolfe, W. D. I., and D. W. Brett
1969 Fossilization Processes. In *Organic Geochemistry: Methods and Results*, G. Englinton and M. T. J. Murphy, editors, pp. 213–44. Springer-Verlag, Berlin.

Scott, Douglas D.
2002 Archeological Investigations of the "Horse Cemetery" Site, Little Bighorn Battlefield National Monument. Midwest Archeological Center, National Park Service, Nebraska.

Scott, Douglas D., and Melissa Connor
1997 Context Delicti: Archaeological Context in Forensic Work. In *Forensic Taphonomy: The Postmortem Fate of Human Remains,* William D. Haglund and Marcella H. Sorg, editors, pp. 27–38. CRC Press, Boca Raton, Florida.

Scott, Douglas D., Richard A. Fox, Jr., Melissa A. Connor, and Dick Harmon
1989 *Archaeological Perspectives on the Battle of the Little Bighorn*. University of Oklahoma Press, Norman, Oklahoma.

Scott, Douglas D., P. Willey, and Melissa A. Connor
1998 *They Died with Custer*. University of Oklahoma Press, Norman, Oklahoma.

Sease, Catherine
1987 *A Conservation Manual for the Field Archaeologist*. Archaeological Research Tools, vol. 4. Institute of Archaeology, University of California, Los Angeles.

Sigler-Eisenberg, Brenda
1985 Forensic Research: Explaining the Concept of Applied Archaeology. *American Antiquity* 50:650–55.

Skinner, Mark

1999 Cremated Remains and Expert Testimony in a Homicide Case. In *Forensic Osteological Analysis: A Book of Case Studies*, Scott I. Fairgrieve, editor, pp. 151–72. Charles C. Thomas, Publisher. Springfield, Illinois.

Skinner, Mark, and Richard A. Lazenby

1983 *Found! Human Remains: A Field Manual for the Recovery of the Recent Human Skeleton*. Archaeology Press, Simon Fraser University, Burnaby, B.C.

Skinner, Mark F., Heather P. York, and Melissa Connor

2002 Post-Burial Disturbance of Graves in Bosnia-Herzegovina. In *Advances in Forensic Taphonomy: Method, Theory, and Archaeological Perspectives*. William D. Haglund and Marcella H. Sorg, editors, pp. 293–309. CRC Press, Boca Raton, Florida.

Sledzik, Paul S., and Marc S. Micozzi

1997 Autopsied, Embalmed, and Preserved Human Remains: Distinguishing Features in Forensic and Historic Contexts. In *Forensic Taphonomy: The Postmortem Fate of Human Remains*, William D. Haglund and Marcella H. Sorg, editors, pp. 483–95. CRC Press, Boca Raton, Florida.

Snow, Clyde C., Lowell Levine, Leslie Lukash, Luke G. Tedeschi, Cristian Orrego, and Eric Stover

1984 The Investigation of the Human Remains of the "Disappeared" in Argentina. *The American Journal of Forensic Medicine and Pathology* 5 (4): 297–99.

Solecki, R. S.

1951 Notes on Soil Analysis and Archaeology. *American Antiquity* 16 (4): 254–56.

Spector, Michael

2000 No Place to Hide. *The New Yorker*. 27 Nov. 2000, pp. 96–105.

Sprague, Roderick

2005 *Burial Terminology: A Guide for Researchers*. AltaMira Press, New York.

Stover, Eric

1985 Scientists Aid Search for Argentina's "Desparecidos." *Science* 230:56–57.

Stover, Eric, and Molly Ryan

2001 Breaking Bread with the Dead. In Archaeologists as Forensic Investigators: Defining the Role, M. Connor and D. D. Scott, editors, special issue, *Historical Archaeology* 35 (1): 7–25.

Thornbury, William D.

1969 *Principals of Geomorphology.* Second ed. John Wiley and Sons, New York.

Todd, Lawrence C.

1987 Taphonomy of the Horner II Bone Bed. In *The Horner Site: The Type Site of the Cody Cultural Complex,* George C. Frison and Lawrence C. Todd, editors, pp. 107–98. Academic Press, Orlando, Florida.

Trotter, M., and R. R. Peterson

1955 Ash Weight of Human Skeletons in Percent of Their Dry, Fat-Free Weight. *Anatomical Records* 123:341–68.

Ubelaker, Douglas H., and C. H. Jacobs

1995 Identification of Orthopedic Device Manufacturer. *Journal of Forensic Sciences* 40 (2): 168–170.

United States Department of Agriculture

1990 *Keys to Soil Taxonomy.* Fourth ed. SMSS Technical Monograph 19. U.S. Department of Agriculture, Blacksburg, Virginia.

United States Department of the Army

1993 *Map Reading and Land Navigation.* Field Manual No. 21-26. Headquarters Department of the Army, Washington, D.C.

United States Department of Justice

2003 *Quick Reference Guide for IBIS Users.* Bureau of Alcohol, Tobacco, Firearms and Explosives, U.S. Department of Justice, Ammendale, Marlyand.

United States Supreme Court

1993 *Daubert v. Merrell Dow Pharmaceuticals, Inc.,* 509 U.S. 579(1993). 509 U.S. 579 William Daubert Et. Ux., etc., et al., Petitioners v. Merrell Dow Pharmaceuticals, Inc. Certiorari to the United States Court of Appeals for the Ninth Circuit No. 92-102.

Van Vuren, Dirk

1982 Effects of Feral Sheep on the Spatial Distribution of the Artifacts on Santa Cruz Island. *Bulletin of the Southern California Academy of Science* 81 (3): 148–51.

Vass, A. A.

1991 *Time Since Death Determinations of Human Cadavers Utilizing Soil Solutions.* PhD dissertation, Department of Anthropology, University of Tennessee, Knoxville.

Vass, A. A., S. A. Barshick, G. Sega, J. Caton, J. T. Skeen, J. C. Love, and J. A. Synstelien
1992 Decomposition Chemistry of Human Remains: A New Methodology for Determining Postmortem Interval. *Journal of Forensic Sciences* 47 (3): 542–53.

Vass, A. A., W. M. Bass, J. D. Walt, J. E. Wolf, J. E. Foss, and J. T. Ammons
2002 Time since Death Determinations of Human Cadavers Using Soil Solutions. *Journal of Forensic Sciences* 37 (5): 1236–53.

Voorhies. Michael
1969 *Taphonomy and Population Dynamics of an Early Poiocene Vertebrate Fauna, Knox County, Nebraska.* University of Wyoming Contributions to Geology Special Paper No. 1. Laramie.

Walker, James W.
1993 *Low Altitude Large Scale Reconnaissance: A Method of Obtaining High Resolution Vertical Photographs for Small Areas.* Rocky Mountain Regional Office, National Park Service, Denver, Colorado.

Webster, Ann DeMuth
1998 Excavation of a Vietnam-Era Aircraft Crash Site: Use of Cross-Cultural Understanding and Dual Forensic Recovery Methods. *Journal of Forensic Sciences* 43 (2): 277–83.

Wettstead, James R.
1988 Forest Fires and Archaeology in the Ashland District, Custer National Forest, Montana. Paper presented at the 46th Annual Plains Conference, Wichita, Kansas.

Weymouth, John W., and Robert Huggins
1985 Geophysical Surveying of Archaeological Sites. In *Archaeological Geology*, George Rapp, Jr., and John A. Gifford, editors, pp. 191–235. Yale University Press, New Haven.

White, Henry P., and Burton D. Munhall
1963 *Cartridge Headstamp Guide.* H. P. White Laboratory, Bel Air, Maryland.

White, Tim D.
1991 *Human Osteology*. Academic Press, San Diego, California.

White, Tim D., and Pieter A. Folkens
2005 *The Human Bone Manual.* Elsevier, New York.

Whitmore, Ann M., Ann F. Ramenofsky, Jacob Thomas, Louis J. Thibodeaux, Stephen D. Field, Bob J. Miller

1989 Stability or Instability: The Role of Diffusion in Trace Element Studies. *Archaeological Method and Theory* 1:205–73.

Willey, P., and Douglas D. Scott
1999 Clinkers on the Little Bighorn Battlefield: In Situ Investigation of Scattered Recent Cremains. In *Forensic Osteological Analysis: A Book of Case Studies*, Scott I. Fairgrieve, editor, pp. 129–40. Charles C. Thomas, Publisher, Illinois.

Willey, P., and Lynn M. Snyder
1989 Canid Modification of Human Remains: Implication for Time-Since-Death Estimations. *Journal of Forensic Sciences* 34:894–901.

Index

absolute date, 21, 22, 25, 26, 27, 221, 234
activity area, 7, 19, 21, 27, 221
ammunition, 34, 184, 192, 198, 199, 221
appliances, dental, 184, 187–88
appliances, medical, 184, 186–92, 199
artifact, 1, 6, 7, 17, 18, 19–20, 21, 24, 25, 26, 27, 51, 95, 96, 105, 145, 154, 166, 169, 218, 221, 222, 223, 228
assemblage, 20, 21, 25, 26, 27, 89, 90, 160, 167, 221
association, 21, 27, 88, 99, 198, 199, 221, 222
attribute, 1, 18, 19, 20, 21, 22, 25, 27, 221
azimuth, 53–54, 67, 221

block excavation. *See* excavation: block
Boas, Franz, 1–2
Bosnia and Herzegovina, 48–95, 109, 121, 173, 174
Bosnia and Herzegovina Federation Commission for Missing Persons, 109, 119, 146, 153, 158, 159, 170, 171, 172, 174–75
botany, 166–67
British Council for the Registration of Forensic Practitioners, 214–15
bullet, 19, 22, 37, 99, 104, 143, 144, 164, 165, 168–69, 180, 192–94, 199, 221, 223

cadaver dog. *See* dog, cadaver
cartography, 51–52, 67, 221
cartridge, 124, 168, 180, 192, 196–99, 221; center fire, 196; rim fire, 196
cartridge case, 19, 21, 22, 24, 25, 59, 124, 144, 152, 164, 168, 192, 196–99, 221
chain of custody, 4, 7, 10, 15, 209, 210, 21, 216; form, 209, 210
clay, 36, 70, 73, 75, 84, 102, 103, 120, 123, 124, 134, 137, 140, 143, 148, 151, 154, 221
clothing: for investigators, 35, 129; on remains, 80–81, 95, 112, 114, 115, 119, 139, 155, 162, 166, 167, 168, 169, 171, 176, 184–86, 198, 199, 200
cognitive map, 21, 27, 221

context, 2, 18, 21, 27, 84, 108, 143, 154, 156, 216, 222
cremains, 101, 105, 222
cremation, 85, 101–2
crowns, dental, 187–88

Daubert v. Merrell Dow Pharmaceuticals, Inc., 12–14, 15, 222
deduction, 13, 15, 222
diachronic, 21, 22, 26, 27, 222
"discovery," pre-trial proceeding, 9–10, 12, 13, 33, 203, 204, 222
dog, cadaver, 5, 55, 117, 139, 140, 176

ecofacts, 19, 20, 21, 27, 222
electrical resistivity, 124, 127–29, 130, 134, 140, 141, 222
electromagnetic induction meter, 123, 125, 141, 222
entomology, 167–68; insects, 5, 20, 71, 80, 86, 100, 101, 167–69
equipment, 14, 29, 30, 39, 41, 108, 115, 169, 172; excavation, 31, 32, 34–38, 60, 150, 154, 202; mapping, 32, 54, 57, 58, 98; mechanized, or heavy, 117, 118, 131, 173; photographic, 32; remote sensing, 5, 120, 122, 138, 140
excavation: block, 162–63; grid, 58–62; mass grave, 3, 6, 90, 121, 129, 147–48, 157–60
excavation equipment. *See* equipment: excavation
expert witness, 11, 12–15, 217

feature: archaeological, 18, 19, 20, 21, 24, 26, 27, 76, 102, 107, 112, 114, 118, 120, 122, 123, 152, 153, 158, 198, 201, 211, 218, 223; definition, 19, 21, 222; form, 205–7; mapping, 51, 53, 63–64
fibers, 9, 183, 185
firearms: discharge residue, 198, 199, 222; identification, 168–69, 192; firing pin, 197
formation process, 19, 21, 69, 76, 77, 222
Frye criteria, 12–14, 15, 222

geotaphonomy, 181, 222
global positioning system, 50–51, 67, 68, 108, 114, 203, 223
GPR. *See* ground-penetrating radar
grid excavation. *See* excavation: grid
ground-penetrating radar, 123, 124–25, 127, 129, 131–34, 138, 139, 140, 141, 223
GPS. *See* global positioning system
groove, rifling, 193–96, 199, 223

headstamp, 197
hypothesis, 13, 15, 223, 225

ICMP. *See* International Commission for Missing Persons (ICMP)
ICTR. *See* International Criminal Tribunal for Rwanda (ICTR)
implant, 101, 184, 186–92, 193; heart valve, 184; orthopedic, 184; pacemaker, 184
indictment, 8, 15, 223
induction, logical, 13, 15, 223
insects. *See* entomology
International Commission for Missing Persons (ICMP), 3
International Criminal Tribunal for Rwanda (ICTR), 3
intrauterine devices (IUD), 192, 195

IUD. *See* intrauterine devices (IUD)

Katyn Forest, 147–48

land, rifling, 194, 196, 223
latitude, 43, 44–45, 48, 50, 67, 68, 203, 223
law of superposition, 76, 84, 223
Little Bighorn Battlefield, 18, 89, 90, 91–92, 101, 109, 185, 186
longitude, 43, 44–45, 48, 50, 67, 68, 203, 223

magnetometer, 123, 129, 130, 132, 139, 140, 141, 223
mapping equipment. *See* equipment: mapping
maps, 54–57; instrument, 56–57; pace and compass, 54–55; polar coordinate, 62; sketch, 54
mass grave excavation. *See* excavation: mass grave
matrix, soil, 21, 27, 72, 73, 80, 222, 223
mechanized equipment. *See* equipment: mechanized
motion, legal, 10, 15, 223
Munsell soil color chart, 71–73, 84, 220, 223

Noggins ground penetrating radar, 125

Occupational Safety and Health Administration (OSHA), 149

palynology, 167
paradigm, 2, 17–18, 26, 27, 223
Paulsen, Brian, 175, 176, 178
ped, soil, 76, 84, 155, 224
pedestal, 103, 105, 109, 152, 153, 154, 156, 157, 162, 163, 164, 179, 181, 224
pedology, 84, 224
pH, 82, 83, 84, 112, 144, 224
photographic equipment. *See* equipment: photographic
PHR. *See* Physicians for Human Rights (PHR)
Physicians for Human Rights (PHR), 3, 78
Plattsmouth County Police Department, 175
pollen, 165, 167
protocols, 4, 7, 15, 24, 30, 31, 41, 210, 214, 216
Prozor, 173–75

range. *See* Township and Range system
Register of Professional Archaeologists (RPA), 213–14
relative dating, 21, 22, 25, 27, 221, 224
remote sensing, 6, 69, 107, 119–29, 139, 141, 222, 224
remote sensing equipment. *See* equipment: remote sensing

sand, 70, 73, 77, 84, 93, 224
scavengers. *See* taphonomy: scavengers
scientific method, 13, 14, 15, 224, 255
screens, archaeological, 2, 36–38, 39, 75, 103, 118, 151–52, 155, 156, 170
shoes: for investigators, 34, 129; on remains, 124, 162, 167, 180, 186
silt, 70, 73, 84, 224
skim-shoveling, 35, 152
Snow, Clyde, 3
Sri Lanka, 4, 35, 78, 157, 195
stents, 192, 194

stipulation, legal, 10, 15, 224
stratification, 21, 25, 27, 134, 145, 224
surveying, 51, 56, 57, 58, 62, 67, 98, 224
synchronic, 21, 22, 27, 224

taphonomy: definition of, 19, 21, 26, 27, 105, 224; grave, 144–48; and scavengers, 86–89; site, 26, 104; surface, 86–96; and weathering, 89–92
testimony. *See* expert witness
tile probe, 114–17
tool marks, 4, 9, 19, 81, 145, 153, 156, 159, 179
Township and Range system, 45–47, 67
triangulation, 61, 67, 225

universal transverse mercator (UTM), 43, 48–50, 67, 225

verification, 15, 211, 225

weathering. *See* taphonomy: weathering
witness, as a grave location technique, 107–8, 140. *See also* expert witness

Yugoslavia, 3

About the Author

Melissa Connor is the director of the Forensic Science Program at Nebraska Wesleyan University. She worked as an archaeologist for the U.S. National Park Service for fifteen years and used those skills in forensic work with Physicians for Human Rights and other organizations. She holds a B.A. and M.A. from the University of Wisconsin at Madison, and a Ph.D. from the University of Nebraska at Lincoln.